LIFE AFTER YOU

SIÂN O'GORMAN

Boldwood

First published in Great Britain in 2020 by Boldwood Books Ltd.

A CIP catalogue record for this book is available from the British Library.

Paperback ISBN 978-1-80048-370-5

Hardback ISBN 978-1-80426-179-8

Large Print ISBN 978-1-80048-366-8

Ebook ISBN 978-1-80048-364-4

Kindle ISBN 978-1-80048-365-1

Audio CD ISBN 978-1-80048-371-2

MP3 CD ISBN 978-1-80048-368-2

Digital audio download ISBN 978-1-80048-363-7

Boldwood Books Ltd
23 Bowerdean Street
London SW6 3TN
www.boldwoodbooks.com

For my brilliant friend, Kaz

If the sun refused to shine...
    I would still be loving you
    Mountains crumble to the sea
    There would still be you and me

— LED ZEPPELIN

1

A low hum of chatter, the odd bray from the over-inebriated, the tinkling of Cole Porter from the grand piano in the corner, the soft lighting, the waft of the kind of perfume that hadn't been bought as an after-thought in Duty Free, the pop of the champagne bottles. Siobhán held up her glass of fizz. 'I could get used to this,' she said, putting on a posh voice. 'I may insist on *always* socialising in the Shelbourne.'

It was early April and there was a touch of spring in the air and we were both a little over-excited. It was a Tuesday which was enough to celebrate on its own, but we were at the launch of a new development for my boyfriend's property company and although Ryan and I had been going out for three months, he and Siobhán were yet to meet.

She'd already peered across the room at him as he shook hands with and chatted to some of the other guests. 'He's handsome,' she said, approvingly. 'The kind of cheekbones that make him look like he's sucking on a lemon or an eighties popstar.'

Siobhán and I had been best friends since our third year of high school when we both realised we shared a hatred of hockey and a love of talking to each other. We'd lived with each other many times over the years, her moving in with me when my then boyfriend, Darragh, left me five years earlier. Her partner, George, was often to be found on our sofa – normally asleep, wrecked from his early starts in a bakery.

Siobhán's arm darted out to nab a handful of canapés as a tray bobbed past our heads. She handed one to me. 'Being a corporate lawyer, you probably eat like this all the time,' she said, mouth full, 'expense-account lunches...'

'I'm lucky if I get ten minutes to buy a sandwich. Normally, it's just me and Catriona working through.' Catriona was my boss, one of the partners at my law firm McCoyMcAvoy. I'd worked there since getting onto the graduate scheme, and had slowly made my way up to being junior to the firm's only female partner. As corporate lawyers, we bent the rules to nearly breaking point, discovering legal loopholes and building cases so rock-solid that we always ensured our clients got their way.

'Lunch is the most important meal of the day,' Siobhán reminded me.

'I thought it was breakfast.'

She held up a canapé. 'No, I forgot. Nibbles and snacks are the best meal of the day.' She grinned at me. 'Can't live without snacks.'

'I'd *die*.'

'We'd die together for the want of a good snack... talking of which, these are very nice, very nice indeed!'

Siobhán was small, with long, waterfall-wavy red hair, and always wore bright red lipstick. I was tall, with shoulder length light brown hair which I tied back for work, with minimal make-up. She wore long skirts and chunky cardigans and dangly earrings, whereas I couldn't remember the last time I wore anything that wasn't sensible. I couldn't remember the last time I had *done* something that wasn't sensible. But, then again, I was the one who'd signed up to be a lawyer and being sensible was part of the deal. Except, I wouldn't mind some fun. It was exactly why I insisted on Siobhan coming tonight. It was at least *something*.

Siobhán, on the other hand, had a far more interesting job editing a feminist magazine, *The Monthly*. But it was stressful and challenging, considering that publishing costs kept increasing and readers diminishing. Her dream was to go to New York, one day. She'd been talking about it ever since I first met her, but her boyfriend, George, wouldn't ever move and therefore Siobhán was stuck in Dublin. Meanwhile, I spent my days fantasising about being sacked and having to get a job with a florist or a newsagent. Any place where I wouldn't have to meet some smooth, overly confident property developer in a suit, like most of my clients.

Ironic really, because Ryan, my boyfriend, was exactly that.

Siobhán looked thoughtful. 'What did you say Catriona's star sign was again?'

'Capricorn.' I'd worked it out when Catriona went to Paris for a long weekend with her husband, Noel, and she admitted that, much as she hated going away, he'd made her because it was her fortieth.

Siobhán nodded sagely. 'Yes, that makes a lot of sense, she exhibits a lot of Capricorn tendencies...'

'What exactly are Capricorn tendencies?' Horoscopes were one of Siobhán's latest passions and in the last few months she'd made me fill out several charts, plotting exactly what my constellation was and she was delighted – 'I knew it!' – to find that we were a perfect match. Siobhán oscillated between several horoscope apps on her phone and her interest had ramped up recently, these days relying on them to guide her through life. I wished I could find something to believe in so wholeheartedly.

'Oh, you know...' she said airily this evening, with the wisdom of a woman who has been around. 'Workaholics, generally. But I'm worried about you,' she went on. 'Being a Libra with multiple moons in Taurus.' She shook her head. 'You need to take advantage of Mercury going retrograde in the next few weeks. Things have been known to go crazy.'

'Oh God...' I had to pretend to take this seriously, that's what friends did, right? Siobhán, after all, had been the very best of friends to me.

'Just be careful.' She smiled at me, and drained her glass of champagne.

'I'll try.'

Siobhán looked around at our fellow guests, most of them corporate bankers, international investment types, all cloned, manicured, preened and primped within an inch of their indeterminate life, faces smoother than a baby's bottom. 'It's like being at a convention for people who are half toddler, half pensioner,' she said. 'It's unsettling.' She drank more of her champagne. 'So, what's this evening all about then? Why are we being plied with free fizz and nibbles?'

'Dublin Investments, Ryan and his mother Carole's company,' I explained, 'is entertaining potential new clients for their new development.'

'You mean apartments?' Siobhán rolled her eyes. 'Like Dublin needs more overpriced shoeboxes. I mean, *our* flat is an overpriced shoebox, but I've seen smaller, and more expensive.'

'No, this is different,' I said. 'They are looking for old properties, heritage sites, that they can buy for next to nothing and then do up. It's all luxury living, with a concierge service and a gym in the basement.'

Siobhán tried and failed to arrange her face into a polite expression. 'I'm sure it will all be very nice,' she said. 'Anyway...' She swiped two glasses of champagne from another passing tray, '... it's just nice to be out of the house. George is probably already asleep on his sofa in front of *EastEnders*, his curried chips cooling on the plate resting on his stomach.'

I laughed. 'But you love him *really*,' I teased.

'Course I do!' she said. 'Who wouldn't love George! Anyway, all I meant was, it's good to be out, having *fun*...'

Fun? I couldn't remember what fun was. Since Dad died, I had worked as hard as I could, spending long hours in the office, going in for weekends. Which was good for my career and meant that Catriona hand-picked me to become her junior, but it meant little time for a social life. It was the beginning of April now, but on New Year's Eve, I'd made a resolution to not work weekends and try and find a boyfriend. And the following week, at a property developer luncheon, a horrible thing where speeches were overlong and everyone overfed and overwatered... I met Ryan.

It was his mother, Carole, who first introduced herself to Catriona and me and insisted we met her son. And the next day, Ryan rang up to ask me out. And I forced myself to say yes. And I quite liked having a boyfriend after all this time. We were taking things very slowly, keeping to ourselves during the week, but normally spending Friday evenings together and then I would stay over at his coach house, which was in the grounds of his parents' (Carole and his stepfather Roger) rather grand house.

'Carole looks absolutely terrifying,' said Siobhán, looking across to where Ryan's mother stood talking to someone.

'Carole's lovely,' I lied, smiling.

'You're not *smizing*,' said Siobhán.

'Smizing?'

'Smiling with your eyes. A smile is only a smile if the eyes are involved.'

I tried again. 'Is that better?'

'Not really.'

'How about this?' I attempted to get my eyes in on the act.

'A little improvement,' she said. 'It's something I have been working on in my quest to be more charming. Not that you need any help in that department.' She winked at me. 'You always look good. It's that smile of yours.'

But I secretly agreed with Siobhán as I too had detected something monstrous about the five foot nothing Carole. In her tight, glossy suits and stiletto heels, with her beady, unsettling eyes, Carole was like a shark sniffing out blood. Just the previous week, she'd presented me with a carrier bag. 'Just a little something,' she'd said, smiling that smile of hers that never quite fitted her face. For a moment, I had been giddily pleased. Maybe she did like me? Ryan and Roger had nodded indulgently as I reached in and pulled out a... hairbrush.

'Thank you,' I had said, uncertainly.

'Just run it through your hair occasionally,' she'd said. 'Your hair could be so lovely, if you only gave it a brush from time to time.' and then she'd smiled again, as though she cared. Maybe she did, I couldn't work it out. But I didn't like to say anything to Siobhán. I was really trying to make this relationship work.

2

'Remind me what star sign Ryan is?' Siobhán said. 'I hope he's Aquarius with Cancerous moons... that would be perfect for you.'

'But I don't want someone with Cancerous moons. It sounds far too ominous.'

'You know what I mean.'

'His birthday is August...'

'August?' She paled. 'As in Leo or Virgo?'

'I'm not sure.'

'When's his birth date?'

I couldn't remember. We hadn't been going out *that* long, and anyway, we hadn't spent the time forensically researching each other. 'We're only vaguely involved in each other's lives,' I explained. 'We haven't got round to those kind of details yet.'

'Vaguely involved?' Siobhán's eyebrows shot up.

'It's casual,' I explained. 'We don't ask too much of each other. We don't live in each other's pockets. We spend some time together, but not every day. He's busy at work, so am I. And his mother monopolises most of his free time. But I like him and he's really nice to me.' Ryan was almost embarrassingly generous. If you half said you liked something, he would turn up with it. Noise cancelling headphones one day, or a Louis Vuitton handbag that was far more than anyone should spend on anything, never mind for what is essentially a glorified carrier bag. Siobhán had stroked the buttery leather of the over-priced handbag. 'It's like a bread roll made by Paul Hollywood,' she'd said, pressing it to her face. 'It's so soft.'

'Have you ever had a bread roll made by Paul Hollywood?' I'd queried.

'No, but if I did, it would feel like this. You are so lucky,' she'd stroked it again. 'I like a man with more money than sense.'

But Siobhán also knew why a half-hearted, vaguely committed relationship might be exactly right for me. She'd been there five years earlier when Dad died and then a week later when my then boyfriend, Darragh, moved to Italy. Just like that. Out of the blue, leaving me in the grieving lurch. We'd been going out with each other for seven years and, of course, I knew he loved Italy, and he'd spoken – dreamily, I thought – about living there. But to do it without me, and that week of all weeks? It was, to put it mildly, something of a blow.

I don't remember much else, except being in such a state of shock that he would choose this week – of all weeks! – to leave. I told him to go, and to never, ever contact me again. I think I threw his book of Seamus Heaney poetry at him, the one that Seamus had actually signed, and deliberately let it land in a particularly deep puddle. I am not proud of that act of vandalism, but I am sure Seamus himself would understand the immense emotional strain I was under.

Darragh *had* tried to contact me over the years – looking for forgiveness? Absolution? There was the letter he left and then the card the first Christmas telling me where he was and what he was doing and again saying he was sorry. But never any real or meaningful explanation. Because, obviously, there was none. Just an act of callous, self-regard. Then, once, he'd phoned when he was back in Dublin visiting his dad and I had refused to talk to him, putting all my energy into moving on with my new life.

'Ladies, gentlemen...' Ryan was standing up to speak, tapping his glass with his Mont Blanc pen. He looked over at me and quickly smiled. Yes, sometimes he came across as arrogant (I was well used to property developers by now), but I also detected an underlying vulnerability. Most of all, I felt sorry for him having Carole as a mother and constantly having to impress her, hoping to be his own man in the family business. He'd been sent to boarding school from the age of eight, and exhibited all the traits of someone who hadn't been loved quite enough. My heart went out to him.

And after being single for so long, I liked having someone to go to dinner with. Or just someone that wasn't a friend, or a relative, or a colleague. Someone just for me. And while we socialised with Carole and Roger more than I would have liked, this was a relationship. I had joined the *successful* people again, the ones who can do normal things and not *still* be grieving for a dead father and a long lost relationship.

Carole stood beside Ryan, her eyes directed on him.

'May I say what a pleasure it is to see you all here this evening,' Ryan continued. 'It's been something of a dream of ours, this plan, this wildly exciting venture. Dublin One will be a place for people who enjoy the finer things in life...' He took a moment to look around at the ancient-baby-faces, dripping in jewellery and smelling of money, before the lights dimmed and a series of glossy, computer-generated images flashed on the large screen behind him, pictures of smiling, good-looking people drinking champagne, or looking serious as they gazed out of a large window at the city outside or sitting in lotus position wearing expensive gym clothes. There was even a photograph of someone carrying a baguette *and* a fabulous bouquet of flowers, as though that was the kind of normal shopping people did every day.

'At the moment, we are viewing some of the city's best buildings,' Ryan was saying. 'We are looking for character, for history. But, of course, because it's a Dublin Investments project, it will be meticulously refurbished, to our internationally renowned standards...'

Out of the corner of my eye, I could see that Siobhán wasn't listening. She was scrolling through her phone.

'... If you choose to invest with us, you will be part of a revolution in development. Instead of apartments with no personality, places in which you exist but not live, Dublin One will prove that there is a different way to live. The building will be within this square mile. It is stage one of what we hope to be replicated across the city. My plan is to make lots of money for you all, to ensure that your investments are repaid manifold times. We plan on a 400 per cent return on investment capital over two years...'

There was a brief ripple of excitement from the tweaked faces of the guests. It was the most animated anyone had looked all evening. Even Carole was smiling. Siobhán, meanwhile, was still on her phone.

'What are you doing?' I hissed.

'I forgot to get *my* horoscope earlier,' she explained into my ear. 'Just checking it now.' She scrolled through her phone. 'I could be in for a few surprises, apparently. An old friend may come back into my life and bring with them a new experience.' She looked pleased.

3

'Ladies...' Ryan said smoothly, handing Siobhán and me a fresh glass of champagne. 'I trust you are having a good evening?' He gave me a quick kiss on the lips which was more on the side of my mouth.

'Ryan,' I said, 'this is Siobhán, my...'

'... Wing woman, mentor, wise counsel,' said Siobhán, grinning, and holding out her hand. 'Lovely to meet you, Ryan. Great speech. Very inspiring.'

'Pleased to meet you, too,' he said, stiffly, boarding-school manners on display. 'Do you work with Milly?'

Siobhán glanced at me, confused. I had told Ryan about Siobhán many times. Surely he hadn't forgotten? Maybe he was just one of those men who don't remember names or details or much of anything.

'No, that's Catriona,' I said. 'Siobhán's my flatmate...'

He nodded. 'Of course, of course...' He smiled at her, a glance taking in the Indian scarf, the nose stud. 'I should have guessed.'

'Yes, I don't look much like a lawyer,' laughed Siobhán.

'More like a gypsy,' said Ryan.

'Yes!' Siobhán laughed again, but uncertainly. 'That's me!'

Ryan turned to me. 'You are looking beautiful, Milly,' he went on, approvingly. 'The earrings look perfect.' he'd given them to me last week while we were out for dinner.

'The fizzy wine is going down a bit too well,' said Siobhán. 'We won't tell him about the canapés, will we, Milly?' She laughed again and winked at me.

'What about them?' said Ryan, not understanding. 'And it's not fizzy *wine*...' He laughed as though explaining something to a child. 'It's vintage champagne.' He smiled at me. 'Only the best for the best.'

'No!' said Siobhán. 'No, I was only being funny... well, trying to be. Unnecessarily and unsuccessfully funny. And the vintage champagne is delicious. Not that I know anything about it, being a heathen about all nice things. And the nibbles were amazing. I haven't eaten this well since I went to McDonald's on my way home from a music festival.' She threw me a panicked look. 'But obviously these are better than McDonald's. I didn't mean to make the comparison.'

Ryan's smile was frozen on his face. 'That's good to know,' he said briskly.

'What star sign are you?' said Siobhán, eagerly.

'Star sign?'

She nodded enthusiastically. 'Leo or Virgo? When is your birthday?'

'August the twenty-fifth.'

'Jesus.' For a moment, she looked horrified.

'What's wrong with that?' he said.

'Nothing... nothing...' she blustered. 'It's just that...' She took a sip from her glass. 'No, nothing.'

The first meeting between Siobhán and Ryan couldn't have gone worse, I thought. 'We've had a really lovely time,' I began, just as my phone started to ring. It was Catriona. 'I've got to take this,' I said. 'I'm so sorry...' I moved to one side while Siobhán and Ryan stood awkwardly.

'Milly!' Catriona's voice teetered on the edge of hysteria, which was unusual as she was known as Elsa in the office because of her Ice Queen demeanour. 'We've got to write a letter for Peter Gregory before the meeting in the morning...' The Gregory Group was one of the biggest property developers in the country and they had been Catriona's client for years. '... You'll have to come into hospital...'

'Hospital?'

'Yes, I've just gone into labour...' She let out a piercing scream worthy of a slasher movie. 'St Patrick's Private!' she managed to yell, before the phone went dead.

Obviously, I'd *known* Catriona had been pregnant, but she hadn't actually *mentioned* it overtly, and I watched in silence as each day she would arrive into work with an increasingly bigger bump. Her jackets began being left unbuttoned, the waists on her silk dresses becoming looser, the heels replaced with flats, her usual double espresso was switched to decaff and then there was the addition of the 4 p.m. Twix habit. But despite it being so obvious you didn't require the brain of Miss Marple, Catriona remained utterly schtum, as though she'd been threatened by the Mafia.

'Maybe she doesn't know she's pregnant,' suggested Siobhán when we had discussed it one night at our kitchen table over a mug of tea. 'Or maybe she's in major denial.'

'Catriona's a highly intelligent woman,' I had said. 'She doesn't *do* denial. Catriona is the epitome of a highly rational, unemotional human being.'

'She obviously doesn't trust you, then,' said Siobhán. 'I hate to say it, but you are not in her inner circle. There can be no other explanation. Was there a baby shower you weren't invited to? Do people go quiet when you go near them?'

I shook my head. 'I think I am the only person she talks to in the building,' I'd said. 'She's not actually *friends* with anyone.'

'Maybe she's just putting on weight,' deduced Siobhán. 'It's happened to us all; a few months of inadvertent carb-loading and next thing you know, you're reaching for the elastic waist and the baggy jumper. Has she been eating more than usual?' Siobhán always loved a mystery drama. In another life, she would have been an old-lady detective and me her sidekick.

But why was Catriona calling me in such a panicked state? She was usually so meticulously organised and super-scheduled.

'I've got to go,' I said, trying to sound calm in front of Ryan. 'Catriona's in labour!'

'So it was a baby!' shouted Siobhán. 'I'm coming too!'
And we raced from the hotel.

4

I left Siobhán at the bus stop, where the bus was just pulling up, while I flagged down a taxi.

'Good luck!' shouted Siobhán, as I ran towards it. 'Let me know what happens? She could give birth to anything!'

Once settled in the cab, I tried to keep calm and focused. Right, I had my briefcase with my laptop and my notebook inside. Whatever work we had to do at the hospital, I was prepared. How quickly did babies come anyway? Would we have time? Didn't they take hours to come? I was grateful that I hadn't drunk very much and had only sipped at the champagne.

Catriona rang again. 'Where are you now?' Her voice sounded low and strangulated, as though something heavy was sitting on her chest.

'I'll be there in ten minutes, I am just going around Merrion Square.'

Catriona let out a low warble, a sound I didn't know a human was capable of, as though she had been taking secret bird-whistling classes.

'I'm on my own here,' she said. 'There was a nurse, but she's gone. I'm feeling... I'm feeling...' Her voice wobbled. Surely Elsa the Ice Queen wasn't scared? Catriona was invincible, never anything less than commanding and in control at work.

We both waited for the old Catriona to reassert herself.

'Anyway,' she said, finally collecting herself, 'that doesn't matter right now, but I didn't expect things to progress as they have. But we have work to do...' She breathed in tightly, as though trying to get a hold of herself. 'An email came in from Peter Gregory about an objection he's received from the council. Typical council, get their arse into gear at the final moment, making work for us. It'll mean having to change our entire defence.' She stifled another unsettling warble, and then continued. 'Peter didn't allocate enough social housing in the new development. I told him about the clause in permission, but he promised me he was dealing directly with his pal in City Hall. He and this pal obviously aren't as friendly as he thought. He needs the defence by tomorrow morning.'

'Is Noel with you?' Noel was Catriona's husband, a high-flyer in finance. I'd never met him, but from what I could tell he was equally driven.

'Noel? What's he got to do with anything? He doesn't know anything about the Gregory case.'

'No, I just meant about the baby...'

'Milly, let's just get the work done. We'll worry about the baby later. So, you've got everything, yes? Laptop?'

Delegation and Catriona had never been introduced. Normally, she had to be involved in everything, but obviously she wouldn't be able to be at the meeting in the morning, and much as I hated taking the lead, I knew I had no choice. I was a good lawyer, I just wasn't the unemotional ice queen you needed to be in order to stand up in court and slay.

'Can I bring you anything...?' I tried to think what she might need. Probably a stiff drink and an anaesthetist. 'Maybe...?' But Catriona suddenly exuded an eardrum shattering shriek which only gained in power and strength, like a hurricane passing over the Caribbean. 'Oh my God...!' She seemed to be now talking to someone who had entered her room. 'What does it take to get a caesarean around here! Things have progressed too JESUSSSS CHRISSSST quickly! I think I am giving birth to a JESSS-SUSSS monster!' There was another long scream and the phone went dead. I caught the eye of the taxi-driver in the rear view mirror. He'd obviously heard everything, he nodded at me, and I felt the car suddenly speed up, skimming the near-empty streets.

When I arrived, the hospital was deathly quiet, the corridors in semi-darkness, just the odd distant clang or bang either from machine or human, the whisper of the ghosts who walked the Victorian wards at night.

'Maternity?' I said to the man on reception. 'St Pat's Private?'

He looked up. 'And in what capacity are you visiting?'

'Professional.'

He looked surprised. 'You're a medical practitioner?'

'No, I mean, I'm a professional visitor.'

He shook his head. 'Nope. No way. You're too late.' He tapped a card sellotaped to a statue of Our Lady.

NO VISITORS AFTER 9 P.M.

'Rules are rules.'

'My boss is in labour,' I said. 'I might lose my job if I don't give her this...' I held up my briefcase. 'She'll kill me if I don't go up.' I tried out my most winning smile. 'Please?'

He surveyed me for a moment, mentally completing a risk assessment for any hints of psychopathy. 'Don't be long,' he said, finally. 'Unauthorised lingering is one of the ten causes of hospital chaos.' I didn't have time to ask him what the other nine were, because he was waving his hand in the direction of the corridor. 'Follow the signs, through main concourse, round by the shop. Lift. Sixth floor.'

I batted away my panic as I bashed at the buttons in the lift and then breathlessly dashed down the corridor to find Catriona's room.

Inside was a banshee with wild hair, smeared mascara, dressed in a long white hospital gown. Surely this woman was auditioning to be Mr Rochester's first wife in a new production of *Jane Eyre*? *This can't be the room of the perfectly and immaculately presented Catriona*, I thought, turning to go.

But this strange and wild woman looked up and for a moment I squinted, thinking I discerned the features of someone I recognised beneath the madness.

'Milly! Thank Christ you're here,' it said, 'I was beginning to give up on you and they promised me the bloody epidural an hour ago.'

It *was* Catriona. It was horrible seeing the office ice queen, the woman least likely to cry in the bathroom, in such a state of vulnerability. But she soon took control, as she always did, talking rapidly and bossing me around. She would stop every now and then and pull a tortured face, clutching her belly or her back, and then, when the moment passed, she would resume her commands.

'Let's get going. Quickly! I'll dictate, you type and we'll have the letter written in no time and ready to deliver to Peter Gregory in the morning. I've got to get this baby out, get some sleep and be in the office for 8 a.m..' She must have noticed my open jaw. 'I don't think I'll be in before 8 a.m., Milly. I know it's later than normal, but I have to be realistic. The bloody epidural team might have arrived by then.' She jabbed a finger towards the chair beside the bed. 'You sit there. Come on!'

I should have brought her something, food or a decent dressing gown and slippers, some good coffee. 'What time will Noel get here?' I was quickly unpacking my laptop and trying to find a plug socket.

'Who knows?' she said. 'He's apparently on his way.' She rolled her eyes. 'Typical. He would miss his own funeral because of work.' But she'd lost interest in Noel and his whereabouts and was utterly focused on her own work. And despite the hair, the gown, and the intermittent wailing, she was almost like the Catriona I knew.

We powered on through, the hands on the wall clock ticking loudly. Catriona paced the room, while I sat on the pleather chair, typing on my lap.

'I will need you to cross-reference and check exactly the contract they signed with the council,' she said, as we got close to midnight. 'And please look up the Housing Miscellaneous Act of 2009 and there is a clause...' She thought for a moment. 'Clause 16c? Double-check that and find out exactly what it says... but it might be the loophole the Gregory Group need.' She broke off to let out a scream, sounding like the victim of some medieval torture and clutched her belly as she slowly fell to her knees. 'I think... I think...' Her voice faltered. Finally, I thought, she was going to see sense and just let me get on with it. I could take it from here. 'I think...'

'Shhh...' I soothed, as she pawed at the bed, trying to get to her feet, as I helped her up and manoeuvred her into the chair. 'It's okay. I'll look after everything. I'll get a nurse in to check on you and the ETA of the epidural team, and I'll get you a cup of tea. I'll call Noel and find out where he is. You just...'

'I think...' she tried again, 'we can defend it under Planning and Development Act 2000. And the clause is not 16c! It's 18f!' She slapped her forehead. 'How could I be so stupid?! Now type! And type fast!'

I sat down again and typed for my life, my fingers flying over the keys like a possessed concert pianist, while Catriona dictated and I added and edited.

Between screams and moans, and the sound of Catriona aggressively bouncing on a birthing ball, we drafted a new document, furiously rebuffing any claims from the council regarding social housing, stretching ethics and morals as finely as possible without actually breaking the law and mentally planning any defence we could make if challenged. I sent the email to Peter Gregory's office. My admiration for Catriona was sky-high. Only she would be able to recollect clauses and have the presence of mind to dictate a word-perfect email. But it would have to be me who would take tomorrow's meeting. And strangely I felt completely calm, all my previous anxiety had gone. Once my mind was focused, I never gave in. Beating it was a matter of staying in control. Except I could never be sure when those moments would be.

5

Finally, we were finished and Catriona lay limp on the bed. 'When are they coming?' she said weakly.

'The epidural team? Soon, I imagine,' I said, getting up. 'I'll just ask again.'

'No! Not the bloody epidural team! Peter Gregory! I just want to make sure that I get this done and am in the office for 8 a.m..'

'Catriona, you can't go to the meeting,' I said, appalled. Surely, even Catriona knew she would have to delegate now?

'I have never missed an appointment with a client in my twenty years as a qualified lawyer,' she said, suddenly sitting up in bed like the bride of Frankenstein, 'and I am not going to start tomorrow. I absolutely refuse to tell Peter Gregory that it is because I'm having a baby. I'd rather tell him I've contracted beriberi.' She turned on me furiously. 'And don't tell him either. Don't tell anyone!' Her face darkened as though there was a cloud overhead. 'Oh Christ...' she began to shout. 'Oh Chhrrissst!'

I grabbed the emergency bell and pressed it so hard I thought I would break it and then ran into the corridor, shouting to a passing nurse, panic cranking up. Being here in the hospital was triggering all sorts of things. Dad had been in and out of St Pat's in the last year of his life. I was twenty-seven when he died and I felt like it was another lifetime. The worst day was when they told us there was no hope. Up until that moment, I didn't even contemplate he wouldn't make it. And it was from then the panic attacks, which had begun when I was a teenager, made a return.

I was working my way up in McCoyMcAvoy, a very junior lawyer, and doing my best to stay calm and focused – which was easy enough but still I had that constant background hum of anxiety. It had really become worse after Dad died, but instead of going away as you might expect *and hope*, it decided to hang around, sometimes spilling over into panic where I had had to keep breathing and stay calm. And if I didn't I would feel it begin in my stomach and then the cold whisper down my spine, the squeezing of my organs, the twist of my liver, the poking of my spleen, the slow, agonising creep up to my heart and my lungs and, by that stage, I was usually hiding in the office toilets gasping for my life, my whole body was being crushed by this... this *thing*. Grief, I suppose.

And now, lately, I could feel it again, stronger and more insistent, as though it was getting restless and I could feel the odious breath of the Black Terror breathing down my neck. *Not now*, I told it. *Not now! Come on!* I roared silently, as I raced back into the room to check on Catriona and then back out to the corridor to shout for help. The panic attack would have to wait. Catriona was on her own and the last thing anyone needed was me on my knees, making a show of myself and drowning in air. Pure willpower and determination kicked in, pushing it away, refusing to give up as I wrested back control.

Suddenly, a phalanx of nurses rushed past me, as I steadied myself and sucked in a breath. And another one. And another. And then that feeling of me being brought back into myself, as though there had been part of me trying to escape, like drops of mercury clinging back together, my skin prickles subsiding, my body warm again. I was back from the brink, feeling utterly foolish. Everyone else I knew just got on with life, they didn't have invisible battles with dark forces, as though I was a living computer game. Grief came and went like a storm. I just wanted the calm missing of someone, where you can remember them without feeling utterly wretched.

Inside the room, one nurse was speaking to Catriona as though she was deaf. 'Hello, Catriona, I'm Sister Mary, and you're now fully dilated. Baby's on its way. Lie down there now, there's a good woman. We'll wheel you down to the delivery suite... I said, we'll wheel you down to the delivery suite and baby will be out before you can say—'

'Epidural.' Catriona was speaking in a tiny voice. 'Epidural.'

'We don't have time for one of those, now,' shouted the nurse. 'It's busier than Moore Street on Christmas Eve here tonight. The yelling and roaring that's going on, you wouldn't believe. You'd think they were being tortured, the lot of them.'

Catriona meekly lay still on the bed, her face grey, eyes scared, as though she was about go into battle but had resolved to go down quietly and bravely.

'I know you,' said the nurse, turning to me. 'Sarah Byrne's sister? How's she getting on? She's never out any more. Never at any of the hooleys or get-togethers.'

Sarah was based in St Theresa's geriatrics ward and as far as I could tell had become a purely nocturnal creature, working nights because she was one of the few nurses on the ward without either children or aged parents. She and her boyfriend, Hugh, had split up a few months earlier, not that Sarah had actually talked about it as she had become increasingly and insanely private about her life and wouldn't ever tell me anything about anything, not even what she was watching on Netflix these days, never mind why she and Hugh had split up. Hugh was like my adopted brother, and Mum and I missed him, but neither of us could say anything, as whenever we did, we were silenced with a frown from Sarah.

'How's she getting on?' shouted the nurse again.

'I'm not sure,' I said, trying to think when the last time I'd seen Sarah was. Maybe last week? Or the week before.

Another nurse bundled a gown and a surgical mask into my arms. 'Birth partner?' she said, without waiting for a response. 'We're going to wheel Mum down now. Follow us.'

'No... I...'

'Don't leave, Milly,' whimpered Catriona, defeated. Her voice trailed away. 'I can't do this on my own.'

What if I had a panic attack in the room? What if I fainted? 'Catriona...'

'I know I should have called one of my friends,' she said. 'But I wasn't meant to be doing this for another eight days. This was not on my schedule...'

The bed was jimmied out of the room and into the corridor, gaining speed as it bobsleighed down the smooth terrazzo. I hesitated for a moment, wondering what the hell to do.

Catriona suddenly sat up as though electrified, and twisted around to shout at me. 'Don't even think about leaving!' she shouted, as the bed rumbled down the corridor. 'I am NOT going in there alone!'

There was nothing else to do but wriggle into my gown and mask and run after them.

6

Twenty minutes later, there was the glorious sound of a tiny newborn human, who was quickly burrito-wrapped and tucked in beside Catriona. Eyes squeezed shut, a button nose, a little hospital-issue stripy hat on its head, the baby was beautiful.

A baby. *A real live baby*. The word miracle is overused, especially on adverts for cleaning products, but here it seemed perfectly apt.

'Ten toes, ten fingers, seven pounds and six ounces,' confirmed the nurse.

'Oh thank God,' said Catriona, nose to nose with the baby, tears in her eyes. 'What is it? Boy or girl?'

'Girl,' said the nurse. 'We've just done six in a row. You'd think there was some kind of feminist plot.'

It was remarkable, after the whirlwind, the calm and the utter amazement that there was now an extra person in the room. And for some reason I thought about the time Dad brought home our dog, Betty, when she was only seven weeks old. He'd heard about the litter of puppies which had been abandoned beside the canal, and without telling us, he brought one home – just to see,' he said, but he'd already fallen in love with the small frizzy white snowball, even before he lifted her out of the car to carry her into the house. As soon as Mum, Sarah and I saw that tiny scrap of fuzz, we too were smitten. Sarah and I swaddled her in blankets, feeding her milk out of a saucer as though she was a cat. And then the first night, she crawled onto Dad's lap, in his favourite armchair, claiming him as her own.

'She's a beauty,' said the nurse, smiling. 'They all are, obviously. But this one's a little angel.'

Catriona nodded. 'I think she might be,' she said. 'I really think she might be.'

'And a name?' said the nurse. 'They're getting more and more unusual these days. A few shockers. There was even a Horatio last week.' she was laying the bed and tucking in the sheets so fast you couldn't see her hands move, wrapping Catriona within the folds so she could barely lift her body.

'Noel had said he wanted to call her Noeleen if she was a girl,' Catriona said. 'Family tradition. They're all Noels or Noeleens – it gets very confusing. But this little one definitely doesn't look like a Noeleen...'

'We're nearly all finished now,' said the nurse, kindly. 'We'll wheel you back to the ward.' She turned to me. 'You say hello to that sister of yours,' she said. 'Tell her not to be a stranger and that we miss her on our nights out. She was always the first one up for the karaoke. Always doing Nirvana. Blessed relief from the usual wall-to-wall Abba.'

The thought that I should go and visit Sarah right now seemed a good one. She would love to see me, I was sure of it.

Back in the room, Catriona asked for her phone so she could call Noel, while I, slightly dazed but elated by the whole surreal experience, trotted down to see if the canteen was open. Amazingly it was but with a lone member of staff, most of the chairs stacked on the long tables and a heavily pregnant woman in a dressing gown eating a sandwich.

'What do you order for a woman who has just given birth?' I asked the woman behind the counter.

'Toast and butter,' she said, unhesitatingly. 'And tea.'

'Twice,' I said, suddenly feeling starved myself. It had been a long time since those nibbles.

As I turned the corner to go back into Catriona's room, a man – rocket-propelled – overtook, panting hard and skidded into Catriona's room. It had to be Noel.

I followed a few minutes later and, after knocking softly on the door, I went in. Noel was holding the baby and gazing down at her face, his face one big beam of love. He looked on the verge of tears.

'Can you believe this?' he said. 'Can you believe how wonderful my wife is?'

'Noel, Milly, Milly, Noel,' said Catriona, weakly.

'Isn't she, though?' he said. 'I mean, we spend ten years trying to get pregnant and my marvellous wife just gets on with it, and even delivers the baby ahead of schedule.' He gazed at Catriona. 'Never one to miss a deadline, are you?'

She rolled her eyes, but she was smiling.

He turned back to me. 'Thank you, Milly, for being here. I can't believe I missed it. I was in my hotel room, long day of meetings, shoes off, watching TV on the bed, all the time in the world... and then Catriona called!' He looked stunned. 'I have never packed so quickly, took a taxi to Heathrow.'

'We thought births could be scheduled like meetings,' said Catriona. 'Turns out, they can't.' she sank back into the hospital pillow.

'She's going to keep us on our toes, this one.' Noel gently kissed the baby's head. 'Look at this girl,' he said, 'look at our little angel.' he smiled at Catriona, a tear rolling down his face. 'I've always wanted this particular variety of baby. The girl kind. We're going to call her Noeleen,' he went on. 'After my Granny, and my aunt and my sister...'

'Over my dead body.' Catriona struggled to sit up. 'She's going to be Lydia, after *my* grandmother.'

'But...' And then he shrugged. 'I think I know when I'm beaten.' he kissed the baby again. 'Looks like that's the end of that particular family tradition.'

Fathers and daughters. A beautiful thing. Watching him hold Lydia so closely and so tenderly, I wondered if Dad did the same to Sarah and me. 'Hello, you two,' he'd say, when he came home from work. 'And how are my sparkling drops of joy?' I felt myself tearing up at the memory. Grief was such a frustrating and all-consuming process. It wasn't something you could walk away from, it kept you locked in, and only when it decided to release you could you join everyone else who had lost someone and were now done with grieving and could keep their memories in their hearts but still get on with their own life.

'Noel,' Catriona, who was recovering fast and back in control, said, 'you'll have to stay here tomorrow morning because I've got a meeting. And I will have to organise the nanny with the agency and it might take a little while...'

'Meeting?' said Noel, nearly laughing.

'Yes, meeting. It's at 10 a.m..'

'You can't go to the meeting,' he said, looking flabbergasted. He was obviously used to Catriona's work ethic, but this was going too far.

For a moment, she looked flummoxed, as though utterly unused to having to explain herself. 'Can't? Can't? Noel, I haven't ever missed a client meeting in my whole career. Milly and I have been working on our response. Peter Gregory is relying on me.'

'I'm sure Milly is more than capable of handling things for a few days.'

Catriona ignored him. 'I'll see you in the morning, Milly.'

'Okay.' I turned to go.

'And, Milly?' she said. 'I can't thank you enough for helping with the Gregory response and also for being there for me... and for Lydia.'

When I got outside the main building, I sank into the silence of the night, like stepping out of a disco, noise and chaos behind me. I held up my hand. There was a slight tremor. But I'd done it, I'd seen off another panic attack and survived.

I felt pretty good as I made my way across the grounds to St Theresa's geriatrics ward, to find the enigma that was my younger sister, Sarah.

7

It was still only April, so the night was cold, and in the dark I could just about make out the dimly lit signs directing me to St Theresa's. I began to make my way across broken pathways and the dark journey to where Sarah worked. I curved around the back of the kitchens and tramped over a scrubby piece of land to Geriatrics.

Sarah had always planned on being a nurse from when she was about nine and became utterly obsessed with *The Flying Doctors,* which was set in the Australian outback and the medical staff flew around in waterplanes and every day there was a new and terrible illness-related drama to solve. Mum had to rearrange our whole lives to make sure we were home for 4 p.m.. As a teenager, Sarah spent every Saturday volunteering at a centre for people with learning and physical disabilities. She'd come home, shower and change, and then and go off to grunge clubs with her friends. She met the lovely Hugh while she was training and when they both qualified – him as a junior doctor – they spent eighteen months working in Senegal in a refugee camp. She was a good person, Sarah was. But, lately, I felt something was up. And she wasn't talking about it. At least not to me. Maybe my impromptu visit would show Sarah how much I was there for her, and how much I cared. Perhaps, she'd open up to me again?

St Theresa's Geriatrics looked distinctly under-loved, its dark green paint was peeling off, the sign outside was missing all its vowels. It was an old prefab, which was as far from fab as possible, and nothing like my gleaming workplace.

I rang the bell and, on the click, pushed open the door and immediately stumbled into a bucket, which was catching drips from a leak in the roof after the recent rain we'd had.

A bleary-eyed nurse on reception looked up.

'Hi!' I said, overly cheerily. 'I'm Milly Byrne, Sarah's sister. Is she here?'

'We don't normally get visitors at this time,' she said. 'Is everything all right?'

'Oh yes!' I said. 'I was just passing and thought I'd drop in.'

I signed the visitor's book she slid towards me. 'She's in with Ollie, I think. Last room on the left.' Her head ducked back down again to her computer screen.

The whole building and corridor was so low lit that you would need infrared goggles to find your way around. Probably, by the time you'd worked here for a bit, you could move around without walking into walls. My pupils refused to dilate to plate-sized dimensions so I shuffled forwards hoping not to bang into any walls.

At the end of the corridor, sitting on the edge of a bed, talking to an old man, I found her. And if it wasn't for the royal-blue uniform, Sarah looked just like her normal self, long brown hair twisted up on top of her head in a messy bun, her tattoo – a smudge of an indiscernible design which she'd had done in Thailand years back – visible above her shoes. She was holding his hand and talking in a soft voice, reassuring him, listening and even smiling. I couldn't remember the last time I'd seen her smile.

'Go to the library and pick it up,' Ollie was saying. 'Life changing.'

'I will,' she said. Her smile so lovely, it was like a reward.

'He's a genius,' the man continued. 'Malcolm Gladwell. Remember that name.'

'I will, Ollie,' she said, still in a low voice and standing up and moving to the end of his bed. 'And I'll make sure you get your tea first in the morning,' she added, checking his chart. 'I know you like it hot.' she picked up a tray of syringes and tiny pots of tablets.

He grinned at her. 'Piping,' he said. 'None of your lukewarm stew.'

'You get some sleep, okay?'

'Maybe...' he said. 'If I'm lucky. I used to take it for granted, but shut-eye is a luxury now.'

I felt like a spy, watching and listening. I shouldn't have come, trespassing on her working life. I took a step backwards, turning round and ready to flee.

'Milly!' Sarah almost dropped her tray.

'I'm sorry!' I mouthed, helplessly, feeling awful.

'Jesus Christ!' she shout-whispered. 'What the hell are you doing here?'

'Sorry... I...'

'Is everything all right? Is it Mum?'

'No, everything's fine,' I said. 'I just thought I'd call in.'

'Call in?' She shook her head at me, as though I'd lost my final marble. 'This is a *social* call? Have you been *drinking*?'

'I've been at a birth,' I babbled, desperate to explain. 'Catriona's had a baby. Lydia. She was working late and then her waters broke and her husband, Noel, was in London, so he didn't make it, but we needed to do work for the morning and so she rang me and I ended up her birth partner!' startled by the reality that I was actually at a birth, I grinned at Sarah's stone face. 'And your friend, Maria, says hello and that the karaoke isn't the same without you. All Abba, apparently. Anyway, I thought I'd stop by for a cup of tea...'

I managed somehow to stop talking, desperately wanting to tell her about the near panic attack I'd had and wishing I could confide in her and she would tell me I was going to be all right and that this wasn't going to be my life forever, that I wouldn't need to keep fighting off the Black Terror and that joy and fun would come back into my life. And I wanted her to tell me what was going on with her so I could give her advice and tell her that everything was all right. And most of all – *most of all* – I wanted to know if she missed Dad as much as I still did, or had she managed to compartmentalise and get on with things. And there was something else: I missed her. I missed that girl who cried when she couldn't watch her favourite Australian soap opera, the person who played Nirvana far too loudly, the woman who used to always make me laugh, my fellow sparkling drop of joy.

'Do you really want a cup of tea?' she said. 'Don't you want to go home? I know *I* would prefer to be in bed rather than in hospital.'

'A quick one?' I said. 'If it's not too much trouble?'

Sarah rolled her eyes and turned away. 'Come on then,' she said, signalling me to follow.

In the tea room, I sank into the chair, wishing I was in my own bed, asleep. And a memory skidded past, the way memories do, like a cloud, of another night, a lifetime ago and being this tired. My ex, Darragh, and I had missed the last bus home and being students with no money, we had to walk all the way. It took hours. I remember that feeling of collapsing into bed, a tangle of us.

'Hospital-issue mug all right for you?' asked Sarah. 'We don't do bone china here.'

I nodded, 'Of course,' letting the memory cloud go again. I'd worked out a long time ago that when they floated in front of you, you could gently push them on. It was when you grabbed them and studied them, as though trying to get inside them, the problems started. Not a good thing for someone with a predilection for anxiety.

I took the mug from Sarah and wrapped my hands around it, soothing and warm.

'I think there's something wrong with Betty,' said Sarah, sitting down across from me. 'Her breathing's weird sometimes and she keeps wanting to sleep.'

'I'm sure she's fine,' I said, dismissing her. 'You're just panicking.'

She shrugged and looked away. 'I just thought you might be interested, that's all.'

'I am!' I insisted. 'It's just that you're always worrying about Betty and she's *always* okay. Remember that time she was limping and you were convinced she had rickets? Or the time she vomited and you were worried she was gluten intolerant?' I was trying to make her smile, but she refused.

'I just love her, that's all,' she said, crossing her arms.

I sighed and tried to start again. 'So, how are you?'

'Fine,' she said. 'Amazing, fabulous, couldn't be better. And I'm moving back in with Mum for a while.'

'Why? Is everything all right? Are you okay?'

She nodded. 'I couldn't afford the flat on my own. Hugh said he would pay for my rent, but it didn't seem fair. Now we're *not* together.'

'What happened?' I asked gently.

'*Sometimes* you can't make things work.' She looked away.

'Sar...' I began. But she looked tired and I decided that now was not the right time for big talk or even small talk. I shouldn't have come. I hugged Sarah goodbye. 'See you at Mum's.' It used to be 'see you at home.'

She hugged me back, 'See you at Mum's,' she echoed.

8

The only thing that got me out of bed after too-little sleep was the thought of coffee. Every day, I bought two from the café across from the office – one for me and one for Catriona.

This morning, Terry, the café owner, almost fainted. 'One?' he said. 'She *died*?'

'She had a baby,' I explained.

'Same thing,' he said. And maybe in the world of corporate law it was.

Obviously she was delirious the night before when insisting on attending the meeting. Although I hadn't heard from her, the thought of her coming was unimaginable. I would have to take charge for the next few days at least. I knew I could do it, obviously. But it was better to be in the shadow of the highly competent Catriona. When I first graduated, I had plans of having my own practice one day, Milly Byrne, Solicitor, but once you are taken on by a huge firm such as McCoyMcAvoy, you tend to get sucked in, and often your confidence that you could do any of this on your own diminishes. You are part of a machine, and the most important part of mine was Catriona. Today, I would have to fake it to make it.

The Peter Gregory meeting was at 10 a.m. and I sat down at my desk and began to prepare for the day. Earlier, at home, when I was dressing, I could feel the slight tremble in my hand again. I had spent the last five years trying to move on. I was a success. I had done it. And yet...

I had to fight again to pull myself away from it. Not again. I couldn't bear to be thought of as that failure, the person who couldn't handle life.

My phone beeped. A text from Catriona.

On my way. If consultant gets here in time. Fingers crossed.

Really?! How are you?

Feeling great. See you at 9.45 a.m.

Okay! See you soon.

A knock on my office door made my heart sink. It was Jarleth, one of my fellow junior lawyers.

'Milly, can you spare a couple of minutes? I know how *busy* you are...' Jarleth had a habit of making everything he said sound deeply sarcastic. 'I don't want to take up any more of your time than is totally necessary...'

Over the years, I had discovered being super-nice to Jarleth was the only way. 'Yes, of course.' I smiled. 'What can I do for you?'

He had a clipboard under his arm. 'I am aware how important you are these days,' he said. 'Catriona keeps you so busy. She doesn't stop and *nor do you*! It's sweet, actually. The only all-female team in the building having to work harder than anyone else to keep up.'

The tremor in my hand had miraculously stopped. Cured by fury and misogyny.

'Heard you won the Fitzgerald PLC case. Congratulations.' He was speaking through his gritted teeth. 'Or rather congratulations to Catriona,' he said. 'She doesn't ever let you lead, does she? I wonder if it's because of trust issues or perhaps she doesn't feel you're ready. We all know Mrs Ice Queen is a control freak and treats you more like her PA. Which is fine, if you're both happy with the arrangement. Which you obviously are. Colm trusts me to take on cases solo. Suits both of us. He gets to hit a few balls on the golf course or imbibe at lunch and I get the kind of experience I need to be made partner. But maybe now she's had a baby, she might take more time off, want to be at home with the brat, not be as focused on breaking the glass ceiling.'

How on earth did he know? But then in Ireland, there was no such thing as a secret. News always got out.

'And we all thought she was busy building an ice palace for one.' He moved towards me. 'May I?' He said, sitting on the edge of my desk. 'Or am I *encroaching* on your personal space? I wouldn't want to have HR on my back or some kind of harassment writ. Men can't talk to a woman these days.' He rolled his eyes. 'It's just that I have important news and I have to take down names.' He picked up my beautiful fountain pen, given to me by Mum and Dad when I graduated. I stopped myself from snatching it off him. 'Is that your sister?' Jarleth had now picked up a photograph of the four of us, taken years and years ago when we all went to Paris for Mum and Dad's wedding anniversary. 'She's very pretty,' he said. 'Very different to you. How does that make you feel? Having such a good-looking sister?'

'I'm fine about it,' I said.

'Not that you aren't *bad*-looking,' he went on, blithely. 'But being attractive is wasted on lawyers, don't you think? No one wants a *beautiful* lawyer representing you, do they? It's distracting. And they are often a bit thick.'

I could feel my hand tremble again. I should tell him where to go, but I wanted as little drama as possible. I shuffled my papers and glanced at the clock to show I was busy. 'Jarleth,' I said. 'What is it you want to see me about?'

'Of course! Sorry, sorry! I just wanted to share news of my promotion.'

'Promotion?' There weren't many opportunities for advancement in McCoyMcAvoy as you usually had to wait for a partner to die, but none of them showed any sign of doing so. They were too well paid. 'You're a partner?'

Jarleth grinned. 'Not yet,' he said. 'But as Mr McAvoy was saying the other day... We had a drink together. He's a great guy, so funny... Ever been out with him? No? Sad, so sad for you. Anyway, he was saying that it was only a matter of time before I was made partner, being the most experienced lawyer at our level.'

I kept my face neutral. Interest would only encourage him. I was normally cool, calm and collected at work and even though I could feel the hum of grief, I could keep it away from the office. But lately, I was becoming thinner-skinned, and less able to hide it. It was as though I could handle it better when people expected you to be grieving, but if after five years, you still weren't *over it* then maybe there was something wrong with you?

'Not *partner*. Not yet anyway. Instead you are looking at McCoyMc-Avoy's brand new *inaugural* director of social affairs. Some might call it social secretary, others minister of fun, even craicmaster or prankmeister... My new role – or extra responsibility – is to increase the happiness levels in this organisation. To bring in more fun.'

'Fun?' The company and I did need more fun, but definitely not Jarleth-organised fun.

'Apparently,' he said, 'we are all working too hard. Too many people on stress leave, burnt out, that kind of thing. Other law firms have already upped the fun factor, leading to a nosedive in stress-related complaints to HR. Those who play together, work better, are happier, et cetera. I'm incredibly flattered to be entrusted in this important life-saving project and the mental wellbeing of the staff. And so I have entered McCoyMcAvoy in the Irish Workplace Craic Awards. All we have to do is have fun! I video us and upload to the site. I just need you to sign here...' He held the clipboard out. 'Permission for us to use your image for the purpose of... blah blah... read the small, print, there's a good lawyer.' Jarleth slid to his feet. 'I'll be sending an email around,' he said, walking out, 'keep everyone informed.'

And that was it, I had let him get under my skin. I had wanted to be a lawyer all my life. This was my *dream*. Everything was going the way it should. All that studying, all the money for my education paid by Mum and Dad, all the times I didn't go out or have fun, because I either had to study or work. And this was the end result. Me sitting at my desk having to remind myself to breathe, just because of a stupid colleague.

My thoughts spiralled and I felt the panic rise. I had to keep breathing, before I was overwhelmed. The photo of the four of us calmed me. Dad's kind eyes looking at me, his arm around Sarah's and my shoulders. *I wish you were here, Dad,* I thought. *I wish you could tell me what I am doing so wrong.*

9

By 9.45 a.m., there was still no sign of Catriona, even though I had got myself more or less back on an even keel by a combination of going to the loo and washing my hands and then making a cup of coffee in the communal lunch room. They were enough of a distraction to keep my thoughts under control.

As I entered the meeting room, I looked at the clock: 9.55.a.m.. Still no sign. Instead Peter Gregory turned up early and typically rushed, as though he had to get through his day as quickly as possible or that he knew we charged by the hour, and there was no way he would let this meeting go on for any longer than it needed.

'Where's Catriona?' he said, after we had shaken hands.

'She's on her way,' I replied. 'Hopes to be here as soon as possible.' I smiled, hoping I looked competent. In the meeting room, we sat on opposite sides of the desk.

'We received your email,' he began, referring to the one I had sent from the hospital the night before. I hoped there weren't too many spelling or grammar mistakes. 'Maybe you would outline exactly how you are going to defend it, and what you think are the chances that we can knock the council's legs from under them... You know how I feel about the council. Interfering little maggots...'

The clock had passed 10 a.m., I could see Peter Gregory looking even more antsy than usual and so there was nothing for it except to get on with it.

And somehow, despite the sweat clinging to my skin, it went well. Everything Catriona and I had discussed was said and I was able to bring in relevant precedents and acted strong and decisive when talking about the council and what we would do. This was our job as corporate lawyers. It was better not to dwell upon issues of ethics or integrity. You wouldn't be able to live with yourself if you did.

After half an hour, I was beginning to wrap things up when there was a sound behind us as the door opened.

'Hope I'm not too late,' said Catriona's voice. 'Peter...' She held out a hand. 'I am so sorry.' I was held up at another meeting. But I'm here now and we can move things on.'

Her hair was brushed, she had on a full face of make-up and was wearing her lovely Max Mara camel coat. She did *not* look like a woman who gave birth less than twelve hours ago. She smiled at us both and slid into the seat beside me.

'I think we've covered everything,' said Peter.

'Everything?'

He nodded. 'Yup.'

'And you're happy?'

'Very.' He smiled.

Catriona looked at me. 'You mean...?'

I nodded, feeling guilty, knowing how hard it was for her to let go.

Peter was standing, ready to go. 'Need to get on. Catriona. Milly, I'll be in touch.' He shook our hands. 'Milly's going to destroy the council for me.' He grinned happily.

'Oh good,' said Catriona. 'And we'll send everything on to their...' She paused. 'Their... their...' She looked at me, helplessly. This had to be Catriona's first ever brain blank.

'... Barrister,' I prompted.

'Yes! Of course! Well, we'll talk soon,' she said.

When he'd gone, Catriona sank back down into her chair. 'I'm so sorry to land you in that,' she said. 'I tried to explain that I had never missed a meeting, but the doctors said there was nothing they could do. I just had to wait. But it was a stroke of luck that I didn't have the epidural because I was talking to another woman in the showers this morning, and she couldn't walk. Okay, so I am leaking... but I've heard horror stories. And I'm feeling fine! I've bounced back!' She looked pretty pleased with herself but still hadn't taken off her coat.

'Are you staying?' I asked.

'Why?'

'Your coat,' I said. 'It's boiling in here.'

'I didn't have a change of clothes,' she admitted, lowering her voice. 'And I have leaked all over my blouse. But I couldn't not come...' Her eyes were dazed as though she was startled by the turn of events. 'Lydia couldn't be in safer hands back at the hospital and I managed to bring the nanny forward by a week, so she's starting tonight as soon as I am discharged.' There was a slight maniacal quality to her grin. But then the colour drained from her face and her eyes seemed to spin around. 'I can't stand up,' she said. 'Would you mind giving me a hand, Milly? My legs have gone wobbly. I knew I should have taken an extra valium.' She leaned heavily on me as I pulled her to her feet. 'Maybe I will head back to hospital now,' she said, sounding a little embarrassed. 'I'm sure I'm fine, but I would just really, *really* like to lie down.'

We managed to get downstairs in the lift without meeting anyone. I flagged down a taxi and bundled her in. Catriona's skin was grey, her make-up had slithered off her face and her hair had fallen flat.

'Thank you, Milly. I will be fine in an hour or so and we can chat through a few things. We have the Fitzgerald injunction to consider and then there's the Treasury PLC papers to oversee.'

'I'll keep everything going,' I promised. 'You get some sleep.'

'Remember, Milly,' she said, sticking her grey face out of the window, eyes wide like a nineties clubber, 'don't tell anyone! There's no baby!'

I didn't like to tell her that everyone knew already.

After I had told the driver where to go, the taxi sped off, with Catriona's head leaning against the glass of the window, eyes closed, mouth slightly agape, already fast asleep.

10

Mr McAvoy was the head of the company. Mr McCoy – whoever he was – was long gone even before I joined a decade earlier. Susie, Mr McAvoy's PA, called me on my desk phone. 'Would you pop up and see Himself? He just wants a little chat about something,' she said, airily.

Of course, my first thought was I was being fired. Why else would the head of the company want to see a junior lawyer like me? Maybe it was the way I hid behind Catriona when even Jarleth was leading on cases and being the new social secretary. Sorry, *craicmeister*.

'Is now okay?' Susie prompted. 'Only he has an appointment in half an hour and can squeeze you in.'

So, it was going to be a rapid firing, I thought, sucking in a breath. My glittering corporate law career finally over. But why then, did I feel something inside that made me feel excited? Why was an imminent sacking stirring feelings of relief? Did I not love my job? I'd worked so hard to get here after all. I climbed the stairs to the top floor.

Susie's desk was positioned just outside Mr McAvoy's office. She stopped typing and looked up. 'How's the baby? Heard you were at the birth and everything. How was it? I can't believe Catriona's a mother. I'm organising some flowers from Mr McAvoy. Not that he knows, of course.

And do you think she'd like a spa voucher? Something like that. Let me know, all right.'

'Yes...' I said, uncertainly, wondering what to say. If the news was out, then there was little point in me denying it. But Catriona had specifically told me not to say anything. I did what any self-respecting lawyer would do, I fudged it. 'A baby is always good news,' I said.

'So, spill,' Susie went on. 'How come you were at the birth? What's the baby like? Lydia, isn't it? Lovely name. Is Catriona around today? I think HR want to talk to her about her maternity leave. I do love babies,' she went on. 'Newborns are ridiculously cute. My sister had one. He's a monster now. Six years old and he has them all terrified. He's like a little Kim Jong Un.'

'Didn't you say I had to hurry to see Mr McAvoy?' I said, not wanting to break Catriona's confidence and also curious to see if I was indeed being sacked.

'Yes, yes of course.' she waved me in. 'Go on in. He's expecting you.'

It was like knocking on the door of a headmaster's office.

'Enter!'

Mr McAvoy's sixth floor office had even better views than Catriona's. From the wraparound glass windows over the city, you could see right up the river Liffey, the city's avenues and Georgian squares laid out like a map of a perfect city. From the other side, you could see the houses petering out and becoming green and then sweeping up to the purple and green of the Wicklow mountains. In college, I was a member of a hillwalking club, and once a month we would head out and brave those paths. It was one of the best things about college, a perfect antidote to all that brain-numbing legal study.

Mr McAvoy, as always immaculately dressed in old-school double-breasted pinstripe, red handkerchief in the pocket, glanced up from his screen and half stood to greet me. His computer screen was tilted a little and I could see he'd been watching a tennis match, I could make out the orange of the clay court and hear that unmistakable sound of a tennis crowd, the clapping, the oohs, the umpire's monotone. 'Ah, Miss Byrne!' he said, briefly clutching my hand. 'So good of you to make the arduous journey to the eyrie, where I am locked away from doing any harm.' He smiled at me.

If he was going to fire me, then I would prefer if it was done quickly. That's what happened in the corporate environment. You were given your notice and you were marched to your desk to collect your things and then marched out.

'Do you follow tennis?' He didn't want for my answer. 'Susie can find me tennis matches from all over the world,' he said. 'Tunes the computer in, somehow, like a visual radio. There's always some match going on some-where. Used to play, of course, until my knee was banjaxed. And then the other one followed suit, as they often do. Two dicky knees is most unfortu-nate. How are your knees? My elbows are the elbows of a twenty-one year old, but that's no use. The knees, you can't do anything with godawful knees. Still waiting for two new ones. But one isn't bad enough, apparently. They want me crawling into hospital before they'll give me one.' He smiled at me. 'Now, I suppose you might be wondering why I've encroached upon your very busy day.'

Maybe he wasn't firing me? Oh God. Not *co*-social secretary then? I really couldn't spend more time with Jarleth. I would prefer to be fired.

'I have, Ms Byrne,' he went on, 'something I need taking care of. A personal matter.'

What on earth was he asking me to do?

'Of course,' he was saying, 'I wish I could do it myself, because I wouldn't mind flexing a few of the old muscles, you know. It's exactly the kind of thing I used to do in the old days, before Mr McCoy and myself got too big for our boots. I was all about David and Goliath in those days, except now we're Goliath. But this little thing came up and I want you to look after it.' There was the sound of polite applause from his computer. 'Peter Gregory spoke very highly of you, passed on his compliments, said you handled yourself very well... I ran into him downstairs.'

'Thank you, Sir. What is it you need me to do?'

'A friend of my mother needs some legal representation. Marvellous woman. A Mrs Mary Murphy. She's my godmother, lovely woman, went to school with my dear old mama. Now, Mary has found herself, at the grand old age of ninety, to be in a spot of bother. None of her making, of course. But at the hands of people we normally defend. The dreaded property developer. They are trying to push her out of her charming little flat on the top floor of Number One, Merrion Square. A forced buyout – and a rather aggressive one at that. Everyone else in the building has been bought out and they've bought the building behind hers as well, going to develop both, merge them into one super-block. But Mary Murphy, being the indomitable woman she is, remains firm. She's lived there for donkey's years and has no intention of leaving behind all her memories. She wants to see out her days in her home. It's all pro bono, obviously, but I have sworn solemnly to her that all will be well and that we will win. Which we will.' He smiled at me. 'Won't we?'

Representing a *person*? Someone's home? Something actually meaningful? I hadn't done that kind of thing for years. That was the old me, who cared about clients and worried about them and fought for them. I liked my facts and figures and unemotional clients.

'Who are the developers?' I asked, just for something to say, and trying to act interested. I would turn it down, of course, say I was far too busy.

'Alpha Holdings. Heard of them? No? Me neither? Well, this shower has a forced-order-to-buy. Show people enough money and they'll take it. But Mrs Murphy is proving a little more intransigent. Her whole life is there. I know we love a developer in this line of work. Deep pockets, easy profits... However – now, keep this between ourselves – but they're not the kind of people I approve of. So, you'll call her and take it on. Thank you, Milly.' Seemingly I was dismissed, Mr McAvoy's eyes were back on the screen. 'Don't make me have to watch that woman moving out into some old people's home. My mother won't be pleased if we don't win this, and we wouldn't want my mother not speaking to me, would we? I knew from very early on, happy mother, happy son.' There was the sound of cheering and even some kind of singing. 'Knife edge,' he said. 'It's all hanging on a knife edge. Break point.' He looked back at me. 'I'll phone Mrs Murphy and tell her to expect your call.'

'I'll go and see her tomorrow,' I heard myself saying.

'Thank you, Milly,' he said. 'Susie will give you all the details and the file. And keep me abreast of developments!'

11

_____

From working with them (and going out with one), I knew property developers were a pretty ruthless bunch. They weren't in the business to preserve the fabric of the city or to make life better for its citizens. They were single minded and focused on only one thing – making money. Which was fine. Except money can make you blind to everything else. It becomes all-encompassing. But what could stop them? Developers forced out vulnerable people all the time. If they had planning permission, there was nothing Mrs Murphy could do. Normally, they bought a property and only then applied for planning permission, knowing with a good firm of lawyers behind them, they were unbeatable. The letter from a Mr Hessling, the lawyer representing Alpha Holdings, stated the company's position and how it expected the planning to be waved through by the council, because of the 'outstanding value such a development would bring to the city'. It was classic arrogance, the kind I had become used to in my work in corporate law.

In response, I drafted a letter stating the facts and legalities and that Mrs Murphy would not be moving out and that the building could not be rezoned and repurposed due to a clause in the 1978 Building Act which claimed that any structure before cannot be repurposed without unanimous agreement of the tenants and that Mrs Murphy would not be giving her agreement.

My phone beeped.

Text from Mum:

Angela and I are in the Westbury hotel having afternoon tea. Come and join us. Xxx

What time?

Now?

Can't. Am too busy. Have a lovely time. See you soon. Love you. xxx

Five seconds later, a text from Auntie Angela:

Life is 4 lvng. U wnt regrt nt wking

I can't.

U can. Will order btl prosecco. Sarah cming 2. Lve u v mch xxx

I could have done without going out after work, especially with the exhaustion just beginning to land after last night's activities. But Auntie Angela was officially the world's most persuasive woman. And anyway, Mum rarely came into town, so this was something of an occasion. I called Siobhán on the way and told her all about the events of the night before. 'So it was a baby!' she said, delighted. 'Why didn't she just say? When are you coming home? Because I need to talk to you.'

'Soon,' I said. She probably wanted to discuss the fact that Ryan was a Leo or whatever. Or that Jupiter was colliding with Pluto and we should be vigilant. 'I'm just meeting Mum and Angela in the Westbury.'

I'd arrived at the hotel, through the revolving doors, up the steps and entered the large lounge, with swaying palms and sinkingly-deep carpet and the tinkling of the grand piano.

Mum and Angela were totally different as sisters, but they had always been very close. Angela had lived abroad for long periods of her life, but she moved back permanently, six years ago, when Dad was dying. It was her, that year, who ferried Mum around and kept her going, discreetly helping, pre-empting anything and everything, even making sure there was always milk in the fridge or that Mum's electric blanket was switched on after she'd spent a long day in the hospital and, later, hospice. Angela had bought a house a few minutes from ours, a small two-up, two-down, and had busied herself in the lives of Dubliners, specifically single ones, having set up Sexy Sixties Singletons, playing cupid to men and women over a certain age. Auntie Angela was a woman with a zest for life, the proverbial force of nature.

I would have to go.

'Yoo-hoo!' Auntie Angela was waving from a chintz sofa in the far corner of the room. 'Milly! Yoo hoo!' She held up her glass of prosecco. 'We're having a cheeky one!' she shouted, making everyone stare at her but not giving a hoot. 'Sarah's on her way!' she roared unnecessarily, as I got closer. 'She's just finishing a double shift. Trojan, that girl. You'll have a prosecco, won't you?' she went on. 'You need one, our high-flyer, after a hard day in the office. I don't know how you do it. When I was working, we all left at five and there was a tea trolley at 3 p.m. every day. And a proper lunch break.' she waved to the waiter. 'Another glass!' she shouted.

Mum was smiling broadly beside her, enjoying Angela's exuberance. She patted the seat beside her for me to sit down. 'You both work too hard,' she said, that old habit of having to be fair to both children, even if it was patently untrue. How could you compare working in a cushy office with working in a leaky geriatrics ward?

'Your mother and I are what is known as ladies of leisure, girls who gallivant,' said Angela, happily. 'Retired but not retiring! So, I'm on a mission to smarten up your mother, get her out of that dreadful gardening waistcoat thing... It's the kind of thing,' Angela went on, 'you couldn't donate to a charity shop. Who needs a waistcoat with huge pockets in it anyway?'

'It's a gilet, Angela,' I said. 'I think some people would consider them very stylish.'

Angela shuddered. 'They sound very practical,' she said.

'And I love it,' said Mum. 'The pockets are very handy for all your bits. You don't lose things.' Maybe it was the glass of prosecco but she was almost giddy.

'Mum,' I said, 'are you wearing lipstick?'

'Is it too much?' She asked. 'Angela said I needed to brighten up my face.'

'It's called Funny Face,' said Angela. 'Which I don't think is the best name for a lipstick, I mean, who wants a funny face? But I think it makes your mother look lovely and, yes, brighter. What do you think, Milly? Doesn't she look beautiful? She was the beauty in the family. I was the brawn.' she laughed, good-naturedly. 'Which is why I have to plaster myself in whatever I can get my hands on these days. A bit of cement may be in order. Milly, have a look... what's different about me? Don't tell her, Kitty,' she warned Mum.

Angela did look thinner, I thought, her cheekbones a little more prominent. 'You've lost weight?' I guessed.

'No, that's not it,' she said, hastily. 'I mean, yes, I have a bit... but there's something else. What is it?'

I couldn't work it out, apart from her hair which was maybe blonder... Mum pointed to Angela's legs.

'Ah! You're wearing jeans.'

She nodded. 'Your mother persuaded me... Thought that, now I have reached middle age, I should give them a go, see what all the fuss is about. Now, you both know me as a woman who likes her glam... I always said I wasn't a jeans girl. But they are far more comfortable than they look and they take about fifteen years off me. And I am also wearing a pair of... trainers.' She held up a foot for me to admire. 'I don't know why I didn't do this years ago. My step count is off the scale. It's quite the revelation... I could have walked around town for another four hours, easily. Now, fill us in about what's new in Milly's world.'

I told them about last night and the birth and then today, Catriona returning to work buzzing on a cocktail valium and morphine.

'She's some woman that one,' said Angela, impressed.

'The poor thing,' said Mum. 'Wouldn't she like a few extra days? I mean, I know some are raring to go.'

'I don't think she wants to,' I explained. 'Work is her life.'

I didn't tell them about the tremor which was still lingering in my right hand and was now spreading to my wrist. Why was I feeling so anxious? If I kept talking and chatting, no one would know but it seemed wrong somehow that life was continuing and all I could think about was that we'd left someone behind. Dad was missing all this. He was missing out of life. Which was obviously ridiculous because he was dead. But it just seemed so unfair. Mum and Angela were laughing about something and I wished I could be like them, happily moving on.

'Oh, here's Sarah!' Angela shouted. 'Yoo-hoo! We'll need another glass!'

Sarah, hair bunched up in a ponytail, dark circles under her eyes, flung herself down on the armchair across the table from me.

'So, what are we celebrating?' She said. 'The meaningless existence of life? The pointlessness of getting up every morning doing the same thing, day in, day out?' The waiter placed two glasses of prosecco in front of Sarah and me. 'Cheers!' she said. 'Here's to sixteen hour shifts!'

We all raised our glasses.

'Well, I would like to celebrate life,' said Angela briskly. 'If you don't mind. And how it never stops giving. One may go to bed thinking that life is terrible, but somehow, with the magic of sleep and subconscious thought, one wakes up and everything is wonderful.' She gave Sarah a look, as though if she stared hard enough, she could make it true.

'That doesn't happen to me,' said Sarah, dismissing her. 'Whatever drugs you are on, I'll have them.'

'You don't want what I'm on,' Angela replied, briskly, waving for the waiter. 'Right.' She turned back to us. 'Ready, Kitty? Ready to tell your news?'

Mum nodded. Breathed in and turned to me and Sarah. 'I have some news,' she said, looking nervous.

'What sort?' I asked, panicked. 'The good kind or the bad kind?'

'It had better be the good kind,' said Sarah. 'I don't think I can stand any more of the bad kind.'

'It's definitely the good kind,' chirped Angela, clapping her hands in excitement. 'It's what you might call *lovely* news.' she nudged Mum. 'Go on, Kitty. Don't keep then in suspense.'

'Well...' She was actually blushing. 'Well...'

'Go on,' I urged. 'What is it?'

'I've been... Oh, I don't know what to call it, but... well, it's Angela's idea... all of it. She's orchestrated the whole thing.'

Angela nodded, proudly. 'Oh yes... Auntie Angela to the rescue!'

'Well...' Mum looked at both of us in turn. 'Well... she signed me up for Sexy Sixties Singletons thing... gave me membership for my birthday.'

'It's the gift of friendship,' said Angela. 'The gift of happiness.'

Sarah and I nodded impatiently at Mum, wishing she'd hurry up and tell us. Mum and Angela were very different people, and Mum was not the type to join a dating group. She was happy pottering on her own in the garden... wasn't she?

'Well, I was starting to feel a little lonely... well, I've been lonely since your dad died. And so...'

'Loneliness is a *disease*,' interjected Angela. 'Except it's the kind that can be cured easily with just a little arrow fired by Cupid.' She patted Sarah's hand. 'And assisted by me.'

'You really want to start dating?' Sarah was saying to Mum. 'You don't know how horrible it is. You might remember it like it was forty years ago, when it was nice out there. People just going to dances, drinking lemonade and having a biscuit. Now, it's awful. There's ghosting, sexting, bread-crumbing, benching, haunting... believe me, you do not want to try it.'

Mum laughed. 'Well, it's a bit late for that because... well... I've met someone.'

Sarah and I exchanged a quick glance.

Mum was blushing and Angela was beaming. 'I have the magic touch,' she said, 'when it comes to romance. I've definitely found a good one for Kitty.'

'He's very nice,' conceded Mum. 'And I really want you both to meet him.'

For a moment, I was too surprised to say anything. Of course I didn't want Mum to be lonely. And, if I thought about it, I certainly didn't want her to spend the rest of her life on her own. But this was real. She had moved on.

'Who is he?' said Sarah.

'Well...' Mum thought for a moment. 'He's a widower with two grown-up children. He's kind, and talkative, and intelligent...'

'Good start,' said Sarah, who seemed unperturbed by Mum's big news. 'You don't want the mean, silent types.'

'I've had a few of those,' said Angela.

'Where is he from?'

'He lives in Sandycove, just five miles from our house. He has two greenhouses.'

'Wow!' said Sarah, teasing her. 'Not *two* greenhouses!'

'He's got a huge back garden,' Mum explained. 'He's passionate about cacti and succulents and grows more than 300 varieties. *And* he gives talks at the Botanic Gardens on exotic plants.'

'I didn't know you could *grow* cacti,' said Sarah. 'I thought you just bought one and took it home to watch it slowly die.'

Mum smiled. 'Well, he would advise you on how to keep them alive.'

'I really need to know how to keep things alive,' said Sarah, picking up her glass.

'What's his name?' I had eventually found my voice.

'Harold Hawkins,' said Mum. 'Retired geography professor. Or is it geology? I can't remember.'

'I think they're the same thing,' said Angela, quickly. 'But we're going to invite him to lunch this Saturday. And we'll *all* be on our best behaviour. No sarcasm, no withering remarks. And I'm looking at you, Sarah.'

Mum looked so radiant, sitting there, with her lipstick now rubbed off, but she was smiling as Angela talked.

And it was so nice to see her like this.

But there was a tug... What about Dad? Was he in her soon-to-be forgotten past? And if we were all expected to move on and forget about him, how did I do it? Dad dying wasn't a surprise. We had a whole year to prepare for it, but with Darragh leaving that week, I hadn't been able to process it as well as I might have done. I should be moving on, as well. Sometimes it still felt as raw as the day five years ago when we said our final goodbyes. I was desperate to get to a point where my grief was manageable, my memories of Dad tidied away, and not spilling over into my daily life, thoughts and feelings all over the place. But I didn't want to lose him. And yet we seemed to be getting further away from the past and into this brave new world that involved Harold Hawkins and his wonderful cacti.

12

Siobhán jumped up from the sofa when I got home. George, her ever-exhausted boyfriend, was, as usual, fast asleep, slumped in the armchair, his feet up on the coffee table. As a baker, he started work at 4.30 a.m. every morning and would come home and sleep on the sofa all evening.

'Hi!' I said to Siobhán. 'How was your day?'

'Fine...' She followed me into the kitchen and sat at the table. She had a slightly weird expression on her face as though she'd seen a ghost.

'Everything all right?' Could she be worrying about the meeting with Ryan. Yes, it had been awkward, but they would soon get to know – and love – each other. I stared into the fridge, hoping something nice would magically appear.

'George brought home some *pain au chocolat,*' said Siobhán. 'They're a little stale, but I've eaten two.'

'Perfect,' I said. 'That's dinner sorted. You're so lucky to go out with a baker. Free pastries. It's every woman's dream.' At least if someone gives you a croissant, you don't feel embarrassed. You can just eat it and get on with it. I would prefer a pastry to a pair of earrings or a posh handbag any day. I just had to find some way of explaining that to Ryan.

Siobhán peered into the living room to make sure George was asleep before continuing. 'I love George and everything,' she whispered, 'obviously, but it wouldn't hurt him to try and stay awake until 9 p.m. and not fall asleep by 7.30 p.m. in front of the television. Every. Single. Night.'

'When he did the patisserie course, you were delighted,' I reminded her.

'I didn't know there was such a thing as too many eclairs, but believe me, there are,' she said. 'And I didn't take into consideration that he would have to keep toddlers' hours. Early to bed, ridiculously early to rise.'

'But you love him really, don't you?'

'Of course I do! Of course!' There was a slight edge of hysteria to her voice.

'Anyway, how was your day?'

'Eventful,' she said. 'Was it eventful? Not really, I was just saying that because one is expected to have eventful days. But really it was quite boring. I read proofs, commissioned an article on toxic masculinity and another on the new codes of conduct in the office, that kind of thing. But...' she brightened, 'my stars were good today. Said I would meet an old friend.'

'Oh yes?'

'And...' She paused, staring at me in a rather weird way, 'I did!'

I looked at her. 'Who was it?'

'Darragh.'

I stopped. The kettle in my hand. 'Darragh?'

She nodded, slowly.

'*The* Darragh. As in Darragh-Darragh?' I wanted to say '*my* Darragh', but he wasn't.

She nodded again. 'He's back,' she said. 'I mean, obviously I didn't go to Italy and bump into him there. I couldn't have. I've been in Dublin all day long. But he's moved home and opened up a wine bar, in the village on Church Street. He's living in the flat above it. They are doing a soft opening, apparently, which means that they are ironing out problems, giving out a few free glasses of wine, introducing themselves to the neighbourhood.'

I had stopped listening at some point, trying to take it all in.

'You know the old grocer's?' she was saying. 'You've seen the builders outside and the endless skips? Well, it's Darragh's. He's taken it over and it looks nice. Really, *really* nice.'

I just stood there. I thought he was long gone, as though him and us and everything had been a mere figment of my imagination.

'Milly. Say something.'

'I don't know what to say,' I said. 'It's just a bit weird, that's all.'

'Weird nice or weird awful.'

She looked so worried about me, that I had to make her feel better. 'It's a bit weird, but good weird.' I was lying. It was definitely *bad* weird. 'So, how did you meet him?'

'There was this impossibly handsome Italian standing there and of course he just caught my eye and he was giving out tiny glasses of wine and little cheeses on sticks. And then we got chatting and then... well, I almost fainted when Darragh turned up.'

I nodded. 'Glad I wasn't there.'

'He's really sorry, you know,' she said. 'I get the impression that he wishes things were different.'

'But they aren't,' I replied. 'He left me the week Dad died.'

She nodded. 'I know. Unforgivable. But...'

'But what?'

'But maybe he didn't mean it.'

'Didn't mean it?'

'Maybe he couldn't help it?' She shrugged. 'Perhaps—'

'He bought a plane ticket,' I said. 'He packed his suitcase. He wrote me a letter. He stood beside me at Dad's funeral knowing he was leaving.'

She nodded, remembering. 'Yeah, he did,' she said. 'But...'

I remember Darragh holding my hand as we stood on the steps of the crematorium as friends, neighbours, colleagues of Dad's... so many faces passed by, so sorry for our loss...

That was the worst for me, that Darragh was planning to leave while making me believe he was my greatest support.

'Look, we don't know what really happened,' said Siobhán.

'Maybe he met someone?' That thought had haunted me over the years, that he had run off with someone else. But it was all just so unthinkable, I didn't know what was worse, that he had met someone or that he just had to get away from me.

'He asked about you,' she went on. 'Said that he didn't know if you would like to see him.'

'I wouldn't,' I said.

'He asked if we were still living together.'

'Oh yes?'

'And he asked after your mum and Sarah and Angela.'

'Oh yes?'

'Stop saying "Oh yes"!'

'Sorry. And what did you say?'

'I told him that we still lived in the same flat, that as far as I knew your mum and Sarah were fine. He was so interested!' she said. 'He really wanted to know. Even asked after Betty. But I also said that you were going out with an amazing property developer called Ryan and you had just got engaged.'

The *pain au chocolat* slipped off my plate onto the floor. 'You said what?'

'That you were about to get married.' She shrugged. 'Listen, I didn't want him thinking you'd been pining...'

'Which I haven't.'

'Obviously.'

'But he behaved badly,' I said. 'He didn't really explain himself. Leaving that letter which didn't say much and just created more questions than it answered.'

Siobhán nodded her head, sympathetically. She was there. She'd pored over that letter, analysing it closer than a literature student reads *Ulysses*. And *Ulysses* was easier to understand. 'Yeah, I know.' Siobhán nodded sympathetically. I loved her for being there for me throughout our friendship, and I loved her for being the person who supported me through those terrible months after Dad's funeral, and Darragh leaving. And I knew for her – for me! – I had to be okay with all this. If he really was back, after five long years, I had to get over it. Any sane person would have moved on. And I suspected I hadn't – not yet, anyway. But I was determined that when – if – I met him, I would be as cool as a cucumber. And maybe it was better that he thought I was engaged. Would make me seem less pathetic.

'I think he's got a girlfriend,' she went on.

'Oh yes?' I said as casually as possible. 'I mean, that's nice.'

Of course he had a girlfriend. And what difference did it make to me, anyway?

'She's called Francisca, I think. Gorgeous she is. Not a patch on you, of course, but beautiful in that carefree Italian long-limbed way. And there's this gorgeous Italian man with them. Looks like a sexy Jesus. Or an even sexier Jesus because I've always had the hots for him. Anyway, this Italian man is called Lorenzo, and for a moment I felt as though I'd wandered onto the set of a perfume ad. It was as though for a moment Dublin was bathed in pheromones. We're not able or used to such sexiness.' She shook her head. 'I should move to Italy. Irish men do *not* look like that.' She stopped, as we both remembered George in the next room. Siobhán tiptoed over to the door and peered out. 'It's okay,' she whispered. 'Still dead to the world.' She turned back to me, as though remembering that the woman she had been describing was my exes' new girlfriend. I arranged my face to look nonplussed. 'So,' she said, 'you're sure you're okay with all this, yes?'

'Of course!' I said, beginning to ramble. 'It's lovely he's back. Anyway, we probably won't see that much of him. I mean, it's not as though we are all going to be hanging out.'

'Well...' she said, awkwardly. 'That's what I was getting to. He's asked us to go to the opening night of the wine bar. And I said we'd love to.'

I would just have to be working late. Or seeing Ryan. 'That sounds great!' I lied.

Siobhán let out a huge sigh of relief. 'Oh, thank God! Because it was actually *really* nice to see him. I was so worried that you might be upset and that it would bring back horrible memories because what he did was awful, but... I can tell he's really sorry. I always thought there was more to it. He wasn't the kind of person to do that. I'd forgotten how lovely he was. Remember?'

He'd become almost mythical in my mind. I tried to remember what he looked like. His hair, dark and wavy, his eyes green... and a laugh which was so infectious that you'd have to smile even if you were across the room.

'Well, he wasn't at the end.'

'No,' she said. 'No, he wasn't. But he's back, so either we avoid him like the plague or we find some way of allowing him into our lives again. I mean, could you ever see yourself forgiving him?'

'Not really,' I admitted.

'Well, then I won't either.' She folded her arms, and nodded at me. 'I shouldn't have even spoken to him. I was caught off guard.'

'No...' Now this was awkward. Damn Darragh and making us both feel bad for talking to him or indeed not talking to him. 'I am sure you should be allowed to talk to him... and maybe I could forgive him.'

'Could you?' She looked so eagerly at me and I realised that it was hard to take sides. Especially as she and Darragh had been such good friends. We all had. 'He was telling the gorgeous Italians about the hillwalking club.'

So many memories. I hadn't thought about the club for years, and now twice a matter of days. Siobhán and I had joined the club in our first year of university and we'd met Darragh while tramping up the mountains in Wicklow. Those Sunday morning walks became the highlight of my month, I'd wait impatiently for the days to go by so I could see that interesting and sexy Darragh O'Toole again, the boy with the shaggy haircut and shy smile. We became a close-knit band of walkers, tackling the fells and hills, frozen in the winter, drenched in spring and autumn and roasted in the summer. It was one of my happier memories of college: the fresh air, the fun we all used to have on the minibus, the other dimension that nature opened up to us, this beautiful world, the seasons changing. It was the one thing that helped me with my perfectionism which bubbled up into low-grade anxiety. I always thought I'd grow out of it, but since Dad died it liked to remind me that it hadn't gone away. Dad's passing and Darragh's leaving had exacerbated it, and now he was back I didn't feel in the least ready to see him. But I would have to pretend that I was over him, like I had to pretend to have moved on in my grief. People expected you to move through the phases and when you didn't, they might think there was something wrong with you.

'Remember the time we got caught in that storm,' said Siobhán, 'and not one of us had brought a rain jacket... and you got stuck on that gate, and I fell in the mud and...'

'It wasn't funny at the time.' But I found myself smiling. A little.

'Now it is,' she said. 'Kind of. Anyway, if it's *really* okay with you, then we could go? So...?' She smiled at me, hopefully.

I couldn't let her down. Not Siobhán.

'Why not?' Give me the Oscar now.

13

At Dad's funeral, Mum wasn't able to make a speech and Sarah hadn't stopped crying for three days, so giving the eulogy was left to me. We, and Angela and Betty, sat in the crematorium, facing the coffin on which we'd placed a photograph of Dad taken on holiday, tanned and glowing, an ice cream in his hand. Mum's small frame in her black dress, her silver pin in the shape of a dog which Dad had given her for her birthday a few years before, shining against the black, being hugged by everyone we knew and everyone we barely knew. I remembered saying to Sarah, 'She's going to be hugged away to nothing.' Sarah was hiding behind her sunglasses, holding Hugh's hand. 'Maybe that's what she wants,' she'd said.

This is the eulogy I planned to give... I wanted to tell a story about when I was eight and I was learning to ride a bike and just couldn't get it. Dad would roll me along, I'd start pedalling and for a brief moment, I'd have it, and then I'd wobble and... fall. This went on for days. I was never going to learn. I was going to be that one person in the whole world who never got it.

'It doesn't matter, Milly,' he'd said, when I lay my head on the kitchen table and sobbed. 'Falling is part of it, you just keep getting back on. And there will be a moment when you just go... and you're riding. And it's not the riding that's the big bit, it's the getting back on with style.'

I had never forgotten it. Falling and getting back on with style. And that's what I was going to say in my eulogy. My dad has lived his life with style, in every way, he didn't waste a moment.

But when it came to it, I couldn't stand up, the words and thoughts locking in my throat, and I knew I wouldn't be able to tell everyone how wonderful and inspiring he was and how lucky Mum, Sarah and I had been to have known him, to be his special people, to be his gang, the people he thought about when he woke and when he went to sleep. And the people who were there when he said goodbye to the world.

But what I wanted to say more than anything was that we may have been his special people, but *he* made us special. And without him we weren't special any more. We didn't even feel like much of a family. Without Dad, we'd always be a bit broken.

'Milly?' Darragh had squeezed my hand. 'Come on.' I didn't want to stand up. I was so afraid that I would open my mouth and nothing would come out or I wouldn't do Dad justice.

Just in front of me were Mum and Auntie Angela. Sarah was clinging to Hugh. And beyond them there were the faces of people I knew. Friends of Mum and Dad's, relatives, neighbours, work colleagues of his... our whole community in one building at this one time.

'You can do this,' Darragh had said. 'I know you can.'

He and I had walked to the front, his hand in mine, and then he'd stood aside, leaving me on my own. You get back on... but you do it with style. And I'd opened my mouth to speak... and I said it all. He was a man who lived his life with style.

I don't think I could have done that without Darragh.

Pity then, that seven days later he'd run off to Italy, without explaining *why*. In the months that followed, I didn't know what to think, there was nothing to go on. Even Miss Marple would have failed to solve that case.

That last year, looking back, Darragh *had* seemed distant. We were living together in the flat with Siobhán and George, and I knew he was going through something, but I was just so sure we'd reconnect, that at the end of it all we'd be okay.

He'd been working in a wine wholesalers', a stop-gap job while he tried to figure out what to do with an English degree. When I called the wholesalers' office afterwards, in my desperation to try and piece together what might have happened, they told me he just hadn't turned up. He obviously couldn't wait a single second longer.

Whatever, he was back now, with a girlfriend and a new business. There was nothing I could do except push all thoughts of him to the back of my mind, and try and get on with my own life.

14

At work, the first thing I had to do was call and introduce myself to Mrs Murphy. I had written to Mr Hessling of Alpha Holdings and I would do my very best, but I knew how determined and ruthless those property developers were and I knew the tricks their lawyers employed to ensure their clients get their way. If this Alpha Holdings had already bought out everyone else in the building, then it weakened Mrs Murphy's position. And if they had also bought the building at the back, their determination was going to be hard to crack. But Mr McAvoy had made it clear that nothing but a win for his godmother would be acceptable.

'Mary Murphy speaking. How may I help you?' Her voice was clear and well-spoken.

'Hello,' I said. 'I'm Milly Byrne from Patrick McAvoy's office. He has asked me to represent you.'

'Oh yes.' She gave a small laugh. 'It's so silly, really. And now it's come to this. I said no, and that I wouldn't sell, and they don't think that's good enough. You would think that educated people would understand a small word like "no", wouldn't you?'

I agreed that you would. But Mrs Murphy, I guessed, wouldn't have come up against many property developers in her life.

'It's only a small flat,' she went on. 'And it won't mean much to anyone else. But it has been good to me and is full of memories. One moment I can be here, like right now, talking to someone on the phone, and the next moment I might go into another room and I am right back in another time, another moment from my rather long, some might say too-long, life, reliving something that happened.' She sounded content, not like someone who was about to lose her home. I had a feeling I was going to like Mrs Mary Murphy.

'Well,' I said, carefully, worried about over promising but already feeling rather protective about this woman, 'let's see what we can do. May I come and see you?'

We arranged to meet the following day. 'Ring the bell, dear, and wait. It takes me much longer than it used to get to the intercom thing. These days, people are gone before I've even managed to get up from my chair.'

I was thinking of Mrs Murphy as I walked home from the bus stop at the end of the day. I thought about how she lived in a flat filled with memories and how everything that happened to her must swim in and out of her mind all day. It must be wonderful to be able to live without pain, to welcome all those memories. I wished I could live like that too. But I couldn't even go into Dad's study because it still made me too sad.

Nearing home, I realised I was close to the old grocer's shop on Church Street which Darragh had taken over. I'd pushed him so firmly to the back of my brain, I had practically forgotten all about him and my determination to stay away. Except, for some reason, I stopped. Curiosity had got the better of me and, for a moment, I stood taking in the building's transformation.

Up until a few months ago, it was shuttered and bordered up and I'd only been half aware of the builder's progress – the skip outside, the noise from inside. Half obscured by the rack of newspapers outside the shop next door, I peered at the building. It looked lovely: the old stone and brickwork cleaned up, the window frames and door painted a dark grey green, the large plate glass windows gleaming and inside were large wooden tables, a long bar at the back and long and low enamel lights. Above the large glass windows, *Teolaí* was written in curly, gold, old-shopfront lettering. My school Irish came back to me. Teolaí was the Irish for cosy.

And now here was another memory floating past. Teolaí had been the name of the wine bar his mother had run in Dublin in the eighties and nineties, and where Darragh had worked throughout his teenage years. *Now* there would definitely be laws about it, but in those days, no one minded, or even noticed, a child clearing tables, taking orders or carrying boxes and stacking the shelves and serving wine. Way back then, wine bars were rarer than a hazelnut whirl once the Milk Tray had been opened. Especially a wine bar run by a woman.

I remembered Darragh talking about her and how she seemed like a goddess when she was in the bar, all eyes on her, moving around the room with a word here, taking an order there, ensuring everyone had a great time. His mother in her realm.

There was a photograph of her and Darragh together hanging up in the family home in Howth: him, maybe five or six, with curly hair and rosy cheeks, his hands holding a bird's nest towards the camera, and this beautiful woman, arms around him, her head touching his, both of them smiling matching smiles. And she looked like a woman who had everything she needed, her tiny boy in her arms.

But she had died before he'd gone to college and he rarely spoke about her. This wine bar, I realised, was for her. Before, I hadn't really understood how he had loved her and must have missed her. After losing Dad, I understood it so much more clearly.

Another memory: Spain, where it rained for ten days and just as Darragh and I were about to attempt another walk, we found a little bar and went there instead. And the man behind the counter didn't even ask what we wanted, just nodded a greeting and poured out two glasses of what looked like wine. It was better than wine, it tangled itself around your taste buds. Darragh looked like he'd had a religious experience.

'I'd like this life,' he'd said. 'A little wine bar in the mountains. A simple life.'

'So, why don't you?'

He'd shrugged. 'Only if you do it with me.'

But I had a big law career ahead of me. I had just finished my exams and was waiting to hear about the graduate programme at the biggest corporate law firm in the city, McCoyMcAvoy. 'We'll do it when I retire,' I'd said.

'I can wait.' He'd smiled at me and we'd sipped our wine slowly, never wanting this moment, hidden in a bar in the hills of Spain, sheltering from a rain storm, to end. Then Darragh had begun to speak about his mother. 'She went to France when she was sixteen on an exchange,' he said. 'Fell in love with everything about it, and then went back when she was eighteen to be an au pair and became obsessed with the food, the culture, the wine. Took a wine course in Paris and was going to stay there forever when she met Dad. He had been working there for a finance company and had had enough of France and was missing Ireland. And so that was their compromise. They'd come home, but she would bring France with her.' He'd held up his wine glass to mine. 'You have to find the right person to compromise with.' He took my hand. 'It would be nice if she was here now. She would have loved you,' he'd said, 'you are exactly the kind of person she liked.'

Standing there in Dublin, I had tears in my eyes. We were happy once and I had really loved him. And more than that, I had really *liked* him. He was the best person I had ever met. But now here he was with his new business venture, back for an adventure in his home town, in his old neighbourhood where we had lived. And Mum was moving on with this Harold. And there was me, who hadn't really done very much for the last five years, just existed. I was still in the same flat, doing the same job. I hadn't much to show for half a decade of living.

'Hey!' there was an Italian voice behind me. 'Don't just stand there, come in for a drink!'

He was the kind of man you don't usually find in Dublin. Hair to his shoulders, tall and tanned, a white cotton shirt unbuttoned low and jeans so skinny they were nearly indecent. It had to be the man Siobhán had described.

'Come on!' he said again. 'You live nearby?'

I nodded.

'Well, come for a glass of wine. Free to our neighbours, yes? Who can say no to a glass of wine?' He shrugged, sexily.

'I can't,' I said, suddenly panicked.

'Why not? Too busy? Too busy for wine? Impossible!'

'Yes,' I said. 'Well... the thing is...' I couldn't go in. With Darragh being back, but I hadn't had enough time to organise my thoughts. Did I forgive him? Or should I still hate him? Or worse – much worse – did I still *love* him? I would have hoped that I would feel neutral about him, but in truth, it was far more complicated. And now I was caught staking him out like a besotted teenager.

But I had to be okay about it, for my own sense of pride. I didn't want Darragh to think that I was still devastated after five whole years, not since he had a new girlfriend.

'Actually,' I said, 'I'm a friend of Darragh's. Well, used to be. We were in college together.' Better face my fears than avoid my local high street for however long it took to book a one-way flight to Australia.

The man's face lit up. 'Darragh! Yes, yes, come in, come in! He is not around right now, but you can wait for him? He won't be too long.' He held out his hand. 'Lorenzo, so pleased to meet you, or as you say here, how's it going?' He grinned and then, still holding onto my hand, yanked me along. 'Come! I will give you a glass of the very best Valpolicella you have ever tasted in your life. And then you tell your friends and they tell their friends and their friends and so on and so forwards. Okay?' He smiled at me again. 'Come on!'

And so I did.

Inside, the room was lit by candles and low lamps on the wall, and Lorenzo placed a glass on the bar, which was the old shop counter, sanded down and oiled.

'There! Try that and tell me what you think.' Lorenzo leaned across the bar, arms folded, waiting for my verdict. 'Good?'

'Very.' It was. Ridiculously.

He nodded, as though he knew I would say that. 'Sunshine,' he said. 'It's the soil, the... what is the word? The insects, the nutrients, thousands and thousands and thousands of years of viniculture... Italy in a glass, no?' He placed a small bowl of olives in front of me. 'Try one of these. From my village in Tuscana.' He popped one in his mouth and signalled for me to do the same. 'Not bad, no?'

'Delicious.' The wine and olives had their usual relaxing effect, and my stomach began to loosen.

From the kitchen beyond the bar, a woman appeared. She was as stunning as Lorenzo, with long dark wavy hair and a face straight form a Fellini film.

'Frankie,' Lorenzo said to her, 'come and meet a friend of Darragh's.'

'Not really a friend,' I said. 'Just an old acquaintance.'

'Francisca,' she said, kissing me on either cheek. 'Ciao, nice to meet with you.' She held my shoulders, studying me. 'Another beautiful Irish woman,' she said with a shrug to Lorenzo, and then back to me, 'you're all so beautiful you Irish girls... your skin, your hair.'

I nearly choked on an olive. 'Us?'

She nodded. 'Why? You don't think so?' She shrugged again, as though I was a lost cause. 'You and Siobhán...'

'She's my flatmate,' I said.

'Ah! Siobhán!' said Lorenzo. 'You know Siobhán? Her red hair. She's like a painting by Botticelli.'

Francisca rolled her eyes at him, but then her focus moved beyond me and her face broke into a beautiful smile. 'Ciao bello!'

I turned around, knowing exactly who it was I was about to be confronted with. Darragh. And he was looking straight at me.

'Hi,' I said, 'Siobhán said you had moved in... back to the old neighbourhood.'

He moved towards us, accepting double kisses from Francisca – obviously his girlfriend – and a hug from Lorenzo. But he was staring at me with an expression on his face that I couldn't work out.

'Hello, Milly,' he said. 'I was hoping you'd come.'

15

'So many friends,' Francisca said, looking bored. 'So many reunions.'

'Sorry,' I said, although I didn't know why I was apologising. 'I was walking home and I met Lorenzo and he persuaded me to come in...'

'She *had* to try the Valpolicella,' said Lorenzo. 'I give it to all the beautiful girls. Especially the ones with blue eyes and smiles like a sunrise. The kind of smile you would wait every day for.'

'Lolo!' Francisca gave him a slap on his arm. 'He's such a flirt,' she said, rolling her eyes. 'He should be locked away.'

'Everyone has to try it... it's the best... Francisca is just jealous because her family doesn't make good wine... it's good, yes, but we make great wine...'

She swiped him with her long arm. '*Stolto...*' she said.

Darragh was still looking at me. Oh God. He didn't want me here, I thought. He was angry or annoyed. Or... what?

He found his voice. 'Apparently it's congratulations,' he said. 'You're engaged.'

I nearly asked him what he meant. And then I remembered. 'Yes,' I said, 'it's very exciting.' It was shocking how easy it was to lie sometimes.

'Great. And Siobhán said you were still working for McCoyMcAvoy.'

I nodded. 'That's right. And you've been...? You've been well?'

'Yeah... yeah, I've been really well. Better, you know...' He opened his mouth to say something and then closed it again.

'I'm going to have to go,' I said. 'But really nice meeting you all.'

'Oh, so sad!' said Lorenzo.

'Thanks for the wine, Lorenzo,' I said. 'Lovely to meet you, Francisca... and... great to see you again, Darragh.'

'Ciao ciao,' Francisca said. 'Come to the opening night? Yes? Friday?'

'I'll see if I can,' I said. 'Bye...'

I walked away, feeling almost sick. After all this time, it was him. He was real. And I wanted to hate him and I didn't. I couldn't.

But at least, the hard bit was over. I had seen him and we had chatted. He had enquired after my wellbeing and I after his. Job done. And if we met again, it would be much easier.

Back at the flat, Siobhán was trying to watch television while the full weight of George's sleeping body leaned against her – all six feet, five inches of him, with the kind of arms made for kneading dough. Or maybe the kind of arms that kneading dough made.

'Thank God you're back,' she said. 'I can barely breathe, my lungs are working at a dangerously low capacity. Help me pull him off. He's the weight of a bus. Is my face blue?'

I managed to pull one arm, and she pushed on the other side and wiggled out. For a moment, she breathed heavily and dramatically.

'I can feel the blood going back into my face,' she said, pinching her cheeks and following me into the kitchen. 'Another fun evening, not so much stuck on the sofa as pinned to the flecking thing.' She flung herself down at the table. 'Put the kettle on, I'm gasping. Anyway, what were you doing? Working late again?'

'I bumped into Darragh actually,' I said, keeping my face straight. 'It's a lovely place,' I went on, ignoring the fact that she was overexcited and gaping at me like a fish.

'Really? How did you feel seeing him again?'

'It was great.' Except it wasn't. I'd spent all this time working on myself, trying to create a new, successful, happy me, but I hadn't made very much progress at all. Okay, so there was Ryan, my pretend fiancé. I thanked God for him, because without him I looked like someone who hadn't moved on at all. 'Darragh asked how I was, I asked how he was, I met Francisca...' My voice was thankfully steady. 'Definitely his girlfriend...'

'I think she might be,' said Siobhán, pulling a face. 'Probably a Gemini. Have you ever met a bad-looking Gemini?' She didn't give me time to answer. 'Thought not.' She paused. 'Anyway, let's forget about her. Did Darragh mention you being engaged?'

'He congratulated me, yes,' I said. 'But don't worry. I didn't tell him you'd lied. I went along with it.'

'That's good. No harm in him thinking it, especially because he's got that gorgeous Francisca.' She paused. 'And what about Lorenzo? Did you meet him?'

'Yes, he's exactly as advertised.'

'Isn't he!'

'He asked after you.'

'No! Get away! He did not!' She quickly glanced at the living room to make sure George was asleep. 'Did he?'

'He did,' I said. 'Said you were like a painting by Botticelli.'

'He did? Is that a good thing? Do you think that's a compliment?'

'It is,' I assured her. 'Do you fancy him? Are you thinking of trading George in?'

'Of course not!' she insisted, going a lighter shade of pink. 'It was just quite nice to be complimented, that's all. George's idea of flattery is to say he liked my trifle at Christmas, and he meant my trifle. He doesn't do euphemisms. And I prefer the euphemistically free Irish male to some handsome, long haired Italian.' She took her glass of water and pressed it to her forehead. 'It's really hot in here... did you leave the heating on? Anyway, we should all go to the opening on Friday. George and I, you and Ryan, and we'll have a laugh?'

'Maybe,' I demurred. 'I don't know what Ryan and I have got planned yet.' We didn't see each other in the week, both being busy with work, and keeping it casual, but Friday night was unofficially the night we spent together so I had stopped making other plans for then.

But later, lying in bed, unable to sleep, another memory floated by. A week Darragh and I spent in Clifden, a little town in Connemara on the west coast of Ireland, surrounded by the sea and islands and mountains and straggly, scraggly sheep. The town is a beautiful, cosy, intimate place, full of small shops and pubs and cafés and in the evenings draws in all the wind-beaten and sun-drenched tourists who have spent the day sailing or fishing or cycling, looking for music and seafood, as the sun slowly sinks behind the mountains.

We had hired a cottage just beyond the village and every evening we would walk home, our journey lit by a canopy of night sky, a trillion stars, and would light the outdoor stove and, wrapped in blankets, we would gaze into the flames, my head on his shoulder.

'Don't ever leave,' he'd said. 'People always leave. Promise me you will never leave me.'

And I'd promised, and we'd laughed and kissed... the universe and life seeming as though they would never end.

16

Friday, bright and early, Catriona was back at her desk.

'Morning, Milly!' she said, as though her valium crash had never happened and the baby was all a dream. She took the coffee I'd bought for her, assuming she'd be in. I'd bought two – and drank them both – the last few mornings just in case she'd turned up. The extra caffeine meant that I worked faster than ever before, I imagined I was a blur of arms and legs. This morning, I'd vowed to donate the extra one if she wasn't there. But Catriona leapt on it like a dog at his water bowl after a long, hot walk, 'I heard about your new assignment,' she said, after she had downed it enthusiastically. 'Let me know if you need any advice.'

'You don't think it's too much work?' I asked. 'I mean, with everything we're doing... it might mean that I wouldn't be able give as much to our other cases.'

'We'll manage,' she said.

'But with the baby, you might need to take time off... parents do, from time to time.' I had to raise my voice a little because of the increasing volume of noise from the corridor. Through my glass windows, I saw a line of office chairs and their owners – our normally serious colleagues, scooting along, Jarleth at the front with a megaphone, singing 'Come on do the conga! Come and join our conga!' Other people were singing the

Macarena and I saw one of the partners with his tie tied around his fore-head and another partner hanging onto the back of the conga line while standing in a surfing position on his wheely chair.

Catriona looked back at me, aghast. 'What the hell is happening here?'

I tried to explain. 'It's an attempt to have more fun...' I'd already avoided an under-desk limbo competition and a lunchtime hopscotch around the desks. Fun was breaking out all over the building.

'Fun?' said Catriona, 'I despair, I really do. I don't come to work for *fun*.' She shook her head in disbelief. 'Anyway, Milly, I will not be putting my career on the back burner. Noel has decided not to take up paternity leave and flew to London this morning. And I am just too busy to take any time off. And anyway, Lydia is being very well taken care of with our lovely new nanny, Josephine, who is actually qualified to take care of babies. I, on the other hand, am not.' She threw back the last of her coffee as there was a loud cheer from the other side of the building – my colleagues had presumedly broken the office chair conga line world record. 'And, Milly, you haven't told anyone, have you? I mean, I am sure lots of people *know* – they always do – but I don't particularly want to be fielding questions about Lydia in the office. Once a woman has a baby, it is assumed that her mind isn't on the job and it doesn't help that McCoyMcAvoy is probably the most male dominated firm in the city.'

Catriona didn't usually disclose her private thoughts. For her to tell me that she was worried about being judged for having had a baby meant that it was a really big deal. Or maybe me being at Lydia's birth meant that I had passed some kind of friendship initiation rite. But that would be quite grandiose for any friendship test. It's much easier to just find people who make you laugh. However, I didn't have the chance to tell her that everyone already knew about the baby because she was pressing on.

'Now,' she said, 'did you go through the contracts for Treasury PLC? And what about the court submission for AGC?'

'They're on my desk,' I said, turning to go, as there was a knock on her door.

'Morning, Catriona! Morning, Milly!' Susie, obscured by a vast bouquet of flowers, walked in. 'Congratulations, Catriona! These are from Mr McAvoy and *all* the staff,' she said. 'Everyone in the entire building has signed the card...' She grinned at us both. 'Everyone insisted on putting long messages,' carried on Susie, 'you know how it is, so it took ages. Anyway, I need to see the baby!' She plonked the flowers down on Catriona's Smythson kidskin leather notebook and propped herself on the edge of the desk, hand stretching towards Catriona's phone, ready to grab it. 'Show me your photos.'

Catriona snatched the phone just in time. 'I don't have any photographs,' she said, looking stern. 'Thank you for the flowers, Susie,' she said firmly. 'But we've got a mountain of work to get through.'

'Okay!' said Susie. 'You'll just have to bring Lydia in to see us all, she has to see the madhouse we work in. We're doing leapfrog around the offices on Monday... everyone has to join in!' Her enthusiasm visibly faded when she saw Catriona's horrified face, and she slipped away.

'Milly?' said Catriona. 'Is it possible to get a double espresso? I think I might need the extra shot.'

Once I delivered the caffeine, I packed my briefcase to go and meet Mrs Murphy, grateful for the novelty of getting out of the office.

Merrion Square is quintessential Georgian Dublin; beautiful doors and fan lights, with basements dropping from the street and windows shooting skyward. Three hundred years ago, the street would have been filled with carriages and horses, but now only the odd Blue Plaque reminded you that Oscar Wilde lived here, or that another poet lived there. Could Mrs Murphy actually be the last person to live on the square, the one flat which was still lit up at night, perhaps a television flickering, a kettle boiling?

Number Two, Merrion Square was a very smart little boutique hotel, but Number One, where I stood, had seen better days. A long column of brass doorbells had names beside them, and at the very top was:

Frederick and Mary Murphy

I pressed and waited.

And waited. And waited a bit longer. Could she have forgotten? My finger hovered over the bell and I remembered what she'd said about giving her time. With my usual clients, everything was itemised to the last second, no one was late, and no one had time for anything but the lightest of pleasantries. And then – finally – there was the crackle from the speaker. 'Hello?'

'Mrs Murphy?' I said. 'It's Milly Byrne. We spoke yesterday? The colleague of Patrick McAvoy...?'

'Of course, dear. Come up.'

A heavy click unlocked the door and, inside, a gloomy hall was revealed and beyond it a sweeping staircase curling heavenwards. Eventually I made it to the top and was welcomed by Mrs Murphy. Small, white haired and wearing a pair of apricot coloured trousers and a man's jacket. I followed her into the flat and through to a long drawing room, which must have had at least eight tables of varying sizes, all displaying china and vases and decorative plates and silver-framed photographs and paintings over every wall.

'So, you work with my godson, Paddy, then,' Mrs Murphy said, after I had collapsed on the small sofa, trying not to breathe too embarrassingly deeply. I really should be fitter. I used to be, all that hillwalking. Now, I was desk bound and muscle free. 'He's a devil, that one,' Mrs Murphy was saying about Mr McAvoy who must be at least in his late sixties. 'Has his mother driven mad. Calmed down a little now. But he's a nice lad, always calls in to see her. She was my best friend since school, his mother, and so that is why you are here today. You'll be wanting a cup of tea, I expect. I asked Daphne to get some in for me. She's some kind of niece or cousin of mine. Her grandmother from Skibbereen was a cousin of my mother. And she knocked on the door one day and introduced herself. She's next door, Number Two, runs a very nice hotel there. I remember when the building was what we used to call a doss house and, before, John Millington Synge lived there. Had a very small dog called Arthur. Used to take him to the square for his walkies. Anyway, Daphne was the one who brought Frederick back to me.' I was losing track of her train of thought when she leaned heavily on her stick and hauled herself up. 'You sit there, dear, and hopefully Frederick will make an appearance to keep you company. He's probably teasing a few dogs.'

17

I took a moment to look around the room. On the mantlepiece, in pride of place, were two large black and white photographs of a couple on their wedding day – Mrs Murphy was exactly the same as she was now, just younger, and beside her, her husband, the name I'd seen on the brass plate downstairs. Frederick. She must have called the cat after him. And in the other photograph was a single shot of Mr Murphy again, looking handsome and happy and smiling into the camera.

'Ah,' Mrs Murphy said, coming back into the room carrying a tray of tea and biscuits. 'You're admiring my Frederick. When he was a man, of course.'

'You mean alive?' I was beginning to think that she was a little bit confused.

'I mean, a man, dear,' she said. 'It was our wedding day. We had all our friends there, my sister was matron of honour, my parents came under duress because they thought Frederick was rather beneath us, but we all went to The Gresham Hotel, where they had made us sandwiches and we danced all night. Even my mother and father had a little spin round the floor. You see, Frederick lived for jazz. His dream would have been to be a musician, but he was obliged by financial constraints to work for the civil service. He had to give his own widowed mother money every week, you see.' She had set the tea down. 'Take one of the biscuits, dear. I think the morning goes quicker when you have a sit down with a biscuit, don't you?'

I obliged, obviously. 'You both look very happy,' I said.

'We were,' Mrs Murphy said, nodding, as though it was the most obvious thing in the world. 'It was a lot of fun being married. Are you?'

'No, I'm not,' I said, thinking of Ryan and wondering if he and I would go any further than where we were.

'Well, make sure you find someone kind and you can make even the most mundane event into an adventure. I think that is what love is, when you are excited just to go to the shop together, or catch a bus. And I'd miss him every single morning when he left for work. But do you know something? His office was just across the square and at 12 p.m. on the dot, every day, he'd wave, sometimes his handkerchief or a piece of paper, and I would be waiting for it. He never missed a day. My very own Angelus.' She laughed, and handed over my cup of tea, her hand shaking slightly, causing the tea to spill into the saucer a little. 'Lovely, lovely man,' she said.

'You were saying that you were best friends with Mr McAvoy's mother?' I had long given up on this being a normal client meeting.

'Ah, well, yes. Now she wasn't so lucky with her husband. I did say that one should marry someone with whom you can adventure, but he had adventures of a different kind, mainly involving a bottle of whisky.' She paused. 'I'm being indiscreet, I know. But what he put her through...' She looked away from me for a moment.

'What happened?' I asked, genuinely curious.

'Well, what seemed like fun at the beginning soon turned into quite a desperate situation. She would go into some of the bars that she knew he would drink in. Doheny And Nesbits was his favourite and there was my friend, Lucy, an alumna of Miss Binchy's Academy For Girls, having to go into pubs.' Mrs Murphy shook her head. 'She was driven quite mad by him, until, thankfully, he fell off a bar stool, his liver having given up on him at the same time as his family and friends.'

'You were best friends?'

'Oh yes, we'd met at Miss Binchy's when we were eleven and have been inseparable ever since. We were always getting into trouble for talking and not listening in Latin. We thought of ourselves as wildly exciting and started a political group in school. It was all after the war, you see, and people were desperate for the world to be different. We'd discuss everything – what was happening in Europe and London, stories from America and then here in Dublin... workers' rights, women's rights, housing conditions... Miss Binchy herself said we were a dangerous influence on the other girls.' She gave another little laugh. 'She didn't expel us though. She couldn't afford to lose paying pupils, I suppose.'

When Mrs Murphy smiled, she looked exactly like the happy girl in the photograph. 'And that is how I found this flat, through trying to find some meaning to my existence. Lucy and I began volunteering at a centre for women, in this very building, two floors down from where we are now. You'd call it a refuge now, but I told my parents it was a women's hospital for genteel ladies fallen on straitened times. They would never have agreed for me to be in an environment they would have regarded as risky. It was run by a rather formidable but terribly kind woman – a Mrs Hackett. She used to refer to it as a sanctuary, which I thought of as a lovely word, it always made me feel safe here, and it became my sanctuary also. Frederick had had an awful time of it growing up and it was a relief for me to get away from my parents. Well-meaning though they were, they were, at best, heavy-handed. So Frederick and I made a nest for two all the way up here.'

It was certainly cosy, you could hardly hear any noise except the call of a seagull or the faint sound of a car.

'Working for Mrs Hackett meant Lucy and I were finally doing something worthwhile,' Mrs Murphy continued. 'We made beds, swept floors, polished the brass on the front door, delivered the washing to the laundry, read books and sang songs to the little ones and helped them with their reading. We learned how to make soda bread and Irish stew and vegetable soup. I can still hear the sounds of the voices of the children playing on the stairs, Mrs Hackett's crinoline petticoat rustling, her voice echoing along the corridors, the women talking to each other. Every time I go up and down the stairs here, it all comes back to me, I can even smell the kerosene lamps we used to light, because we couldn't afford electricity. And if I look out of that window, I can still see Frederick waving to me. At 12 p.m. every day, and I promise you, as clear as day, there he is. Memories don't go anywhere, they just float around until you need them again. I find the stairs

rather a trial these days, but when I am making my slow and plodding journey, it all comes back to me and I'm there again, *right there*.' She smiled, and
I noticed that a white cat had entered the room and was rubbing himself
against her legs as she stroked his head. 'I'm being long-winded,' she said,
'but I am getting to my point, which is how we came to be living here.' She
stroked the cat. 'It was perfect for us, wasn't it, Frederick? More tea?'

She topped me up while going on with the story, just as the cat jumped
up onto her lap. 'It was just being used as the storerooms, then. And when
Mrs Hackett heard that Frederick and I were getting married, she said she
would rent it to us and later, when the sanctuary moved to a better building
down by the river, she sold this building as separate units and we bought
this flat. She set up the Women's Place of Care and Rehabilitation on
Poolbeg Street.' She leaned down to the cat and spoke in its ear. 'We were
so lucky, weren't we darling?' she said. 'Our first and last home.' The cat
miaowed as though in full agreement. 'Well, I hope it will be my last home,
anyway.' The cat miaowed again, more forcefully.

I felt it was time to bring the conversation to a more conventional area.
'Would you have deeds to the flat, proof of the sale from Mrs Hackett, that
kind of thing? And also would you have the letters sent by Alpha Holdings?
They've written to me at the office, but I would like to see what they have
said to you.'

Mrs Murphy nodded. 'The deeds are somewhere with Frederick's
things... he had a trunk with all sorts of things in there. I will have a look.
And I have kept the missives from those dreadful people... one of them
knocked on the door. Very smartly dressed, you know, and nice as the King
of Siam. He explained very politely, and in that loud and slow voice people
use when you are over a certain age, that the rest of the building was sold
and I had to go too. He tried to come inside, to show me plans, he said, and
that the council would find me somewhere to live, even put his foot in the
door, but I threatened to call the Guards, and he was all nice as pie again,
even said they would give me money if I left. Money! As if that would
change anything.'

'May I see everything – the letters and the deeds?'

She nodded. 'Yes, I'll find them.' She got to her feet again, pulling
herself up on her stick, as the cat jumped elegantly to the ground. 'I think

they are on the table, under the fruit bowl. I think that's where Daphne said she put them.' After a moment's riffling, she waved an envelope in the air. When I took them from her, the words Alpha Holdings were emblazoned in garish purple and gold at the top of the paper.

Scanning the letters quickly, they were what I had imagined; the usual notice to vacate, all jargon and legalese, worded to intimidate and frighten. Horrible things. I knew them well, having drafted a few in my time. I looked up at Mrs Murphy, who was leaning on her stick watching me. And weirdly, I felt the old me return, the wide-eyed, idealistic graduate; I could feel a tingle, a passion I hadn't felt in years. This wasn't about money. This was about love. And passion.

'This must be defended, Mrs Murphy,' I said, 'and I think we will have to be as aggressive as they are. We must stand up for you and your right to remain in your home. And I would be delighted and honoured to represent Frederick and yourself.'

Frederick miaowed in agreement.

18

It was a lovely spring evening as I walked across Merrion Square to meet Ryan for dinner. We normally spent Fridays together, and I would stay the night at his house, and then leave early as he usually had an appointment with his personal trainer. I never hung around the following day in Ryan's house – which was basically in his parents' garden – and anyway I much preferred heading home on a Saturday to have breakfast with Siobhán. It wasn't the world's most passionate relationship. No sonnets or love songs would ever be written about us, but passion wasn't something I wanted. I'd had that kind of ardent relationship with Darragh and it ended in heartbreak.

The blossom hung heavy on the trees, and at this time of year, the city opens up, as though everything – the people, the trees, even the buildings – has been longing for a little heat in their bones.

Ryan had already started eating when I arrived at the restaurant. He had a bowl of soup in front of him and a plate of bread and butter.

'Hope you don't mind,' he said, his mouth full of soda bread and after giving me one of his half-lips-half-face kisses.

'No, it's fine,' I said. And it was, we were only meeting casually, and in a half-hearted relationship how could you demand that someone waits for you if they are hungry.

'I had to eat something,' he went on. 'My blood sugar was dangerously low and I started feeling a little shaky and light-headed. I didn't want to go into hypertonia.'

'What's that?'

'It's when your blood-sugar is dangerously low.' He smiled at me, as though my being slow on the uptake was endearing. 'I wouldn't normally eat this...' His soda bread was held up in the air, exhibit A. 'But sometimes you need a quick-release carb. But you'll be glad to know I feel much better now. My isotonic levels have stabilised.'

I wanted to make a joke, something lightly teasing. But I stopped myself. A half-hearted relationship doesn't allow for quips or leg pulling. But it did, it seemed, allow for small bags being pushed along the table towards me, Cartier swirled in gold on the outside.

'Thought you might like this,' he said. 'Just a little something...'

It was like a scene from some terrible Hollywood film. His smile had taken a rakish turn. I hesitated.

'Go on,' he urged, slightly impatiently. 'Open it!'

There was a large square box inside and there, on a velvet cushion, was a necklace, the diamond glinting and twinkling like Liberace in Las Vegas.

'Oh, Ryan...'

'I know,' he grinned, happily. 'I know...'

'It's...' What was it? Beautiful? To some people. Expensive? To most. Unwanted, unwarranted, unnecessary? To me. Oh God. 'Thank you.'

'The best for the best,' he said. 'Put it on. It's twenty-four carat gold...'

'It's too much,' I protested. 'I can't accept it.'

'It's a present, Milly,' he said. 'I bought it for you. Mum always says diamonds are a girl's best friend, and I thought you could do with some new best friends. I mean your real one...' He stopped. 'It's beautiful, like you.'

I swallowed. 'Thank you.'

'You and me, *we're* the best. And we deserve the best.'

A memory landed in my subconscious. Being with Darragh on the Ile de Ré, off La Rochelle, cycling and swimming, the air warm and the light golden. And the way he kissed me one evening as we walked to find a bar, our skin salty and roasted like peanuts, his hair with newly bleached highlights, my freckles making their annual return. 'You're the best,' he'd said, pulling me close.

My ghosts were visiting me, just like Mrs Murphy's. I held my hand under the table to hide the tremor from Ryan.

'I'm going to put it on later,' I promised him. 'I'm just worried I might drop it or lose it. But thank you.'

'Suit yourself.' He looked annoyed.

'I think I'll have the soup,' I said. 'Keep my isotonic levels up.'

He smiled, but it seemed he couldn't tell if I was teasing or not. I was, but I didn't mean to. It just came out.

'It looks really nice,' I said, hoping he wouldn't be insulted. My hand which held the necklace was still trembling. I had to manage this situation or I might spiral.

But thankfully Ryan was fiddling with his phone. 'I had this timer to remind me to alternate my carb with my protein snacks...' he was saying. 'I think I must have not heard the alarm...' He stopped. 'Are you listening to me?'

'Yes,' I said. 'Go on.'

'I was just wondering if I had your full attention? I mean, I give you a hugely expensive necklace and you not only don't listen but you don't put it on.'

'I am listening.' My hand tremor began to creep up my arm. 'I was just thinking about the necklace and how lovely it was. And how generous.'

'I'm glad you like it,' he said. 'I took a bit of time choosing it.'

'It's incredible.'

He nodded, agreeing.

I could feel a whisper of cold breath on the back of my neck, making me squirm. *Oh no. Keep away. Please keep away.*

'Is it carrot?'

'I told you, twenty-four carat...'

'No, the soup.'

He sighed. 'Sweet potato and turmeric, but it's far too salty. I only got it because my beta-carotenes are low...'

I focused on my breathing and trying to look interested in what Ryan was saying. The energy it took to keep things together was exhausting.

'I'm feeling a bit panicky lately,' I admitted. 'I don't know why... but losing Dad... and... well, I know it was a long time ago, but recently, I keep thinking about him.'

He blinked at me, uncomprehending. 'It's sad,' he said. 'People die. I get it. But you have to move on...'

'I'm trying...'

'But Milly,' he went on, 'you have got to count your blessings. *I* should be anxious, being self-employed, running a business. *You* get a pay cheque at the end of the month, we only get paid depending on how hard we've worked.'

I should have known better. In a half-hearted relationship, you don't bring up mental health. You had to be whole-hearted for that. He'd never signed up for the real me, the *whole* me.

'You're right,' I said, 'I'm just distracted. I think I need some of that soup. I think I could be in danger of becoming hypertonic!' I laughed and waved the waiter over in a bid to move things on and smooth them over. My hand was still trembling, I noticed, so I quickly hid it under the table again.

'*You're* not hypertonic,' he said, just as the waiter hovered beside us. 'You shouldn't make fun of those of us who are.' He glanced at the waiter. 'I'll have a glass of wine,' he said. 'Isoflavins and electrolytes are good when you are depleted of energy.'

'I'll have the same,' I said, 'and some soup and bread and a bowl of chips.' I smiled at Ryan, when the waiter had gone. 'I'll be fine once I have some food.'

He gave me a look, but then he softened and smiled. 'I've got a lot on my plate at the moment,' he said. 'Work. Travelling. Keeping everyone happy. Meetings. And now Ken, my PT, gives me a new food plan. It's like, what else does the world want from me? I can't give any more!'

'I know,' I soothed. 'It's not easy.'

'No,' he agreed. 'It's not.'

'But, by the way,' I went on, 'an old friend – acquaintance really – has opened up a wine bar. Siobhán's mad keen for us all to go. It's the opening night.'

'A wine bar?' He spooned the last of his soup into his mouth. 'Sounds a bit old-fashioned... not what people want nowadays.'

'His mum used to run one in the eighties and so...'

'Tell him the eighties are over,' he said. 'People want drinking clubs, cocktails, luxury. Not wooden tables and olives in bowls and tea lights everywhere.' he looked at me. 'I'm right aren't I?'

'Okay, so you don't think it's very fashionable, but it has nice red wine and...' I thought back to Teolaí and the twinkly lights, and orange glow, the gentle ambience and the taste of those olives. '... It's got a really nice atmosphere.'

'WholeFoods has a nice atmosphere,' he said. 'But it's not a place I'd like to hang out. You know me, some old wine bar doesn't really sound exclusive enough. And anyway, Mum and Roger are having a drinks party. I said we'd drop in before going to mine. That okay?'

I felt in some way that I was being bought with the gifts and the presents, and that if I accepted them I would have to do what Ryan wanted.

'Sounds lovely,' I said. I was relieved not to be going to Teolaí and not having to face Darragh and his beautiful girlfriend. But there was also a tug at my heart when I would have liked nothing more than talking to him again, and being friends. But it was all impossible. I was with Ryan now and drinks at his mother and step-father's house awaited.

I texted Siobhan.

We can't make it.

Sad face.

Sorry.

You tried. See you later.

See you later. Have a good time xxx

19

Roger, Ryan's stepfather, had made his usual beeline for me and had cornered me on the window seat of his and Carole's Blackrock house. Across the room, there was the whisky-infused guffaw of a man easily pleased, and the bored tinkle of laughter from a woman who was like one of those toys where you press a button and they react. Laugh. Sympathise. Look interested. Flirt lightly.

From the drawing room, the views out to sea were amongst the best in the city. The house was a huge mock-Georgian mansion with manicured grounds with a dolphin fountain and the coach house where Ryan lived, and inside the house it was all dark panelling and chintz upholstery. In the downstairs loo, the taps were gold swans. I had taken a photo of them the first time I saw them for Siobhán to marvel at.

This evening, Roger was on his favourite subjects: his health. 'It was excruciating. My consultant said he had never seen one so big,' he explained. 'Called in his team to witness it. Jaws were on the ground. You know what these medical people are like, the worse something is, the more excited they get. Practically salivating they were. I was the possessor of the largest hernia ever recorded in the Clinic. They weighed it and said it was the equivalent of a chicken. Plucked and oven-ready. Some of the doctors were snapping away on their phones. Bright red and purple, like a Quality Street, my consultant said, and too big to cut out!' Roger looked particularly proud at this moment. 'Oh no! They had to chip it out, they did, shard by fleshy shard. Amazed they were that I had managed all those years with the equivalent of an oven-ready chicken inside me. It was almost bulbous,' he was saying. 'Quite glorious it was. You'd think at my age that there were few opportunities to feel proud about one's body, but when they showed me the pulsating mass of flesh, I felt a stirring I hadn't felt for years.' He patted his inside jacket pocket. 'I have a photograph on my phone... wait one moment.'

Ryan joined us, smiling. 'Everything all right? Roger, top up? Milly, more wine?'

'Marvellous,' Roger drawled. 'My man, my doctor fella, says I should lay off the old firewater, but I told him I would rather drink my own urine than anything healthy. He was suggesting tap water! I haven't drunk that for thirty years. Filthy stuff. Full of bacteria and viruses. Goes around the insides of every person in the country and it's barely cleaned.'

Whenever I saw Ryan in this house – which was more like an expensive but unstylish hotel than a family home – I felt a bit sorry for him, as though he didn't belong here. His father and Carole had spilt before he was even born, but when she married the exceedingly rich Roger, she and Ryan moved in to this large pile.

'I was just telling Molly here about my hernia,' Roger explained. 'Magnificent beast of a thing it was...'

Ryan's eyes glazed over. 'Fascinating, Roger,' he said. 'Maybe you can tell her more about it another time.'

From the windows, a beautiful view of Dublin bay was spread out, the flashing of the lighthouse on Howth Head, the ferry beetling its way across the Irish Sea, determined to make it to port by dusk.

'I haven't told you about what happened on the golf course, have I?' said Roger, suddenly, as though he'd been racking his brain for conversational matter and thankfully had forgotten about showing me the picture of his hernia. 'Well, it was a funny thing all right...'

Carole appeared beside us. 'May I borrow Milly, Ryan?' she said, slipping her arm into mine. 'Just for a moment. I would like to have a little word. Girl to girl.' She pulled me over to the faded yellow velvet sofa and sat me down beside her. 'My dear,' she said, 'I just thought I hadn't spoken to you all evening, there are so many friends just needing attention from me. But as Ryan's beau, I am only too happy to give you some of my time. Now, I hope you like the necklace, but he said you wouldn't put it on? Is there a problem? Don't you *like* it? We put a great deal of time into choosing it... without mentioning the expense, of course. We couldn't talk about how much something like that costs, could we? And Ryan wanted to go for something more expensive, but I thought modest was more your style. Am I right? But he insisted. We almost had an argument in the shop. But in the end he went with my suggestion. The *single* diamond.'

'It's beautiful,' I said. 'But far too generous.'

'Yes,' she said. 'Yes, it was. People give gifts, Milly, for a reason. Loyalty, usually.' Her lips were pursed as she studied my face for a moment. 'Tell me, how is work? What are you doing at the moment...?' She smiled at me.

'A few bits here and there.'

'Right. Well, any time you want to talk, pick my brain, let me know. I am always here.' And then she was looking at my hair, as though it horrified her. 'Milly,' she said, laying a hand on my arm. 'Now, please don't think me interfering, because you are a very beautiful young woman, it's just that I am rather evangelical about a few things, and I like to spread the message.'

'Okay.' Oh God. I had to galvanise myself for any kind of discourse with this woman. What passive-aggressive put-down would she come up with this time. After the hairbrush incident, I had learned to nod and smile at everything she said.

'Now, please, dearest Milly, do not take this the wrong way...'

Here we go.

She smiled at me. 'It's just that I don't think you put enough effort into your appearance. You could be so much more beautiful than you are. And I wouldn't say this to someone I didn't think wasn't worth it...' She smiled over at Ryan, who had moved away from Roger and was chatting to another guest at the fireplace. 'You have a pretty enough face... but your hair? It's nice enough. But it really needs a restyle. A radical one, to be honest. Or any style at all.' She smiled. 'I hope you don't mind me suggesting such a thing, but it's just that I have a great hair guy. A few lowlights, a better cut... and get those brows done. You have the eyebrows of a mountain sheep. And also I was going to suggest my face man for a few little touches around the eyes... and between here...' She patted between her eyebrows. 'It must be all that straining over documents and whatever it is you do that has made you look a little tired... How old are you now?'

'Thirty-two.'

'Really?' She looked flabbergasted. Carole herself was of an indiscernible age, oscillating between sixteen and sixty, all signs of a life erased by an expert syringe. But sometimes you would get a flash of her real age, which would appear like a hologram and then disappear just as quickly. 'I would have said much, *much* older. I hope you don't think I'm rude. I've often been accused of being blunt. But, as I said, it's just friendly... even maternal, advice. A little freshening up, that's all. Nothing that can't be sorted.'

I was quickly learning that Carole and her poisonous advice should be ignored.

She was studying my face again, the slightly disgusted look had returned. 'And is that hair on your top lip?'

My hand quickly covered my mouth. I hadn't had time to spend on personal housekeeping.

'You know what I am going to do?'she said. 'I am going to give you the number of the salon I go to. Now, they are expensive, but they are top-notch... give them a call and tell them Carole Kingston sent you.' She smiled at me, a less disgusted smile now. 'All right? Isn't that exciting?' She stood up. 'And you have to do something about your slouching!' She gave a laugh. 'It's almost comical, the way you lounge about. You didn't do ballet as a child, I presume?'

'I did actually,' I said, 'but not for very long.'

'Ah, there we have it. Mystery solved.' Behind her, Roger hovered. 'Roger darling, Milly was just saying how much she longed to continue talking to you.' Roger sat down heavily beside me. 'I'll just go and mingle,' she oozed.

I looked out of the windows and out to sea. Across the bay was Howth
Head, a spit of land stretching out to sea, as though it wanted to run away.
Howth was where Darragh had grown up and where his dad still lived.
Darragh spending his childhood looking out to sea, dreaming of a life away
far away even then. And right now, I could see the appeal of running away.

20

I had left Ryan's early the next morning, taking a taxi home, and had got into my own bed with a cup of tea. I was reading the paper, finally feeling safe and unbothered, my stomach unknotted. And then Auntie Angela called.

'Now, you know Harold is coming for lunch today,' she said.

'Yes, of course.'

'We need to have everything shipshape by 1 p.m. precisely. Table laid, tea made. They don't have long, you see, they're going to a talk later at the Botanic Gardens. It's called... Now, where is the booklet? Here it is, "The Wonders of Echeverias"... whatever they are.'

'You don't think it's a bit formal, Angela? I mean, it's a bit *Meet The Parents*.' I wasn't sure if I was up to meeting Harold. The rest of the family might be moving on, but it was happening a bit too fast for me.

'It's the right thing to do,' she said, firmly. 'Believe me, a bit of formality never hurt anyone. When Kitty first brought home your father, well... our mother put out her lovely Donegal lace tablecloth, we used their wedding china... and... I just want to do the same. Now, Sarah is making her scones.' Angela, I noted, had no problem with delegation, unlike Catriona. 'She tried to protest and say she would buy some, but there is nothing like home-made, is there?'

Sarah had once made a very successful batch of scones when she was fifteen in Home Ec. She absolutely hates all forms of cooking and baking, but at every family occasion, she is obliged by Angela to make some. It's Angela's way of making us all feel involved.

'And you're making the sandwiches,' she said. 'I am thinking nice ham. Will you pick up some nice ham on your way? I'll be making my world-famous pavlova, of course,' she went on. 'Such a crowd pleaser that one. Always goes down well. A scene stealer, if you don't mind. Like myself!' She hooted.

Angela's enthusiasm for her own life was undaunted – and her enthusiasm for my mother's life was even more resolute. For some reason, she had taken it upon herself to encourage Mum's moving on from Dad far more vigorously than even Mum.

When I eventually got out of bed, Siobhán was still wrapped in her dressing gown, fluffy slippers on her feet, her hair a matted halo, sitting at the kitchen table, having emerged from the gloom of her bedroom, silently drinking a strong black coffee.

'I can't risk anything else,' she explained, 'or I might throw up after last night at Teolaí. George had to go home early – *quelle surprise* – so I stayed on my own, chatting to Lorenzo... Do you know, he's called Lolo? Isn't that the sweetest name you've ever heard? Anyway, Lolo's grandmother makes her own grappa and, my God, I didn't realise it was so strong. I thought it was just like an Italian alcopop because it tasted like strange sugary water but...' She quailed. 'It's basically Italian rocket fuel.'

'So you were drinking with Lorenzo? Just the two of you?' I began making tea, boiling the kettle, taking down a mug from the cupboard.

'No! Don't be silly! There were loads of us. Francisca and some of their Italian friends. I was the only non-Italian there.' She paused. 'Except for Darragh. But he was working.' She looked up, pushing aside her hair so I could see her face. 'You don't mind, do you? You know, me hanging out with Darragh...?'

I put a tea bag in a cup, and read the small print on the box. 'I told you, didn't I?' I was aware of Siobhán looking at me.

'He asked after you again,' she went on, carefully. 'I think he might feel guilty about the way he treated you.'

I found my voice. 'He should try Confession. I hear there's plenty of room there these days.'

'I think he just wants us all to be friends.'

I busied myself making some toast and pretending to adjust the temperature gauge on the side of the toaster.

'So, how was *your* night?' Siobhán asked.

I really didn't want to tell her I had spent the evening discussing hernias. It didn't exactly make it sound as though I was living my very best life. 'We had a lovely time,' I said. 'Carole was having a drinks party, so we went along. It was really fun.'

'Lorenzo is so lovely,' Siobhán resumed. 'He's up for the hillwalking. So's Francisca, so's Darragh. You and Ryan and me. George is too unfit. And tired. But it's important, I think, to show people around when they come to Ireland.'

Did Siobhán really think me going on a walk with Darragh and his new girlfriend was a normal thing to do? Or maybe it was? Maybe normal people did hang out with old boyfriends five years on? They forgave them for past mistakes and were happy with the new lives they had made. And I should be happy with my life. Who wouldn't want to be a corporate lawyer and to have a handsome and generous boyfriend like Ryan?

Normal people, I thought, didn't have panic attacks at the age of thirty-two, their hands didn't shake so much that they had to hide them just in case anyone noticed.

But Siobhán was miles away, thinking about something, twisting a curl round and round her finger. 'Do you think I need to change my life?' she said suddenly.

'What do you mean?'

'Well, I think it's time. I mean, everyone says that Mercury retrograde means it is time to revaluate your life. I mean, am I on the right path? Am I with the right person? When Mercury goes backwards, one should be prepared to make a few changes. A change of scene. My own horoscope said it and I've been thinking about it *non-stop*.' For a moment, she looked utterly thrilled with the prospect. 'A change of scene... a new adventure...'

'You mean move out of the flat?'

'Never!' she said, and then, as though it was an idea she had already mused upon, 'You might move in with Ryan?'

I couldn't see myself living in the coach house, under the eye of Big Mother, aka Carole. 'Maybe,' I said. 'Or you with George?'

'Maybe.' She sounded less than enthusiastic. But she soon perked up. 'You see, when Mercury is back on track in a few weeks' time,' she said, eyes alive with possibility, 'I have to be in the blocks, ready to go.'

But for me the thought of her leaving, and having to find new flatmates filled me with horror. I sat on my hand to stop it trembling, until I was ready to go and meet the other arbiter of change, my family's very own Mercury – Harold.

21

Sarah was making her scones and Angela was dotting strawberries onto her pavlova when I arrived at Mum's house in Dun Laoghaire, the house I'd grown up in. Betty, our dog, gave me a wonderful welcome, licking all the parts of me she could. Maybe she could sniff out the posh ham I'd bought for the sandwiches. Or maybe she was just pleased to see me. Being in a needy state of mind, I hoped it was the latter.

'If I say so myself,' Angela said, licking a finger, 'even Nigella would be proud of this. What do you think, girls?'

'Stupendous, Angela,' Sarah said. 'A work of art.'

Angela beamed. 'I don't know why it came out so well. Even the peaks are particularly impressive, aren't they?'

Sarah put her scones in the oven. 'You make one thing once and it turns out edible,' she said, 'and then you have to make them for the rest of your life. I would have let them burn if I'd known they would become my albatross, the cross I have to bear.'

'But you do them so well,' said Angela. 'Like my pavlova. Perfection.'

'I'm too tired to bake,' said Sarah, taking Betty from me, sitting down. 'I'm just so tired lately...' She stopped speaking and nuzzled Betty's fuzzy head.

'What's up?' I asked.

'Nothing,' she said. 'Doesn't matter. I'm fine. I mean, who isn't tired these days?' She pulled a face. 'Aren't we all meant to be burned out, running on empty... I just...' But she stopped again.

She did look utterly exhausted. Sarah cooed into Betty's ear.

'How is she?' I said, sitting down beside her. But I really meant, 'how are you?'

'I can't tell,' she said, kissing Betty's head. 'She's kind of slow and doesn't eat very much. I bought some chicken breast for her as a treat.'

'Sarah!' I laughed. 'And you a vegetarian!'

She scowled at me. 'But Betty isn't.'

Mum came into the kitchen.

'Give us a twirl, Kitty!' said Angela. 'Let's have a look at you! Thankfully you are not wearing that awful pocket waistcoat thing!'

Mum was wearing a new linen blouse and had new highlights in her hair.

'You look lovely,' I said.

'Thank you.' She blushed a little. 'Angela chose the blouse.'

'I always said Kitty looks pretty in pink,' Angela piped up. 'On me, it makes me look like a big fat baby, but Kitty looks pretty. Our father used to say, pink to make the boys wink. Well, Harold will be winking!'

Whenever Mum wore something new or nice, Dad used to say, 'You're a sight for sore eyes. Even in your old gardening clothes.' I wished I could hear his voice in my head. The memory was too far away to grab it and hold it close.

'Angela,' Mum said. 'It's a talk on succulents! Not a night out at the opera!'

'Well, it doesn't hurt anyone to make an effort,' Angela replied. 'Now, come with me for a moment and I'll put some of that Funny Face on you.'

I waited until they were well gone before I said anything. 'Don't you think Angela is being a bit controlling?' What I really wanted to find out was if Sarah minded Mum having a boyfriend and moving on.

Sarah pulled a face. 'You mean after all these years, you haven't noticed Angela's meddling, controlling tendencies? We're her hobby.' She went back to stroking Betty. 'Did I tell you Angela even went to see Hugh?'

'Hugh?'

Sarah nodded. 'Tried to find out why we split up.' Sarah rolled her eyes. 'Can you believe it?'

'Why *did* you split up?'

'Oh God! You're just as bad! I know! Why don't *you* go and ask Hugh? Just what I need, another interfering relative!' She closed her eyes as though I was the very last straw. 'I can't believe I have to spell it out to both of you. It's none of your business!'

'Sorry,' I said quietly.

'It's okay,' she said, eventually. 'Anyway, Hugh was unfailingly polite to Angela, as he always is. He told her that he couldn't tell her, but that he appreciated her concern. She actually came to the hospital and waited until he came out of surgery.' She shook her head.

'How did you find out?'

'He told me of course! What do you think? You spend a decade of your life with someone and then, just because it's not working out, you never see them again? We still talk, see each other. We're just not... *together*.'

'Sorry,' I said again.

'Stop saying sorry.'

'I just worry about you, that's all,' I said.

Her expression softened. 'Well, I worry about you as well.'

I laughed. 'We've got to stop being people that people worry about,' I said.

'Would make a good start.' She smiled at me. 'Make life easier.'

'By the way, Darragh's back in Dublin,' I said. 'For good.'

'Darragh? Your Darragh?'

I nodded. 'Just opened a wine bar near the flat. So now I am in constant danger of bumping into him, and I'm trying to pretend to everyone that I'm completely cool with it.'

'Don't be,' she said, suddenly animated. 'Never be cool with being treated badly.' She turned to me, a fierce look on her face. 'Ignore him. Stay well away. God! When I think about what he did to you!'

I was slightly stunned for a moment. I had no idea that Sarah even remembered what had happened.

Then she suddenly screamed, Betty jumping off her lap with fright.

'The scones! The bloody scones! They're burned. Maybe now Angela won't ask me to make the fecking things ever again.'

* * *

When he arrived, Harold was very short – smaller than Mum, and even with his wire-rimmed spectacles, he squinted at us, blinking. His suit was slightly creased and he sported a bow tie which was dotted with tiny cacti and he was holding a cloth shopping bag. He couldn't have been more different to my dad.

'Harold,' said Mum, 'these are my daughters, Sarah and Milly.'

'*Salve*,' he said, holding up a hand in greeting. 'Or for those who are not Latin enthusiasts, hello. My children call me a Latin nut, but I like to think of myself as a lover of Latin...'

Out of the corner of my eye, I could see Sarah was grinning. 'You mean a Latin L...' she began, but Angela gave her a hard stare, and she stopped.

'Indeed,' said Harold, seriously. 'I am determined to keep the language from death's door. Not on my watch will it die. *Non hodie moriar!*' He beamed at us and then took my hand in both of his, and grasped it. It felt like being greeted by a mole. Albeit one who spoke ancient languages. He then grasped Sarah's hand as well in his paws, but then suddenly let go as though he'd just remembered something. 'Gifts! I bring gifts!' After digging around in his bag, he handed us both a small succulent in a tiny clay pot. '*Echeveria agavoides sirius*,' he explained to Sarah. And then to me, 'And this one is *echeveria elegans*. Good for air purifying, mind focusing, increasing oxygen levels. Now, don't thank me as they are cuttings. I spread succulents like confetti. I think every desk should have one, every windowsill should have several, and every home should be overrun with them.' He beamed again.

'It's lovely,' I said.

'Thank you,' said Sarah. She looked at me. What do you think? She was saying.

I ignored her. I wasn't sure what I thought.

22

'Come on, Harold,' said Mum, 'I'll put the kettle on and we'll have a sandwich.'

'Ah, sandwich!' he said wistfully, scuttling after Mum, as though it was a dreamy, far-off substance.

'And Sarah's done her lovely scones,' said Angela.

'Oh! A scone!' he enthused. 'Now, that's clever!' He turned back to nod encouragingly at Sarah.

'Not really,' she said. 'They are literally the only thing I can make and they are a little overdone.'

'With a cup of tea, they'll be perfect,' said Angela.

Harold sat at the head of the table, his legs dangling and feet not quite touching the floor, but Betty, I noticed, sniffed around at his shoes for a while, and then settled down beside him.

'She likes you!' said Mum, pleased.

'Most dogs do,' said Harold. 'It can be an affliction. I can't walk through a park without attracting quite the pack. It can be embarrassing.'

'Pheromones,' Angela offered, knowingly. 'You must have a surplus. I once met a man in Dubai who told me a fascinating story about the time he encountered a tiger... they were on safari to Namibia and when they had set up camp he – being the alpha male type and refusing to take instruction –

ventured further than the perimeter which the guides had marked. And, lo
and behold, a tiger began to step stealthily towards him, saliva dripping...
This man, this *alpha male*, was understandably terrified and lifted up his
arms in fright or in surrender, and the tiger caught a whiff of his under-
arms. The man said he could see its nostrils twitching and the tiger stopped
still, dropped to his front paws and rolled over, submissive and tame as a
kitten.'

'Are you suggesting Harold is sweaty?' Sarah teased.

'Of course I wasn't,' said Angela. 'I was being complimentary. Not
everyone has an impressive pheromone level.'

Sarah laughed. 'So, sweaty, then.' She grinned at us.

'Do you live around here, Harold?' I said, changing the subject, knowing
how much Sarah loved Angela's conversational ambulations and would
quite happily egg her along until nothing sensible was said at all.

'Oh yes,' he said, 'just down the road. Sandycove. Or what I would call
Sinus Sabulo, the cove of sand.' He gave a little laugh.

Mum placed the pot of tea in front of him.

'You like just a drop of milk, don't you?' she said. 'And first from the pot.'

He nodded. 'If that's not too much trouble.'

'None at all.' She smiled at him, and he blinked back at her, shyly, but
pleased, the two of them already seeming together and it was obvious that
they didn't need our approval or acceptance. 'Well, this looks nice. I am
very glad I left home for this wonderful array. It's a roman banquet,' Harold
commented, peering out from behind the tower of sandwiches. 'Are you
responsible for these, Milly?'

'And Harold,' Angela interjected, 'there's my *pavlova* to come.' There
was the touch of an Italian accent. 'And *Wexford* strawberries.' She nodded
meaningfully at us all. 'Only the best on such an occasion.'

Harold didn't seem to mind this scrutiny or pressure. He'd survived the
pheromone awkwardness and was handling us all with aplomb.

'It's so good to meet you both,' said Harold to me and Sarah. 'Your
mother has told me so much about you. I already feel very familiar with
you. I have two children of my own... one is thirty-five and the other thirty-
six. So not children, per se. They keep me on my toes, I can tell you. When
my wife passed away, they found it hard, naturally. We all did. But they

have both made excellent lives for themselves. One is a geologist, the other works for bands as a sound engineer.'

Sarah's eyebrows lifted in interest. 'What sort of bands?' she asked.

'I think the word is *electronica*,' replied Harold. 'I am not sure exactly what that entails, but I assume electricity plays a role.'

'And Harold is a lecturer,' said Mum, pouring us all some tea and sitting down beside him.

'*Was*,' said Harold. 'I am now a man of leisure. Or, I think, in Latin one might say, *via otium*. I taught geology, geography and... of course, Latin. Until it became *obsoleta*.' He paused. 'I do go on, you must forgive me. My own two children are always saying that I tend to hog the available oxygen and that I am overfond of my own tones.'

'Not at all!' said Angela, stoutly. 'Far better be a chatterbox than sit there with your tongue all tied up. We like talkers in this family, don't we?'

Sarah gave a half-shrug as though it was debatable. 'Depends on the talker,' she said.

'Everyone help themselves,' said Mum. 'Harold, jam and cream with your scone? Or start with the sandwiches?'

'Hmmm,' he mused, taking it all in. 'I think start sweet, veer towards savoury, maybe a U-turn back to sweet, and then a handbrake turn to savoury, and a screech into sweet, thus oscillating my way through this thoroughly delicious-looking repast.' He smiled charmingly at her, his little glasses bobbing on his nose. 'As Hippocrates says, let sandwiches be thy medicine and medicine be thy scone.' He beamed again at Mum, who laughed just as heartily as him. It had been a long, long time since I had seen her so happy. I had to be happy for her.

This lovely non-axe-murderer, Harold, was delightful, but there was a feeling in the pit of my stomach that I couldn't quite explain. I wasn't anchored, I thought, there was nothing pulling me to earth, no gravity, no tug of home. I was floating in space.

I felt a shiver down the back of my spine. We were all on the same page of grief, I had thought, and were all reading at the same pace. But it turned out Mum was nearly finished and I couldn't get past chapter one. You think you're all together, all losing the same incredibly well-loved person, but grief is different for everyone, I was realising. Mum had had to deal with all that loss – her husband, her future, her retirement. Her whole life was wrapped up in Dad's and his with hers, and in a way, her loss was greater. And yet, she was doing better than I was. She had had to recalibrate far more than I had. All her life plans had ended the day Dad died. I couldn't admire her more.

Mum and Dad's grand plan was to hire a motorhome and travel from Ireland, through France and into Spain. They planned it for when Sarah and I had left home and all they had to think about was themselves. They had talked about it for years, sticking a map to the kitchen wall, the two of them planning different routes and poring over their Michelin road guides. Mum had already taken early retirement from Blackrock Community College and they were waiting for Dad to step down from the accountancy firm he'd worked in all his adult life. Finally, he retired and the motorhome was booked, the ferry paid for, Betty's pet passport applied for.

Except... there was the small issue of the pain in Dad's chest. A routine GP visit was followed up with a trip to a consultant, which was followed up by scans and tests and then the hospital stays began. They should have been packing and writing lists and issuing instructions on watering the tomatoes in the greenhouse, but instead he was enduring weeks and weeks of tests followed by hospital appointments, overnight visits, blood tests, scans, elimination diets. Eventually, he was diagnosed with chronic heart disease and he was put on the waiting list for a triple bypass. The European Tour was put on hold while we waited for the recovery that never came.

'We should have gone years ago,' he'd said to Mum, towards the end, holding her hand, Sarah and I hovering behind her in the hospital room. Angela was there too, I remember, a quiet presence, making us all tea, pre-empting any needs. 'We spent too long planning.'

'We still will,' Mum had said. 'We'll just go next summer. She had developed a new smile, the one she plastered on when she needed to look as though she wasn't worried about anything. 'We'll just get you out of here and we'll go.'

'Won't be long now,' he'd said, looking beyond her to us, as Sarah and I quickly rearranged our faces from total devastation to happy and optimistic daughters.

'Just don't eat too much bread and cheese,' said Sarah. 'Or drink too much wine.'

He did come home eventually, but it was to say goodbye. Betty slept beside Dad's bed, on the floor, refusing to move, and we had to drag her out for walks.

'Maybe we should have just gone. Years ago. Not waited,' he'd said.

She'd held his hand. 'Maybe.' She'd looked at us. 'Maybe.'

'I'm glad we didn't,' he'd said. 'We had everything we needed right here.' He'd looked at me, then Sarah, and we crowded him, holding his hands. 'I was the richest of them all. I had you three.'

We'd had each other.

But there was one last present for Mum, which he had planned to give her on the ferry on the first night of their adventure: an eternity ring, a slim silver band with a tiny pearl. 'Pearl for happiness,' he'd explained, 'for my happy pearl.'

Mum had slipped it on and she'd wiped away a tear.

And in that one tiny moment, I realised she was giving up. She knew he wasn't going to make it. And, of course, he didn't.

The rest is a blur. All I can remember is Mum calling to tell me to come to the hospice. And driving there, battling with my anxiety, refusing to let it spoil this last moment with Dad. I would not let it stop me from getting there.

I abandoned the car outside the hospital, not even shutting the door and racing in, my heart about to explode, seeing Mum, seeing Sarah, already crying... as our family of four became three.

The end.

The end of life, I suppose. The end of our family. The end of ever feeling normal again. Sadness and pain slithered over me.

Leaving him behind in the hospice was the hardest thing – his body wouldn't be brought to the house until the next day – and then going home to our house, which felt different, as though the ions in the air had been altered, the world fundamentally changed. Betty didn't make a noise, not a squeak or a whimper, but sat as silently as us, and then, when we sat at the kitchen table, she laid her head on Mum's feet.

We tried to reconfigure our lives, no longer that strong and stable square but now a rather rickety triangle. Not until the end, did I believe that Dad was dying. And not until a week later, when Darragh – my rock, my constant, my soulmate – had gone to Italy, did I realise that life wasn't always on your side. From stability to chaos to despair in a matter of months.

23

'Hold the lift! Wait!' Susie was clutching her coffee and was trying to run in heels towards me. 'Wait!'

It was Monday morning and I had a coffee in both hands but managed to slam on the open-doors with an elbow. I'd spent the previous day getting ready for the week, like I did on most Sundays. Washing and ironing and preparing any work. Sundays were the least fun part of my week. I liked to be organised, always had five days' worth of office attire hanging up and ready to go.

'Thank you!' she said. 'I'm so late. Couldn't get out of bed and I am just too tired.' She chugged her coffee, as though it had magical healing properties. Which, you might argue, it did.

'Late night?'

She nodded. 'Maybe 3 a.m.? I was too exhausted to look at the time.'

At least, I thought, Susie was having fun and there was one person in this entire building who still went out and drank too much and staggered home in the early hours.

'Where were you?' I asked.

She looked at me, puzzled. And then, 'Oh, I wasn't *out.*' She laughed at the absurdity of the idea. 'I was at home, working, writing my dissertation.'

'You're studying?'

'Yes! Law, of course! Now, I know all you fully qualified lawyers always say the same thing: don't become a lawyer, it's too soul destroying, go travelling, and have a proper life or become a zoo keeper or a hairdresser, get out while you are yet to be corrupted...'

'Do they say that?' Maybe we all thought it, and only said it to non-lawyers, so as not to appear weak.

She nodded. 'I still want to be a lawyer, though.' She grinned at me, sipping her coffee. 'There is literally nothing that makes me happier.'

'You're like a young Catriona,' I said. 'I bet she was like you.'

'I wish,' said Susie. 'I'd do anything to be like her. She's so brainy. And scary.'

I could only nod in agreement.

'So, you're doing your...?'

'My law degree. I've been doing it for three years as a mature student. Well, mature-*ish*.' She gave a little dance with her shoulders. 'I wasn't one of those swotty kids at school. I had too much fun. Smoking, parties...' She pulled a face. 'My poor parents. Didn't do a stroke of work...'

'I *was* one of those swotty students,' I said. 'Had zero fun at school. The fun only got going at university.' And had utterly petered out now.

She nodded. 'Of course you were a swot, everyone in this building was. I'm still playing catch-up.'

The lift stopped on the first floor and Nora, one of the other secretaries, stepped in. 'Morning, Susie, morning, Milly.'

'How's it going, Nora?' said Susie. 'Anyway,' she said, continuing our conversation, 'so major cop-on situation. The party had gone on far too long. And... well, there were a few things I had to confront. I remember thinking that this was all my life would be, working the night shift in a cash and carry. Until...' She paused. 'I went back to college – which was humiliating and got my Leaving Cert in a year. That was hard. And now I've been doing a law degree at night. That's even harder. And this solicitor who once represented me when I was up in court for something...' she pulled an embarrassed face, 'put me in contact with Mr McAvoy and that's how all this came about. So, no more fun for me.'

'Apart from the muffin roulette competition later,' said Nora. 'That's going be a hoot.'

'Muffin roulette?' I said.

'Jarleth's organised it,' Nora explained. 'You each choose a muffin and one is filled with a burn-your-head-off hot chilli and the others are just normal. Basically, if you choose the wrong one, you could actually die. We're going to have the fire extinguishers at the ready, aren't we, Susie? Jarleth says that we are definitely going to win the most craic office in Ireland. There's a doughnut hoopla next week.'

The doors opened on my floor. 'Hopefully,' said Susie, 'one day, I'll be doing what you do. Corporate law. It is literally my dream. The thought of...' The door began to close and Susie leaned on the button. 'Nearly got you compressed there!' she said.

I was about to make a weak joke about it being the story of my life, when, somewhere beyond us, we heard the sound of a baby crying. Nora, Susie and I looked at each other. Catriona? Susie hopped out after me and Nora was elevated away.

We both quickened our pace down the corridor. 'She's brought her in?' said Susie, wide-eyed with excitement. 'I thought she said babies and work didn't mix? Or maybe something's *happened*?' It struck me that work was impossible being just work. It had to have drama or intrigue, or even muffin roulette. Susie was practically running now and I broke into a jog to keep up.

Pacing up and down, a crying Lydia on her shoulder, was Catriona.

'You've brought the baby in!' squealed Susie, but one look from Catriona shut us both up. Hers was the face of a broken woman. The sound was deafening.

'She won't be quiet,' said Catriona, near to tears. 'I don't know what to do. I've tried feeding her, changing her, jiggling and rocking. I've changed her Babygro thinking that perhaps the other one was too itchy. I even gave her a lick of a chocolate biscuit – my grandmother used to do that with me when I was upset – but that didn't work. And I even tried singing, but that made her worse.'

'Where's Josephine?' I said, absorbing some of Catriona's panic.

'She's gone to see her mother,' she said. 'She's very ill apparently, and the agency don't have anyone else. And so we were awake all night.' And Catriona began to cry. It was unnerving to see someone you had considered emotionally rock-solid crying, but today, standing beside her desk, wiping her eyes with the sleeve of her beautiful beige silk dress, she looked human. Maybe *I* could take her and rock her to sleep. Maybe I had heretofore unnoticed baby-whispering talents, was the woman with the magic touch. I put the coffees on the desk, ready to display my Supernanny skills.

'Maybe I could take Lydia and try to soothe—'

Catriona practically dropped her into my arms, collapsed into her chair and closed her eyes. 'It's just so piercing,' she mumbled. 'My eyes are hurting from the sound... how is that even *possible*?'

With the tiny bundle close to my chest, I made shushing sounds and swayed a little, but still Lydia screamed. My shushing sounds began to get louder, competing with Lydia's howls. My swaying became deranged.

'What am I going to do?' Catriona said. 'It could be a *week* until Josephine comes back. A week!' She looked at us in disbelief. 'I can't ring her up and make her come back because her mother isn't well and she wants to make sure she's comfortable and the doctor's been and everything.' She paused. 'And so, I'm in charge. Of my own child. And I don't think I can do it as well. Josephine is brilliant at it. But me...? And who can't look after a baby? But no one tells you how difficult it can be. My friend, Louise, potty trained her Hamilton when he was *six* months old. And Hamilton never cried, she said. Even when the cat scratched him and drew blood.' She shook her head. 'I push Lydia in the park and I see other people with babies who don't cry, who are sitting there looking around with little hats on, smiling. The good mothers, the capable ones. The women who are meant to have babies.' She began to cry again. 'For the first time in my life, I don't know what to do. I am delirious with lack of sleep. I thought imposter syndrome was for successful women. I didn't realise that you could feel like an imposter mother. I shouldn't be allowed to do this.'

On cue, Lydia let out a roar filled with renewed energy.

Catriona went on, her voice trembling, 'I didn't really think it was going to be like this. I didn't think it would actually be hard. You know you think how hard is it to look after something you can fit in your handbag, but it is hard, it's really, really hard.' She took her coffee and drank it back as though it would magick her into someone who could stop a baby crying. I nodded my head, trying to understand, but feeling as helpless as she did, realising that being good at exams, training as a lawyer and wearing a suit all day did not qualify you for anything other than working in an office.

'My friends all breeze through being a mother,' admitted Catriona. 'One of them, Sorcha, gets her children up at 7 a.m. to do Mandarin. Another has a child who has just represented Ireland in the World Spelling Bee. She's only eight and came fifth... which they were more than a little disappointed with. Tripped up on the word logorrhea. No, me neither. Had to look it up. It's verbal diarrhoea which is ironic because the child does not stop talking. I had to discuss the American elections with her last time. And Becca has fecking twins. They can already make their own breakfast. They are two years old! And now Sorcha wants us all to go to Lisbon for a girls' weekend. Told me to leave Lydia with Josephine... but... I don't want to go... I just want to get this right...' She paused for breath, while Lydia's screams continued with the gusto of an Italian tenor.

'I think I might be able to help,' Susie said, holding out her hands to take Lydia. 'May I? I have four younger siblings and I nannied in New York for two years.'

Catriona nodded. She would have done, I suspected, if Rasputin had offered to take the baby, but we watched as Susie turned Lydia so she was facing down and balanced her on her arm. For a moment, Lydia teetered a little, and wobbled, but then she released a burp so huge, the three of us laughed.

'Wow,' we breathed in unison.

Open mouthed, we waited for the vibrations to cease... and then there was silence, glorious, wonderful silence.

'I bet Hamilton couldn't burp like that,' I said, and Catriona grinned.

'I don't think he has ever burped or farted,' she said. 'He's too busy going on about the solar system. He knows every planet, and every bloody moon.' she stopped. 'I shouldn't be mean,' she said. 'He's a sweet little boy. He just likes the sound of his own voice. Takes after his father.'

Susie efficiently righted Lydia and held her close to her as the baby closed her eyes and went straight to sleep.

'Oh my God,' said Catriona. 'What witchcraft is this?'

Susie shrugged modestly. 'It's nothing.' She basked in the glow of success.

'It's genius,' I said.

'Would you mind putting her in her pram, please?' whispered Catriona.

Susie placed the sleeping Lydia down and tucked her blanket around her, a woman of many wonderful talents.

'I'm going to phone Little Dumplings, the crèche down the street,' I said. 'They open early and I'll see if they can take her for the week. Okay?'

Catriona nodded.

'And I am going to make you one of Mr McAvoy's secret coffees from his special supply. It's *very* expensive. Flown in from London once a month,' said Susie, heading upstairs. 'And I'll put a tot of whisky in it as well. I go on the basis that the dustier the bottle, the better the whisky.' She winked at us both. 'And Irish coffee before 9 a.m. is officially designated as medicinal.'

In no time at all, Catriona was sitting on the low, leather couch in the corner of the office which was normally reserved for informal client meetings, drinking an Irish coffee.

'I think every day should start with one of those,' said Susie.

Catriona slipped off her shoes and sank into a lying position, her legs curled up, as Susie covered her with her Max Mara cashmere coat.

Within moments, there was the sound of soft snoring from both pram and sofa.

I switched off the overhead lights and closed the door.

'I'll pop back down in half an hour to see how the two madams are getting on,' said Susie. 'And put Little Dumplings on the expense account. If some of the male partners can expense all those meals and endless drinks and bottles of Bollinger and Midleton Very Rare Whisky, I think a week of emergency childcare could be equally expensed, don't you?'

I felt quite humbled, safe in the superhero hands of young women like Susie. Ridiculously capable and ambitious. And kind. The sort of person the world of corporate law needed more than anything. I hoped she would hurry up and get qualified and then change the world.

24

Mrs Murphy opened her front door of the flat with the white cat sitting at her feet, as though he was welcoming me too.

It was Wednesday and I had spent the last couple of days researching the rights of Mrs Murphy, along with all my other work with Catriona.

'Good afternoon, Milly,' said Mrs Murphy, 'we've been waiting for you.' The cat slunk in a figure of eight around her ankles. 'Kettle is boiled and Frederick has had his fur brushed for the occasion. He didn't like it very much, did you, Freddie?' She smiled down at him. 'Never were keen on fuss, were you?'

'He looks very smart,' I agreed, following her into the living room, where tea things had been laid out ready on a tray. 'Who else is here?' I said.

'Just us,' she said. 'Why?'

'It's just that you said *we've* been waiting. I wondered who you meant.' I smiled at her, hoping she didn't think I was being rude.

'We?' she beamed back at me, as she lowered herself into the armchair. 'Why, Frederick and I, of course!'

The cat looked back at me, and seemed to give a smug little nod, as though to say, 'There you go.' He gave his bum a waggle as he moved around and sat down on the ground beside her feet.

'Shall I just run through a few things?' I said. 'Just bring you up to speed on everything, your rights, the choices we can make, our chances of winning and what direction I think we should bring the case?'

'Up to speed?' she said. 'We don't know what that means, do we Frederick?' Two pairs of eyes – human and feline – waited for my answer.

'Just update you,' I said, 'that's all.' I went on to talk her – *them* – through everything. 'So,' I ended, 'I hope to build a strong enough case so that when we face Alpha Holdings in court, it will be immediately dismissed.'

'What do you think, Frederick?' she said to the cat. 'Do you think it will? You always knew so much, so full of good advice and wisdom, what do you think?'

The cat looked at her, a very serious expression on his face.

Perhaps it was better if Mrs Murphy didn't stay in the flat, I thought. I was beginning to think that staying here, on her own, with a white cat for company, wasn't the most sensible of plans.

'Mrs Murphy?' I said. 'The cat...?'

'Yes?' She gazed at me beatifically.

'Do you think the cat is...?'

'Do I think the cat is what? You mean, Frederick?'

I nodded. 'Your husband.'

'Ah!' she said, smiling benignly. 'Another disbeliever. Daphne was the same.'

'It's not that I don't believe...' I insisted, 'I'm just curious.' But I felt even more protective of her, thinking about how grief can make you believe all sorts of things. I wish I could believe as fervently that Dad could return.

'Until it happens to you,' she said, 'how can you be sure?' She gave me a small smile that nearly broke my heart.

Whatever it took, I thought. Whatever you need to get you through. Dementia or not, believing the cat was Frederick wasn't hurting anyone. In fact, it was helping her and it wasn't any of my business.

'It's so comforting to have him back again, after all these years and thinking I'd lost him for ever. Turns out, he was next door all the time. I was wondering why this little cat would leave his comfortable home with Daphne, get in somehow through the basement and come all the way up the stairs, and then I realised – Frederick has come back to keep an eye on me.'

Frederick was purring contentedly, stretched out, eyes closed, perfectly happy, as though listening to this love story.

'He's my guardian angel,' she went on. 'My sister used to come back, after she had passed. She used to tell me the most interesting things about life in the afterlife. Although that sounds like a double negative. She'd met Michael Collins himself, and Queen Victoria. Thought she was a bit snobby, but Mick, she said, was a real gentleman. Which is just what you would expect. But when I married Frederick, she didn't come back again. And I missed her, but he was my pal. And then when he left... I hoped she'd return, but instead, this little chap turned up. The only fly in the ointment is that he isn't much of a talker. Rose was a chatterbox, in this world and the next. Used to have wonderful chats with Mr Oscar Wilde and, you'll be glad to know, he was universally loved and adored up there. A comforting thought, is it not?'

I had seen people with dementia before, but this wasn't quite it. Mrs Murphy's grey eyes were as clear and focused as anybody's I'd ever met.

'I kept waiting for him to come back to me,' she was saying, 'and then, last year, he did. I always knew he would.' She looked across at me. 'Who is your guardian angel? Anyone passed over that watches over you?'

I shook my head. 'Not that I know of.'

'There's always someone, a grandmother perhaps? The nice, kind ones come back to make sure their grandchildren are fine. But some of the more selfish ones like to have the kind of fun they didn't have when they were on this side of the divide. But I knew it was Frederick the very first time he came slinking in here. My Frederick had white hair, you see. Went white while he was still in his twenties, would you believe?' She bent down to kiss the cat. 'Didn't you, Frederick. Didn't you, my sweet?'

'We were never able to have children,' she continued, 'but instead of being sad and defeated, Frederick saw it as a blessing, because we would mean more to each other, we were all each other had. Of course, I thought that if we didn't have a child, we weren't quite a proper family, and that just one child would have completed us, but Frederick didn't let me think for a second that *he* was disappointed. He made me feel as though we needed nothing else. And do you know something, Milly, maybe he was right.' She held the cat's head in both her hands and pulled him to her lips where she placed a very gentle kiss on it.

'It's the little things that make marriage wonderful. The 12 p.m. wave, the cup of tea in bed, listening to jazz records. Yes, there were sadnesses because we couldn't have children, and that was a great disappointment to both of us, but the wave, just as the bells of the Pepper Canister rang, righted the world.' She smiled at me and then struggled to her feet, using her stick to winch herself up.

I tried to help, but she ignored my hand, eventually wobbling to a standstill.

'I think,' she said, 'I will put on some music. Louis Armstrong? He's one of Frederick's favourites. Isn't he?' The cat's tail swayed in response. 'We played him at our wedding.'

She went over to an old record player and carefully put the stylus on the edge of the record, and then there was the crackle and the first note of that unmistakable trumpet.

'Dublin was full of jazz clubs then,' she went on, after she had settled herself and Frederick back into the chair. 'No one had very much money, and you'd go to somewhere like The 44 Club on Gardiner Street and make a drink last all evening. Or we'd have parties where people would bring their instruments, or others would recite a poem. Life flew by.' She paused for a moment and took another sip of her tea. 'Do you know, Milly? After he died, for years I kept looking out of the window, expecting to see his little white handkerchief from across the square.' She stopped, one hand stroking the cat, the other looking over my shoulder, lost in her thoughts. 'The shock of not seeing it surprised me every day. Silly really, but I forgot he was gone, he was so inside me. I was having conversations and making all these plans as though he was still here, physically. And then I'd look, expect the wave... and then nothing.' She looked back at me. 'It takes a long while for the mind to let go... the heart never lets go... but the mind takes its time to catch up with events. It's like some kind of reconditioning. I had to teach myself he was gone, like learning a language. And then...' Mrs Murphy and the cat looked at each other. 'He came back.' She gave a small laugh. 'But until he turned up again, I was speaking the language of loneliness fluently, I wondered what was the point of it all.'

Frederick was looking at her face, listening as intently as I was.

'When you have someone in your heart. When they are deep down, tucked away, looked after and warmed by you... well, they don't go far. You don't forget them. You don't really move on, whatever people say.'

I thought how much I wished Dad would come back as a cat. Or a dog. Anything. I was almost jealous of Mrs Murphy and her Frederick, the white cat.

25

The house next door was a mirror image of Mrs Murphy's building, but this one hadn't been sliced and segmented into separate units, it was one large and imposing hotel; smarter and grander, with a red-painted door, flanked by topiaried bay trees. I rang the bell and waited.

A woman in overalls splattered with white paint opened the door.

'I'm sorry,' she said. 'We're closed.' She smiled at me. 'No guests for another month.'

'Daphne?'

'Yes?'

'I'm Mrs Murphy's solicitor and representing her in the case against Alpha Holdings.'

She squinted at me, as though disbelieving. 'Would you mind showing me some ID?'

I riffled in my bag for a business card, handed one over and Daphne read it carefully and then looked back at me.

'I need to make sure,' she said. 'There's been a few others who've knocked on the door.' She stood to one side to allow me to pass. 'Would you like to come in?'

Inside was white and airy, with a chequerboard-tiled floor, a large side-

board with a row of tiny vases filled with violets, and pots of trailing gera-
niums on each step of the sweeping staircase.

'Beautiful place,' I said.

'It's a labour of love,' Daphne said, as she led me downstairs to the basement kitchen and motioned for me to sit at a large and long, scrubbed pine
table. 'It was crumbling and damp when we bought it about eight years
ago,' she said, filling the kettle. 'Slowly, room by room, we've been bringing
it back to its former glory. Pierre, my husband, said I was mad to take it on,
but we'd just moved back from Paris, and I needed a project. My parents
ran a hotel for years back home in Skibbereen, and I'd run away from it all.
Looking after people all the time, the cleaning of bedrooms and the endless
tea making... talking of which, will you have one?'

I nodded. 'Thank you.'

'And then my mother died, and there was this strange niggling feeling and I
couldn't work out what it was about, or what the universe was trying to tell me.
Pierre thought I'd gone mad with grief. I kept saying, I don't know what it is I
am meant to do. But when the fog of grief began to clear a little, I knew the only
thing I wanted to do was to run a hotel. And when we came back to Dublin, we
bought this old house and... well... I've never been happier. Running away and
becoming an architect, trying so hard to be something different to my mother
took so much out of me. I feel so much more peaceful now.' She smiled at me.
'Except the wolves are at the door. Alpha Holdings. They've bought the
building behind us, and they are trying to buy this, but I'm not budging. But
Mary is vulnerable. Well, they think she is. Do you know anything about
Alpha Holdings? Have you come into contact with them before?'

I shook my head. 'None of us have. Even my boss hasn't heard of them.
They were only registered in Companies House last year. The director is
someone called Bernard Hessling, there's a co-director a Mr R De Vere.'

'R De Vere,' she repeated, 'like something out of a Bond film.'

'Isn't it? And tell me about the white cat... I think that Mrs Murphy
thinks he's her husband?'

Daphne smiled. 'Well, actually he's called Pussy Galore – another Bond
reference!' She laughed. 'But Mary rechristened him. I've only had him for
a year, but he kept disappearing for hours at a time. After a while I gave up

worrying about him, because he would come back every so often, looking plump and happy. Then, I was in Mary's house, taking her evening meal...'

'I was going to say, it's really kind of you...'

'It's nothing. I have to cook anyway for myself and Pierre, so a small plate of food for Mary is nothing.' She shook her head. 'It makes *me* feel better. I don't think I would be able to sleep if I thought of her not eating. She's in great health, for her age. It's just not the most age-friendly flat.'

'But she wants to stay?'

'Of course! It's her home. I'm an architect by training, and I have done a few drawings to make it more age-friendly, such as changing the bathroom, simplifying the kitchen... but that's a lot of upheaval for her. And you know something, it's a point of principle. What they are doing is wrong. We can't just let them do it. Whatever Mary decides at the end of the day will not be because some bullies forced her into leaving. And if she wants to believe my cat is her husband, then what's the problem?'

She was right. There was absolutely no problem at all.

* * *

I walked back to the office and found Catriona eating her afternoon Twix at her desk, her phone in her hand, as though she didn't want to miss a single message.

'Noel has Lydia today,' she said, when I went to drop something to her. 'Decided that he had to get better at it all, and took the day off and said Lydia wouldn't be going to Little Dumplings. We've been muddling through, us both desperately googling or asking Alexa everything. I don't know how people did it before Alexa's wise advice. Noel asked her how warm a baby's bottle should be, and it turned out we were two degrees too warm.' She paused. 'Two. Degrees.' She shook her head. 'He asked her to sing the baby a lullaby and it sent him to sleep faster than Lydia. She was still awake when I went in at 7 p.m., but he was curled up in the foetal position.' She smiled. 'It's quite the adventure.'

'It sounds like you are at least coping,' I said.

'Coping!' She let out a hollow laugh. 'Oh, we're not coping! Oh no. We're *surviving*. And arguing. And not eating very well. Noel has given up ironing his shirts and even left the house with baby milk on his tie yesterday and didn't even notice. The man used to be meticulous about the way he looked. But even his hair has taken on a life of its own.' Her phone rang. 'Noel? Yes, okay. They're in the bag. The baby bag, the leopard print one. No... yes. The pink bunny. It should be in the other bag, the Orla Kiely one. Really? Try laying her on your arm and she should be okay. Yes? Try it now. Did it work? Yes? They would have heard that on the Aran Islands. Okay, see you later. Love you. Yes, still.' She smiled. 'Bye.' She looked up. 'Back to work. Now, Milly, I need the notes on the Fitzwilliam acquisition. Did you find the details on the capital allowances? Good. Will you print it off for me and we can decide how next to move for them?'

She popped the last of her Twix in her mouth. And smiled.

26

I had managed to avoid Darragh over the last two weeks, but Siobhán had been spending time in Teolaí and making plans. One of which was the idea to bring her new Italian friends to Wicklow for a walk on the mountains. She was absolutely determined the hillwalking club would be resurrected but I suspected it was just a cunning ruse to spend some time with 'Lolo', but she fiercely denied it.

'I have George,' she reminded me. 'I am just being a good citizen. Showing foreigners our beautiful country.'

'If you say so.'

'I do say so,' she said. 'But you are coming. You can't let me bring them on my own. So, it's you, me, Lolo, Francisca and Darragh. And Ryan?'

I shook my head. Ryan and I hadn't developed as yet into the walks in the countryside part of a relationship. And anyway, I didn't think he was a walker. He took exercise seriously but it had to involve machines that beeped and personal trainers who shouted.

But maybe, I thought, I could bring Betty as a foil. She would be something to concentrate on and hide behind. Mum was on a day trip to some garden somewhere with Harold, and Siobhán seemed rather desperate that I go.

'Okay.'

So, on a damp, grey Saturday morning, at the end of April, the Hill-walking Club was reborn. Siobhán, Betty and I stood on the corner of our street, waiting for Lorenzo, Francisca and Darragh.

Siobhán wearing eyeliner and mascara and her posh perfume that she only wore for special occasions. 'Hair up?' she said. 'Or down? Which looks better?'

'We're hillwalking,' I replied. 'It doesn't matter.'

She sighed and tied it up, and then a moment later, let her long hair drop.

I'd avoided Darragh quite successfully, taking the long way home and bypassing Teolaí altogether. Instead, I was trying to concentrate on making things better with Ryan. I felt that I needed to at least try to make it work, and prove to myself that I was capable of having a relationship. We got on fine, he had many good qualities, and he was kind and generous, and was sweet to me. I liked him. And it was just nice to have a boyfriend after so long.

'Do I look like an idiot?' Siobhán was still tugging at her jacket. 'Do you think the fleece ear-warmers are a good idea or not? I think I might overheat in them, but they are good at keeping my hair off my face. And I think I've had a revelation about my water bottle. It has to go in my ruck-sack.' She began pulling at the water bottle, which was diagonally across her body. 'I think I'm a massive eejit.' The belt became tangled in her hair.

'You look great,' I said, untwisting it. 'Like a proper mountain climber. Ranulph Fiennes or someone like that. Now, wait a minute, stop moving, you're making it more tangled.'

'I think I might be in fancy dress as a hillwalker,' she said. 'It wasn't like this in the old days, was it? I think I was usually hungover and in jeans. And didn't I once climb the Galtees in a pair of flip-flops?'

'I think that was the time you twisted your ankle. Now, stop wriggling. I can't reach.'

Siobhán fell to her knees to make it easier for me to loosen the hair around the belt.

'My God, it's really tangled.' I had managed to pull away some of her hair strands and had begun gently pulling some of the rest away. 'So are you just trying to look nice for the sheep?' I teased. 'Are you making all this effort for maybe a nice farmer we might bump into?'

She glared at me from her twisted position on the ground. 'Are you suggesting that I might fancy Lolo?' she began, but a sound of a car and a cheery '*Buongiorno!*' made Siobhán scream and scramble to her feet. 'They're here!' she shouted, yanking her head from my hands and pulling the belt from her hair so hard a clump was attached, making her yowl in pain.

Darragh was driving, Francisca beside him and squashed in the back seat was Lorenzo.

'We follow you? No?' Lorenzo leaned out of the back window. 'You drive, we go after?'

'Okay!' Siobhán began pushing me into the car. 'Come on, Milly!' she screamed, panicking, the pain of the hair removal making her hysterical. 'We can't keep them waiting!' after pushing me into the front seat, she ran, arms flapping, around to the other side.

Our convoy wound its way towards the Wicklow mountains, the city flattening out, before the road started to twist and ascend past farms and sheep and through villages and past the little handwritten sign at a particular bend in the road:

Duck Eggs For Sale

Once, years ago, when we were driving home after a morning walking in the mountains, Darragh had parked up just beside the sign. In the farmyard, there was a table and a bucket of these large and beautiful white eggs, a few cardboard egg boxes and an old Quality Street tin.

Leave what you like

said a handwritten sign. 'It's the nicest way ever of buying eggs,' Darragh had said. 'I will only shop by honesty boxes from now on,' he'd declared. He'd kissed me and put down a ten euro note.

After my car croaked its way to the top of the mountain, Siobhán shouted at me to stop. 'We're here!' she yelled, and then leaned out of the window and waved her arms around, signalling for the car to pull in behind us. She turned to me, her face glowing, as though she'd already been on a five mile walk. 'I can't believe we're here,' she said. 'After all this time.'

From the other car, Francisca's long limbs revealed themselves. 'Ciao! Ciao!' she called, coming and kissing us on both cheeks.

Darragh gave us a wave before going to the boot of their car to take out his rucksack.

'Today,' said Francisca to us, 'we are all explorers. No?'

'Yes,' said Siobhán and I in unison, both rather dazzled by her ability to look so good wrapped in a scarf.

Francisca bent down to say hello to Betty, while Lorenzo kissed Siobhán and I on both cheeks.

'It so good for you to take us strangers out for the day,' he said, holding my gaze. An Irish male would rather miss the All-Ireland final than make eye contact.

Siobhán was in an excitable mood, talking non-stop, taking out her map, offering water to everyone, and putting on and taking off her ruck-sack. Darragh was still at the boot of their car, fiddling with his.

Francisca was now clutching Betty. 'She reminds me of my parents' dog. But she's not able to walk the mountain? She's not a...' She broke off to say something to Lorenzo, and then back to us. 'A St Bernard?' They both laughed, and I noticed Siobhán was laughing a little too hysterically along with them.

'Betty is very hardy,' I said. 'You shouldn't judge a dog by its size or its fur.'

'She is very fluffy, no?' said Lorenzo. 'My mother had a hat like her once. She would wear it for *la passeggiata*!'

They all laughed again, Siobhán the hardest.

'What's that?' Darragh trudged towards us. 'What are you all laughing at?' And then he spotted Betty. 'Hello, little girl! Oh Betty!' He dove for Betty and put two hands around her head and tickled and stroked her behind the ears. Betty proceeded in desperately licking Darragh's face as though it was a dropped ice cream. 'She remembers me!' Darragh pulled himself away from Betty's frantic kissing and looked at me, smiling. 'I can't believe she remembers me!'

'I had to bring her,' I said, ignoring his delight in being reunited with *my* dog. And there was I thinking that dogs were meant to be loyal. 'Sarah's working and Mum's out.'

He nodded. 'Can't leave her on her own, now can we?' He picked her up and looked at me. 'It's so lovely to see her!'

'I'd better take her,' I said, stiffly. 'We don't want to get her overexcited, you know, with all the sheep around.' I extricated Betty from Darragh's arms and put her down on the ground, holding tightly onto her lead.

'Sheep!' Lorenzo laughed again. 'I don't think the sheep have anything to worry about.'

'I think they are more likely going to think she is one of their lambs,' said Siobhán, sniggering.

'She's well capable of mauling a sheep,' I insisted, which just made them all laugh even harder.

'Right,' said Siobhán, still grinning, 'we should get going. Francisca? Lorenzo? Welcome to Wicklow. Darragh, welcome back. Let's go!'

We followed her march up the hill, through a pine forest, and on the path which took us along the top of the mountains for miles. Francisca walked beside me and Betty for a while. Ahead of us, Siobhán, Lorenzo and Darragh were deep in conversation.

'Your dog is gorgeous,' Francisca said. 'How old is she?'

And so I told her the story about when Dad came home with a tiny puppy for me and Sarah and how the very first night we put her basket on the floor between our two beds, Sarah measuring to make sure that she wasn't more on my side than hers. But in the morning, I woke up to find her in bed with her. 'She must have climbed in!' Sarah had said, radiating smugness.

'Sounds like me and my sister,' said Francisca. 'She and I would argue over anything... she used to steal everything of mine and sell them to her friends. She sold a pair of shoes of mine once for a couple of euro.' Francisca laughed. 'She's now a very successful businesswoman in Milano. Every time she receives another award, she thanks me.' She smiled at me. 'And I'm still just a waitress, no?'

'What's wrong with being a waitress?'

She shrugged. 'It's not very... I don't know...' She searched for the right word. 'My parents wonder when I will go and get another job. They always wanted me to be a lawyer.'

'*I'm* a lawyer,' I said. 'Sometimes I would prefer to be a waitress.'

She grinned at me and looked even more beautiful than ever and it was obvious what Darragh saw in her. She was lovely.

'No! Don't say such a thing. Not after all the studying and hard work,' she said. 'My best friend from home is a lawyer. She has worked so hard. But she loves it... she lives in London now and works eighteen hour days, never sleeps or eats or drinks wine or comes home. But she says she's happy. But I wonder. Don't we all say we're happy when we're not, because we don't want to worry people?'

We were edging towards the top of the mountain, the ground falling away into a valley. The colours of russets and golds, the tiny dots of sheep, green swathes of woodland.

'You have a boyfriend?' Francisca asked.

I nodded. 'Ryan.'

'And he couldn't come? Is he a lawyer too?'

'It's not his thing,' I said.

She nodded. 'He gives you freedom,' she said. 'Better than being... what is the word? Controlled?'

'Controlling.'

She nodded. 'This is freedom, no? Up here on this mountain? No one to answer to, no one to please except ourselves? You, you please yourself?'

I wanted to say yes, that I did exactly what I wanted to do, when I wanted to do it, but I tried to think of anything I had done in the last year – the last few years – which was just for me.

'I do what I please, when I please,' Francisca was saying. 'I learned that no one was going to look after me but me, yes? No one is going to make me happy but me. It took me a long time to learn that lesson. Back at home, I...'

'Back at home, what?' said Lorenzo, who had hung back to wait for us.

'Nothing,' she said. 'I miss home, but Ireland is beautiful. If it was warmer I might want to stay.' She smiled at me. Did that mean she didn't want to live here? Would she and Darragh return to Italy? I tried to push it all away. It was a bit much when I was still trying to untangle my feelings. I was still optimistic that we would be friends, and all of us be able to hang out without the noose of history around us.

'Ireland is beautiful,' agreed Lorenzo. 'It's so different to Italia. The colours are so rich.'

'We are so lucky,' Francisca said. 'To be here, far away from home, seeing this beautiful place.'

Siobhán walked up to us. 'Shall we stop for something to eat?' she said. 'It's an Irish tradition to have tea and fruit cake on the top of a mountain.'

Darragh and I turned to each other. 'Is it?' We suddenly laughed together, and for a moment, we'd gone back in time, laughing about something we both found inexplicably funny.

'Yes, yes it is!' insisted Siobhán. 'Well, *something* to eat, it doesn't have to be fruit cake. It's just that I made it myself. And I thought it was something that our Italian friends might like to try. Fruit cake made with Irish whisky.' She flicked open the rug and shook it onto the ground. 'Lorenzo said he liked whisky, didn't you, Lorenzo?'

'Lolo likes everything,'said Francisca, drily. 'There's not a thing he doesn't like.'

Lorenzo shrugged. 'I can't help it. I like nice things.'

'Sit down everyone,' said Siobhán, who was unwrapping a huge fruit cake and handed round cups of tea. Betty drank some water from my water bottle and then went over to Darragh and sat down beside him.

'Milly? Cake?' Siobhán held out a slice for me.

'Thanks,' I said, biting into it and realising it was basically whisky in cake form. 'Wow! That is strong!' I wheezed. She'd made it yesterday evening, and I had noticed the flat had taken on the air of the Jameson's distillery.

'How much did you put in to it?' Darragh's eyes were watering.

'As much as the recipe said,' she said. 'Is it not nice?'

'It's delicious!' pronounced Lorenzo. 'The more whisky, the better. My mother always says a light hand with bread, a heavy hand with alcohol.' He laughed. 'I think the cake could do with even more whisky. It's the taste of Ireland. And I like this tradition, whisky cake on mountains.'

'It's amazing, Siobhán,' said Darragh, obviously feeling bad that his initial reaction hadn't been as charming as Lorenzo's. 'I just wasn't prepared for it.'

'*Delicioso*,' agreed Francisca who slid the rest of her cake onto Lorenzo's knee when Siobhán was pouring out more tea.

'So why couldn't your fiancé come today?' Darragh turned to me, so utterly nonchalantly you wouldn't ever think it was anything but a casual question. Which perhaps it was.

'He's too busy,' said Siobhán. 'With his boot camp. He goes at 6 a.m. every Saturday morning.'

'He isn't a hillwalking type.' Everyone was looking at me, and I concentrated on my slice of cake.

'He's a captain of industry,' said Siobhán.

'A captain of what?' asked Francisca.

'Industry,' repeated Siobhán. 'Master of the universe.'

'He's just a business person,' I said, feeling Darragh's eyes on me.

'Like our Darragh, yes?' said Lorenzo. 'He's a business person. He came to Italy with no Italian, no money and no friends, and he returns to Dublin with all three.'

'He's nothing like Darragh,' said Siobhán pointedly. 'He couldn't be more different. He's...' But she quickly clamped her mouth shut.

When I looked up, Darragh quickly looked away. There was a sound from far away, making us look up. There was a couple with a large dog bounding around them as they made their way down the mountain.

'Ah!' said Lorenzo. 'We are being invaded. We no longer have this mountain to ourselves! This is how Native Americans must have felt.'

'Or the Irish,'said Darragh, making me and Siobhán laugh.

'More cake, Lorenzo?' said Siobhán, passing over a slice.

'I think getting drunk on cake on a mountain might be my favourite way to die,' he said, accepting it.

'Darragh? More cake?'

He shook his head. 'I think my liver might not be able to handle it,' he said, smiling. 'I don't have Lorenzo's constitution.'

'No one does,' said Francisca, lying back on the ground, her head on her rolled-up jacket, eyes closed.

'Maybe I was a little too heavy handed with the whisky,' Siobhán admitted.

'How's it going?' Darragh raised his hand in greeting as the couple with the dog – a Rottweiler – passed us. Betty was on her feet and ran to their dog. And then it was a blur.

27

All I can remember is snarling and then a flurry of bodies, saliva, teeth, tails and fur as I realised that Betty was being attacked and was clamped within the jaws of this dog.

'Betty!' I yelled. 'Betty!' There was a strangled, screeching yowl from Betty, the whites of her eyes imploring me to help. 'Oh my God!' I screamed, launching myself at the dogs as Betty was shaken like an old shoe. 'Get your dog off my dog!' I shouted at the owner. 'He's killing her!'

I tried to grab hold of Betty, my arms flailing at her tiny body. I felt a shower of hot liquid as Siobhán threw the rest of the tea at the dogs while I had managed to grip the Rottweiler's collar and was clinging on, fuelled by adrenaline and fear.

Beside me, on his knees, was Darragh, both hands wrenching open the salivating jaws of the dog. Everybody was screaming in two different languages – Italian and English – Siobhán even released some Irish swear word that she reserved for the most trying of circumstances. Darragh's hands were shaking with the effort as he prised open the crocodile jaws, and finally poor little Betty fell to the ground.

'Oh Betty.' I flung myself on her, crying.

The other dog had been pulled away, Siobhán was shouting at the owners, urged on by Francisca and Lorenzo, but all I could feel was Betty's tiny lifeless body as I buried my face against her fur.

'I shouldn't have brought you here,' I said into Betty's velvety ear. 'I am so sorry, little Betty. I love you.' I kissed her face.

Darragh, kneeling on the damp ground beside me, was taking off his jacket to fold under her head.

'She's dead,' I said, my voice shaking. 'Betty's dead.'

'Look!' He pointed with a bloody finger. 'Her chest.' There was the slightest little movement, a fluttering of Betty's tiny heart. One of her eyes opened, as though she was looking around to see if that horrible dog had gone. And then she closed it again.

'Give her some water,' Darragh said, pulling his scarf off and laying it over Betty.

Her breathing was laboured, but then I felt a little lick on my hand.

'She's alive!' I shouted, like something from a film, but the cheering turned to screaming as the Rottweiler had pulled free again, bounded over to the cake which had been lying unwrapped and wolfed it all down.

We all glanced at each other, not wanting to tell the owners that their dog had consumed at least a triple of whisky in one huge cake-shot. But they were full of profuse apologies and dragged their horrible dog away down the mountain. Betty lay limp but breathing in my arms. I checked her body, everything seemed okay, not very much blood but a lump of fur gone from her back leg, she was in shock more than anything.

'That big dog is going to die,' I heard Lorenzo say. 'My aunt had a dog who drank a glass of Amaretto. He knocked it over and lapped it up. He lasted only two hours before he laid down and died. Just like that.'

'Would it be manslaughter?' wondered Siobhán. 'I mean, we didn't *mean* to kill him.'

'But the intent was there,' I said. 'I mean, if he did die, I wouldn't be *that* upset.'

'You'd have to defend yourself, Milly,' said Darragh. 'Stand up in dog court and plead your case. Yes, you are happy that he died, but no, you had nothing to do with it.' He smiled at me and I noticed he was holding one hand with the other, as though he was in pain. I looked at his hand and saw the indentations of a hound's fangs.

'My aunt's dog was the size of her handbag,' Lorenzo was saying. 'I think that big dog will be okay.' He paused. 'Unfortunately.'

'You'll need a tetanus,' I said to Darragh. 'That dog probably has rabies.'

'That's all I need,' he said. 'A frothy, foaming-at-the-mouth death.'

'I'll take you to A&E,' I said. 'You'll need an injection.'

'No, you're all right,' he said.

But his hand was already looking bruised. Francisca and Lorenzo didn't know where the hospital was, and Siobhán didn't drive. It had to be me.

'Come on,' I said. 'If we go now, we'll miss the evening A&E rush.'

'We'll be fine,' said Siobhán. 'Francisca can drive Darragh's car. We could meet in the bar later?'

'Maybe,' I said, thinking it was highly unlikely.

'We will work for you,' said Francisca to Darragh, as Lorenzo nodded. 'You take the evening to rest, yes?'

'Why don't you bring Ryan down later to Teolaí?' said Siobhán.

'Your captain of the universe, no?' said Lorenzo, making Siobhán laugh a little too hard. At the car she hugged me, knowing how worried I was about Betty. 'She's going to be okay,' she said. 'That dog is a trooper.' We both looked at Betty who was smiling again, her tongue hanging out of the side of her mouth.

'She's Lazarus,' I said. 'The Lazarus of dogs. Back from the dead.'

'Well, she's an Aries, isn't she? Born in April, didn't you say? They are fighters... so there was no way she was going down.'

* * *

Betty stayed on Darragh's lap all the way to the hospital and during the journey she slowly returned to her normal self. By the time I was parking the car, she was wagging her tail but still trembling a little. Her big brown eyes looked from me to Darragh and back again.

'We can't leave her here,' said Darragh. 'She'll be scared.'

'But you can't bring a dog into A&E.'

We looked at each other.

'No one will know,' said Darragh. 'Just tuck her under your jacket.'

'You sure?'

'If we get arrested for hygiene or bringing A&E into disrepute,' he said, 'I'll go to prison.' He gave me a look, one I hadn't seen for years, one that used to make me laugh.

'You're so heroic.'

He flexed his muscles. 'I know, right?' And winked.

For a moment, it was like the old days, as though, like Mrs Murphy, I was transported back through time. I could have been the Milly of five, six, ten years earlier. I felt light as air.

Betty seemed to like being tucked inside my coat, hidden in the dark, and by the time we sat on the plastic chairs of A&E was fast asleep.

'Sorry about this,' I said, as Darragh and I sat side by side.

'Not your fault,' he said, his bloody hand resting on his scarf now it wasn't needed for Betty. 'Mine, for trying to impress...' He stopped.

Francisca, I presumed he was going to say. For that moment, I'd forgotten about her. And I'd forgotten about Ryan. And everything that had happened in the past. It was surprisingly easy to forgive, when you realised how much you liked someone. Maybe we would be able to be proper, genuine friends?

'You must have missed the delights of an Irish A&E,' I said. 'The chaos, the people in pain, the old ladies on trolleys.'

Darragh gave me a rueful side-glance. 'It's amazing what you miss when you are away.'

'Like what?'

It felt weirdly normal sitting there with him, almost as though no time had passed, no heart was broken.

'Oh, you know...' He sighed. 'Everything. Like Guinness and Tayto crisps or a Supermacs on a long drive home...?'

'You go to Italy and you miss beer, crisps and takeaway burgers?'

He gave a laugh. 'They taste of home,' he said. 'And the radio – there is nothing like Irish radio anywhere in the world. I used to listen in Italy, but it just made the homesickness worse. And Irish politics and the kind of conversations you might have with some random person sitting on the bus or in a shop. Just the kindness of people, the way they talk. And Dad, of course. And my friends and... well, lots of things.'

'And the rain... bet you missed the weather.'

'Yes, I missed the rain.' He held my eye for a moment. 'So kill me. Irish rain!' He laughed. 'It's beautiful. The other day it was a gentle mist, it was glorious, like the whole city was being misted. And then we had the other type. The great splashing kind. And I was the only one who seemed to be enjoying it. It was like sparkling drops of...'

'Joy.'

'Yes!' He laughed. 'Sparkling drops of joy. So, yes, I missed the Irish rain.'

'You're a weirdo.' I smiled.

'I know.'

And we sat in silence for a while, not speaking, allowing everyone else in A&E to fill the world with conversation.

'That's what Dad used to call me and Sarah,' I said suddenly.

'What?'

'His sparkling drops of joy.'

His face changed, from interest to a flicker of something else. Sadness. 'I'd forgotten,' he said. 'I remember him saying it now.'

'Ever since we were little. He'd be holding her in one arm and me in the other, and that's what he'd say, how are my two little sparkling drops of joy?' I stopped. 'I cannot cry in A&E.'

He smiled. 'No, there's enough going on there. But... he was a really great dad, if you want my humble opinion.'

I remembered how well they used to get on and how we'd go for Sunday lunch with Mum and Dad and the two of them would talk about all sorts... they were similar in so many ways.

We sat again in silence, me keeping my feelings as steady as possible. Betty was a comfort, as though she was a relic from Dad, keeping me safe and warm. But what was I doing chatting with Darragh, as though nothing had happened? Everything had happened. This was the man who had run away at the lowest point in my life and had caused everything to go wrong. Whatever his reasons, I didn't think we could just be friends.

'And I'm sorry about... you know, leaving.'

'Let's not talk about that,' I said. 'I'm not ready... it's been...' I didn't know what else to say, and I didn't want to talk about anything heavy, not after the adrenaline of the day. 'But I'm glad that everything's worked out for us both.'

He nodded. 'And your fiancé, and your job...'

'Francisca's nice,' I said.

He nodded. 'Very nice,' he agreed. 'And Lorenzo. They were good to me in Italy, when I needed people to rely on. They didn't ask any questions or demand anything from me.'

I didn't say anything in response. I mean, what was there to say? *I'm glad you had friends to look after you when you went off and broke my heart in the process?*

'That's nice,' I said.

'Yes, well...' He seemed to be about to say more, when a nurse called his name, and I was left alone.

28

Are you at work?

I texted Sarah.

I am in A&E.

She texted back.

WTF?

Fifteen minutes later, she walked in. 'Who's ill?' she said, sitting down beside me. 'Why are *you* here?'

'Darragh's having a tetanus,' I explained. 'This horrible rabid dog tried to eat Betty and Darragh managed to pull her out of its jaws.'

She paled. 'Where's Betty? She's all right, isn't she?'

I opened my jacket and inside, in the dark, was a tiny face with a shock of white frizz and two huge chocolate eyes.

Sarah gasped, and then looked around furtively. 'You will get arrested if anyone sees a dog in here,' she said. 'But the poor little thing. She's not hurt, is she?'

'I thought she was dead initially, but it's like the second coming, the dog with two lives.'

'Thank God, she's all right. Super dog, I told you.' She smiled at Betty. 'Best dog in the world.' She looked back at me. 'Not *Darragh*-Darragh? I thought I told you not to have anything to do with him.' She eye-locked me. 'Milly. Have some *pride*, all right?'

'I know,' I said, pathetically. 'I didn't want to go on a hike. It's Siobhán.'

'You can say no,' said Sarah. 'It's only a very small, two letter word. And it's even a complete sentence.' She shook her head, exasperated.

And on cue, Darragh walked towards us, his hand in a bandage, his face a shade of off-white.

'Well, well, well,' said Sarah, all smiles. 'If it isn't Darragh O'Toole...' She stood up and they hugged. 'Heard you were quite the hero today. Thank you for saving my little girl... I feel like I am the only one keeping her alive these days. Thank God,' she said, dramatically, 'there's someone else who cares.'

Darragh laughed. 'You haven't changed,' he said, grinning.

'So, you're back... what are you doing with yourself these days?'

'I've just opened a wine bar,' he said. 'In Ranelagh... you should come down sometime.'

'I'd love to.'

'And you're well otherwise?'

She shrugged. 'Clinging onto life by a thread, that's what I'm doing, Darragh,' she said, breezily. 'I think I might be having some kind of existential crisis, but it would take too long to tell you all about it now.' She smiled at him. 'And I've got to get back to work.' She turned on her heel. 'See you, Darragh.' She threw me a look. 'Bye, Milly.' And she was gone.

Darragh and I looked at each other. 'Shall we go?' he said. 'Or do you particularly like being in A&E?'

'Well, it is exciting. The fluorescent lights, the smell of antiseptic and the fact that you never know what's going to turn up next. A broken leg, someone who has ingested something they shouldn't...'

'Like what?'

'I don't know... anything. I swallowed a coin once.'

'A coin? You never told me that.'

'I was five. I just remember popping it in my mouth and swallowing it. I mean, how do you swallow a coin? I can't even swallow an aspirin without a full glass of water.'

'That was impressive.'

'Have you ever done anything dangerous.'

'No,' he said. 'I think you know all my childhood scrapes.'

And then we looked at each other again, but this time there was an intensity, a longing, a draw... like we were being pulled back together. It was so easy to go back in time and be the people we were six years earlier, the same easy conversations, the thought that the next moment he would reach for my hand, and my body would sink into his, and we would continue on, the two of us together.

And here in the hospital he held out his hand, reaching for mine as though it was the most natural thing in the world, to take my hand, our fingers curled around the other's and we stared at each other and it was only the teeniest, most infinitesimal moment, but we looked away, and the hand was dropped.

'Come on,' I said. 'We should be getting back.'

* * *

I dropped Betty at Mum's and when I parked in the driveway and carried her in, Darragh followed me into the house.

'It looks the same,' he said, walking into the hall.

I didn't say anything, not knowing quite how to respond and not quite sure how I felt about him being here, after all this time.

'I always liked this house,' he continued, walking behind me into the kitchen. 'It was always a house full of things happening.'

I placed Betty onto her bed, filled up her water bowl and put some food out, which she sniffed at vaguely, and then fell back into bed, happy to be home. She didn't need the vet, I was sure of it, and anyway, Mum would be back soon to keep an eye on her.

'There was always some drama,' he said. 'Usually involving Sarah, or Angela. Or you. And there was your mum trying to make everyone happy and your dad...' He stopped.

'Go on,' I said. 'My dad what?'

'He was always so happy, being surrounded by all these interesting and brilliant women. He called it the swirl. He said to me once that he loved his swirl of girls.'

'I never heard that.' I smiled, hearing his voice so clearly and, for the first time in years, if I closed my eyes, I could see and hear him. His swirl of girls. For a moment I knew exactly what Mrs Murphy meant about the voices on the stairs, I had time travelled.

Darragh was looking over at me and sighed. 'He always struck me as a man who had enough,' he said. 'I don't mean he'd had enough. He had enough. He didn't need a single extra thing. You, Sarah, your mum...'

'Betty.'

'All of you. He was a happy man.'

'Yes.' Tears filled my eyes.

Darragh started speaking. 'Milly—'

'We should be getting back,' I said. Francisca surely would be wondering where he was and this was too weird. 'I'll drop you off,' I said.

'Okay.'

* * *

Driving away from the house, I felt relieved. I would be dropping Darragh back at Teolaí and need never see him again. I could go back to my half-hearted life and he could go back to his wine bar and Francisca. Today had been confusing, a sandstorm of emotions... and I was under the impression that he was as confused as me. But there was the reality of the last five years, and Ryan... and Francisca. The past was the past, and I had a future to fight for.

We sat in silence for a while. And then he asked, 'You said your mum was out for the day, where is she?'

'She's on a day trip,' I said. 'To some garden, a stately home and café, you know the kind of thing.'

There was silence and then I couldn't help giving him more information.

'With *a man*.' I glanced at Darragh.

'A *man*?' He gave me an amused look.

I nodded. 'Yes, *a man*.'

'Well, now.'

'Exactly. She's having a romance. With a man called Harold Hawkins.'

'Now, that's the name of someone you could trust.'

'He's obsessed with cacti and Latin.'

'Of course he is!' Darragh smiled. 'He sounds adorable.'

'It's all Angela's doing,' I said. 'She set Mum up at her dating club.'

'Ah! Of course! Angela! She always was – how shall I put this – instrumental.'

'She's become worse,' I said. 'It's like we have all become her special projects and that she knows what is right for us... and Mum has met Harold and she's happy, except...' I stopped.

'Except what?' he asked.

I'd forgotten how easy he was to talk to. He was the kind of person who wasn't afraid of silence, who gave you space to think and to talk and who listened to you with all of himself. It was as though he listened to you in every dimension. He heard you... Except, of course, when he left the country. He really went out of his way *not* to listen, that time.

'I don't know,' I said.

'Do you feel that she is leaving your dad behind?'

I kept my eyes on the road ahead. 'A little,' I admitted.

'As though he doesn't matter any more?'

I nodded. 'Something like that. I've just got to cop myself on and deal with it,' I said, 'but... I don't know. It just makes me really sad and I don't know why exactly...'

There was silence between us.

And then Darragh spoke. 'When Dad met Shirley, I was exactly the same. I mean, hypothetically, *rationally*, I was pleased. It meant he had someone to go out with. You know they go ballroom dancing together? They are now Leinster Over 65s Champions.'

I laughed. 'Amazing.'

'I'm really proud of them,' he said. 'He wears a suit with these long tails... they call each other Fred and Ginger, it's very sweet.' He paused.

'Mum had only been gone a year when their eyes met across a glitter ball lit dance floor. I hated it. Wasn't too keen on Shirley.'

'You never said.'

'No, I know. I was just *trying* to be a grown-up. But on the inside, I wasn't handling it very well.'

'And they're married now?'

He nodded. 'They got married in Rome and came to me for their honeymoon. Shirley is a lovely woman. And they are happy. Mum would never have gone ballroom dancing, but it suits Dad. But they've taken down all the photos of Mum and they got rid of the old orange kitchen with those horrible brown tiles, but I remember Mum sitting me up on the work surface and asking me about my day in school, and the radio would be on, and... Oh I don't know... it was the safest place in the world.' He let out a sigh. 'And they are right, of course. You can't live in a museum to a dead person. Except... if it was me, I would do. So, what I'm trying to say is that I understand.'

We looked at each other, a moment of recognition. He saw me, more than he'd ever seen me before, but more than that, I saw the seventeen year old Darragh who lost his mother.

'You poor thing,' I said.

'Don't feel sorry for me,' he said. 'Not after what I did.'

He was right. I shouldn't feel sorry for him. Except I did. 'Sorry,' I said, 'it's delayed shock, from seeing Betty attacked.'

He smiled at me. 'Thank you for not hating me,' he said.

'How do you know I don't?'

'I was hoping you didn't.'

'I oscillate,' I said.

'Well, I'm glad I've caught you on a non-hating day.'

'Tomorrow might be a whole different story.'

We were close to Teolaí. Perhaps this would be the last time I would ever talk to him, our only chance at closure.

'So, when's the wedding?' Darragh asked.

'Mum and Harold? They've only just met.'

'No, you and...'

'Ryan. I don't know,' I said, evasively, hating having to lie. 'We haven't...
we haven't set a date yet.'

We pulled up outside the bar, and I waited for him to get out. But he
stayed.

'It's good being back,' he said. 'For so long I wondered how I'd feel,
seeing everyone again... Italy was good to me, but I had to come home... I
missed...' He stopped and looked at me. '... Everything.'

Through the glass windows, I could see Francisca sweeping the floor
and Siobhán lighting the candles on each table.

'Is Siobhán working in the bar?'

He glanced up and saw her. 'She comes in most evenings,' he said. 'Says
she leaves George asleep and comes down for a chat. Frankie must have put
her to work. Why don't you come in, stay for a drink?'

'I can't,' I said. 'I'm meeting Ryan.' I wished it wasn't all so complicated.
A drink in a bar with an old friend would have been nice.

'Of course.' He paused. 'Why don't you bring him sometime? I'd really
like to meet him.' He paused. 'I suppose what I'm trying to say is that I want
you in my life and I want us to be friends.'

'Maybe.' Sarah was right. I needed to remember how he'd treated me.
Yes, he may have been confused but I was beginning to think that we
shouldn't ever see each other again. A clean break would help us both.

He got out of the car, and hovered for a moment, leaning in through the
open window. 'It's just... it's just I missed you,' he said.

'Yeah, well...' I looked at him. 'But you really. really hurt me,' I said.

'I know,' he replied. 'I knew at the time. I'm sorry...'

'It's fine, Darragh,' I said. 'I'm not hurt now. But it's pointless you going
on about missing me. It's not relevant. You hurt me. I got over it. We
move on.'

He stared at me, as though a million thoughts were forming and
popping like bubbles in his brain. Or maybe there was nothing. Maybe,
maybe, he just didn't care.

'See you, Darragh,' I said before he could say anything else and I drove
away, suffused with an overwhelming sense of loneliness.

29

'The most important thing,' Mrs Murphy was saying, 'was to have a nice drawing room. Mrs Hackett insisted on it.'

It was Wednesday afternoon and I was beginning to enjoy these unorthodox meetings at Mrs Murphy's flat. Usually in meetings I was worrying about all the work I had yet to do, or the pile of files on my desk or having to avoid Jarleth's latest fun-filled scheme or wondering if I should go to the vending machine in the kitchen for a second Twirl at 4 p.m. and all the other million thoughts I had during office hours.

'She said that you couldn't think straight without a room full of books and a nice view. And how were her Ladies going to make better lives for themselves if they couldn't plan? There were books and comfortable chairs and the big windows overlooking the square. All the children had to be as quiet as mice in there. Mrs Hackett said a lady couldn't be a lady if she didn't have somewhere to go and think. She called it a thinking room.' She smiled at me. 'A library of calm. We get so caught up in the world that you need somewhere to just be quiet and to allow it all to rest, all those thoughts and ideas and things that whirl around.'

I nodded, understanding. The luxury of _just being_. 'Life can be challenging,' I said.

'And it was for those women,' went on Mrs Murphy. 'Go into the *thinking room*, dear, Mrs Hackett would say when one of her ladies was having a bad day. Gather yourself and allow the atoms to settle.' Mrs Murphy gave a small laugh. 'Good advice, don't you think? Gather yourself and allow the atoms to settle.'

I nodded. 'Most of us do neither.'

'We're all too harum-scarum. Of course, when you get to my age, one's only choice *is* to gather and watch the atoms of your life fall slowly to the ground, like snowflakes. All your memories and all your thoughts and everything you've ever done floats gently down, giving you time to examine it and reabsorb it once more.' She smiled. 'It's to be recommended,' she said, 'reliving one's past in the stillness of one's old age. I wish my Rose would come back and talk with me. My word, how I idolised her. Like a film star, she was. The family favourite, and, of course, I wasn't a bit jealous because she was my favourite too. Such a sweet person, the kindest heart. She would have given you the coat off her back if you'd needed it. Mother used to say she could have been the double of Lilian Gish, all little lips and tiny hands, like a china doll. Of course, I was nothing like her, couldn't dance, clumsy and loud with big feet. I'd have tripped over my own shadow.'

'When did she die?'

A shadow flickered over Mrs Murphy's face. 'She was only sixteen... hit by a tram and thrown into the path of a horse... she always loved horses, passionate she was, used to spend hours and hours in her room drawing them. Father bought her a special set of pencils and a beautiful sketchbook and she filled it with horses. So, I always felt sorry for the horse who ended her life. *We* were all devastated, needless to say. Mother didn't speak or cry for a whole month and then she cried solidly for another month.' She sighed. 'We were all much more silent afterwards, all of us making room for our grief, getting to know it because we knew it was going to be with us for the rest of our lives.'

* * *

As I walked back to the office, I thought of Mrs Murphy and how she was able to examine her life in great detail, and how she conveyed a sense of peace and calm. Would I have to wait until I was ninety to be the same? Was life just a waiting game, a succession of tumult and turmoil until finally you were able to glance back once again before the final curtain?

Susie was standing outside the building dressed in running gear. 'I've been looking for you everywhere!' she said. 'I've been trying to call your phone.'

'What's the problem?'

'It's the around-the-building relay race. It starts in five minutes. You're on my team...' I looked around, there were other colleagues dressed in shorts and lycra, some either warming up with jogging on the spot or taking the opportunity for a fag, and some doing both.

'But...' I couldn't exactly recall signing up for this. I had joined corporate law so I didn't have to do anything but be boring. And now, I was being forced into fun and activity as though I was on some awful hen weekend which showed no sign of ever ending.

'Have you got your stuff?' Susie pressed.

'You mean trainers?'

She nodded.

I did have some that I could change into but they had remained under my desk for a year and a half, brought in when I thought that maybe I could be that person who went to a spinning class after work, the type of person who drank water competitively and made *and kept* new year's resolutions.

'Go and put them on,' ordered Susie. 'We've got to win!'

Lycra wasn't something in which I had any desire to appear in front of my colleagues. And running was something which I thought should only be undertaken when you had no choice, such as being chased or on the first day of the Brown Thomas January sales.

'I am way to busy.' Susie was looking increasingly unimpressed. 'I've got to write up a report,' I went on, desperately. '*And* I've got this thing wrong with my Achilles heel. The doctor said that I shouldn't put any pressure on it. I really shouldn't be walking at all. I am already taking a risk. And also...' What other plausible reason could I give? 'And also I really, really, don't want to.'

Susie gave me that look that I was beginning to recognise, the one that told me that she would one day be running this country. It was the kind of look that put the fear of God into the inadequate, the incompetent and the liars. And I was definitely at least two out of three of those.

'Milly,' she said. 'We're all busy. We've *all* got things to do. I've got a three hour lecture later on that I need to read up for. I'm back in work for 7 a.m. and I've got to finish my dissertation by Friday. But I am making the time for my colleagues because I don't like letting people down. This is for charity. All the money raised will be going to the homeless. *Five* minutes, Milly, that's all. Five minutes of discomfort for the homeless and for office morale.'

'Well,' I said, suitably mollified, 'when you put it like that...'

'Go on then, and get changed. I'll see you back here in three minutes.' She checked her watch, as though she was actually going to time me.

I began a little jog into the office to change into my kit.

30

Upstairs, in her office, Catriona had her head on her desk and her eyes closed. She lifted her head when she heard me.

'Are you all right?' I said, quietly.

'*All right* might be going too far,' she said. 'I have survived. I am surviving. I will survive.'

'Can I get you anything?'

She shook her head. 'I thought we were doing okay, but it's as though a bomb has just exploded in my life, and it's just chaos. Did you know that the only thing I have eaten in six days is Sugar Puffs? I've become addicted to them. At first it was nice, it gave me this beautiful, comforting feeling in my stomach, this warm rush, as though all was well with the world. But I am worried that I will never eat anything else ever again,' she admitted. 'I felt I had totally got this parenting thing. Everything was timetabled: nappy changing, feeding, sleep, play, fresh air. But it couldn't last. And so, I just had another bowl, and then another, hoping for the high of that first one. And then another, and then another, and you never manage to reach it again. And now, I'm on something like fifteen bowls a day.' She turned to look at me, her pupils were dilated, her hands on the desk trembling.

'Oh my God,' I said, 'you poor thing.'

And then she started to cry. 'Don't be nice to me,' she said. 'I can't bear it when people are nice to me. When we used to go and stay with my grandmother, she would make such a fuss of me. My granny, Lydia, would bring me breakfast in bed, and make me apple pies and she taught me to knit.' She held up a trembling hand. 'I still miss her every day,' she went on. 'Granny would have been able to sort this out. She would know exactly what to do. We lost TV reception one Christmas Day and she got up onto the roof with a coat hanger and it worked.' She sniffed. 'She wouldn't let me eat Sugar Puffs, she'd make me eat a roast dinner or a baked potato.' She groaned. 'A baked potato. What I would give for a baked potato.'

I let her cry, and talk about Granny Lydia, as the tears and memories came in waves. And when she eventually had calmed down, I ushered her over to her office sofa, helped her to lie down, took off her trainers which revealed odd socks, one a man's sports one, the other a chenille slipper sock.

'You should go home,' I said.

'Too tired,' she slurred.

'I'm going to go and run in this race and when I come back, I will sort this out for you.'

'Okaaaaaay.' And her eyes closed and she went back to sleep.

Downstairs, back outside on the street, Jarleth was on fire.

'Burpees!' he shouted. 'Explosive energy! Let's go! McAvoy's Are Go! Give me star jumps!'

I stood at the start line of the round-the-building relay race. Beside me were my colleagues, now fellow competitors. Some of them were actually doing as Jarleth ordered, jumping up and down, with rather differing skill levels, ranging from spritely to the desk-bound whose main form of exercise was opening a new packet of biscuits in the tea room.

'I'm missing the Knitting and Stitching Show for this,' said Nora, leaning into my ear. 'It's starting today at the Arena. I go every year, stock up, get some supplies. The demos are unbelievable. We had Kirsty Allsop last year.'

'Okay!' Jarleth's voice silenced everyone. Oh God. It was starting. 'Are we ready to rumble? Are we ready to tumble? Are we ready to run for our lives, for our self-respect, for our offices? Are we ready to have FUUUNNNNNN?'

There were whoops and yeahs from some of the more enthusiastic (younger) members of staff.

'ON YOUR MARKS!'

'What are we meant to do?' said Nora.

'Hand this...' I waved my baton to her, '... to the next person along. Who's on your team?'

'Brian in accounts, Philippe on reception and Darren the caretaker.'

'So, hand your baton to one of them.'

'GET SET!'

'Bless us our saints,' said Nora.

BOOOOM! Jarleth had fired a starting pistol. I was sure that you had to have an actual licence to use one, but I didn't have time to think about it because we'd all started sprinting wildly, as though we were being chased by Freddy Krueger.

'Run!' I screamed, panicked into pedalling my legs. I was a career woman, I thought. I had studied hard, gone to law school, and somehow, along the way, I had been forced into running around my office building, because someone deemed we weren't having enough craic.

And on and on it went. My breathing was hard, and I felt the same kind of dread one might feel if they are being chased by some cannibal tribe, fear and pants-spoiling panic, combined with the will to survive.

Oh my God, I thought. This is horrible. Beside me, the pounding bodies of middle-aged office workers, pasty of skin, weak of heart and weary of soul. The younger members of the teams had already peeled off to the front, leaving the unfit and forgotten behind, as though it was a Darwinian fight to the death.

As I pegged around the full length of the block, I saw Susie holding out her hand. And I suddenly realised that I didn't want to have this kind of fun. I wanted the kind of fun that wasn't organised by an eejit like Jarleth, or anything prescribed by anyone other than me. I wanted more fun in my life – I couldn't remember the last time I had a laugh, or did something silly or went to Paris or drank alcohol in the middle of the day or did anything that didn't involve having to behave myself. But I wanted to organise it myself.

'Come on, Milly!' Susie screamed at me, and the sound of passers-by and the rest of my colleagues who hadn't been dragooned into running like fools pounded in my ears. 'Milly!' Susie wrestled the baton out of my hand and off she ran, sprinting as though her life depended on it.

Nora was still in her red coat and was panting nearly as heavily as me. 'If I'm quick,' she said, 'I'll make it down to the Knitting And Stitching.'

'Aren't you going to stay to see who wins?'

'Nah,' she said. 'I'm sure someone will tell me. Got to dash.' And off she went, nipping into the crowd like a Russian spy.

I need to be a bit more Nora, I thought, and a little bit less like Milly. Or rather, I need to find the old Milly. The only thing was, I wasn't sure she was still there.

* * *

Afterwards, Susie walked back upstairs with me. 'That was mega,' she said, glowing. 'Now, what's next?'

'Catriona,' I said. 'I have to make a few calls for her.'

In the office, Catriona lifted her head and looked around groggily. Susie and I had spent the last half an hour organising Catriona's life.

'You're awake!' said Susie. 'We were getting worried.'

'I'm just so tired,' Catriona said. 'No one told me...'

'Everything's fine,' I said. 'You're going to go home, and sleep some more. Susie has called Josephine, who says she is very happy to take your suits and blouses to the express dry-cleaners. Lydia's fast asleep in her pram and she says they are due for a walk.'

'Thank you.' She seemed near tears.

'And I've ordered a delivery from The Irish Kitchen,' said Susie. 'Stew and apple pie and custard. It will arrive at 6.30 p.m.. Make sure you're in your pyjamas for when it arrives.'

Catriona gaped at us, as though we'd produced a rabbit out of a hat. 'What kind of stew?'

'Lamb,' Susie said, 'with carrots and barley. And they've won an award for their apple pies from the Irish Countrywoman's Association.'

Catriona began to cry properly. 'Just like Granny Lyddie used to make.'

'We've ordered you a taxi to take you home,' I said. 'And Josephine is going to start running the bath as soon as she hears the key in the lock.'

At this, Catriona started to sob. 'Oh God,' she blubbed. 'A bath... a bath and some...' she could barely get the words out, 'and some proper stew!'

Susie looked at me, a satisfied smile on her face. The world of corporate law was going soft. And it felt good.

31

On Saturday afternoon, Sarah was sitting at the kitchen table at Mum's, the crossword open in front of her, Betty in her lap. Betty opened one eye and looked at me, her tail gave a weak wave.

'How is she?' I went over and bent down beside her and stroked Betty's front paw, hoping that she might crawl into my arms.

'She's doing okay,' Sarah said. 'She's been a bit quiet and I have to lift her on and off the bed.' She bent down to kiss her head. 'She's on probiotic yogurt twice a day. And I gave her an acidophilus earlier.' She grinned. 'I never thought I would be nursing a *dog*.'

'I'll take her,' I said, pulling Betty towards me, but Sarah had her clamped to her chest.

'Don't disturb her,' she said. 'She needs to rest.'

'What made you the expert?' I said. 'How do you know what she needs more than anyone?'

'I *do* know what she needs!' she said. 'I love her more than *anything*. Even more than Kurt Cobain and Dave Grohl... Betty has never let me down. Kurt *died* for God's sake...' She closed her eyes with frustration. 'And by the way, Ollie died.' Her voice broke. 'They always die. Why do people keep dying on me?'

'Ollie?' And then I remembered. He was the man Sarah was talking to that night I went to see her. 'I'm sorry.' I put my hand on her arm.

'He was old,' she said, wiping her eyes with her sleeve, steeling herself. 'It's not as though it's a surprise, it's just that being old doesn't mean people will miss you less. Just because you've had a long life or a good innings or whatever stupid things people say, it's not easier for the people you leave behind. It's worse, if anything. It's like I am surrounded by death, everywhere! I feel like the Grim Reaper. It's just... it's just... it's just shit.' And she wiped her eyes with her sleeve.

'I can't imagine how difficult it must be,' I said, trying to take it all in. 'I'm sorry.'

'It builds up,' she said. 'The grief. You think you are managing it, but then it comes out in different ways. Some people drink too much, some people turn to food. I think I just turned into a massive bitch.' She pulled a face.

For some reason, we'd never weathered the loss of Dad together. We'd had to be strong for Mum, and the two of us retreated into our own lives and worlds, maybe not wanting to upset the other. But we'd never really talked about how we felt about Dad dying.

'Do you think the house is different without Dad?' I said.

She looked surprised. 'In what way different?'

'I don't know.' I felt foolish suddenly. 'The energy. That it changed when he died. I felt like I knew he was gone, even though he wasn't here.'

'What do you mean?' She spoke quietly.

'The morning after the funeral, it was like something had changed in the air. The ions or something.'

'Ions?' I could tell she was about to make a joke. But then she shrugged. 'Yeah,' she said. 'Everything's different. Even the *ions*.' She gave me a half-smile. 'Sometimes I think Betty might be the only connection I have left with him. It's like if I don't keep her alive, there'll be nothing left.'

'Me too,' I said. 'He's slipping away from us.'

'Well, he's dead, so he's kind of slipped away completely. It's called *dying*.' And sarcastic Sarah was back.

'I know that, I just meant...'

'I know what you meant,' she said, more gently. 'But there's not much we can do about it. You can't bring someone back to life. But I do other things.'

'Like what?'

'I've been reading *David Copperfield*.' She rolled her eyes. 'I know. It's a far cry from Stephen King. But you know how much Dad loved Dickens. And before that it was *Bleak House*. And *Dombey and Son*.'

I nodded, remembering how every January the first, Dad would start on a Dickens novel, which he always said was the very best way to start the year. And there was Sarah, my sleep deprived, grunge loving sister reading Dickens to conjure up her father. I felt my heart break a little.

'And other things,' she said.

'What kind of things?'

'Since I've moved home, I bring Betty to Killiney Hill. Just like Dad did. We start in the car park and loop round. You know Mum couldn't go there after he died. It was too sad for her, but you should have seen Betty the first time I brought her back. She almost lost her mind. She kept looking around, and she ran up to one man and started sniffing him, and I realised that the man looked a little like Dad. He had a tweed cap on. Betty's face, though, when she realised it wasn't...' She stopped. 'It was *awful*.'

'Poor Betty.'

'It's worse for dogs than people,' she said. 'It must be so strange for them. At least we know what happened. Poor Betty must be traumatised.'

We both looked at Betty, who didn't look tortured in any way, it had to be said, sitting snugly against Sarah.

'Sometimes,' Sarah went on, 'I can feel Dad with me, as if he's on the walk with me and Betty. It's quite weird.'

'Really?' I felt quite envious, I would love to feel him somewhere. 'Wish I did,' I said. 'I can't find him anywhere.'

'Maybe you will,' she said, smiling at me. 'I really hope you do.'

Later that evening, Siobhán was straightening her hair in her bedroom, talking to me with the door open. 'Come down to the wine bar. Lorenzo's got some photos from the walk he wants to show us.'

'I can't,' I said, going in and sitting on the bed. 'I'm going over to Ryan's. He couldn't meet me last night, so suggested tonight instead.'

'Well, bring Ryan! He doesn't know how *nice* it is there...' She stopped. 'Or are you awkward about your *ex* meeting your *present*?'

'No... I just don't want to see Darragh.'

'I thought everything was cool?'

'It is.' I shrugged, not able to explain. 'I wish he was still in Italy. It was easier then. And it's not that easy to just be friends.'

'You okay?' She looked concerned, her hair half straightened, half curly.

'I'm fine,' I said, smiling.

'You're not okay,' she insisted. 'I can tell by your lack of smize!'

I tried again. 'Is that better?'

'Yeah. I suppose.' She stared at herself in the mirror. 'What do you think? I am going for something different. My horoscope said not to be afraid to present an *unfamiliar* side of me, so what do you think?' Her red hair was even longer without the curls. 'What does unfamiliar even mean?

Unfamiliar to my family, or unfamiliar to myself? Or unfamiliar to strangers! It's so confusing.' She looked genuinely upset.

'You look gorgeous,' I said. 'So, that's good...'

'You're always going to say that because contractually as my best friend, you have to. But am I gorgeous generally?'

'Of course you are!'

'But I'm not,' she said, upset. 'I'm not one of those women who can walk into any room and—'

'Siobhán, it doesn't matter...'

'It didn't,' she said. 'But sometimes it does...' Her voice drifted off.

'What are you talking about? George thinks you're gorgeous.'

'He doesn't count, though,' she said. 'Look, will you come tonight? Beg Ryan, if you have to. I just wouldn't mind having you there.'

'I'll ask him.'

'Will you? Please?' She seemed quite desperate.

'But George will be there, won't he?'

She nodded. 'But he'll want to go, and I'll want to stay and... well, it would just be nice to have a friend, that's all.'

'Is it Lorenzo?'

'What do you mean?' She blushed bright red.

'I mean, you fancy him, don't you?'

And now angst spread over her face. She nodded. 'I feel slightly crazed by it,' she said. 'Like I'm possessed. I've been trying to talk myself down, but I just can't stop thinking about him. It's awful.'

'George?'

She nodded again. 'I wish I could fall back in love with him,' she said. 'I wish I could just transfer all the passion and excitement I feel for Lorenzo onto George. That would make life so simple. I mean, if I was being rational, I wouldn't fancy Lolo, I would fancy someone nice and sensible like George, but I don't feel like being rational. He makes the hairs on the back of my neck stand up. He makes my whole body shiver when I think of him touching me.' Her eyes were practically spinning around. 'I wish I could wake up and it would all be over, and no one was hurt. I just wish I could love George again.'

'Okay,' I said. 'I'll come. I'll make Ryan come.' Siobhán needed me, and as much as I wanted to avoid Darragh and Ryan won't be happy slumming it in a neighbourhood wine bar, I had to do this for Siobhán.

* * *

I met Ryan in the Atlantic Club in town, one of the swankiest (Siobhán would say *wankiest*) bars in town, men in suits and expensive cocktails and Japanese bar snacks and ambient jazz.

'I thought we should fly to New York,' he was saying. 'You've never been, so I took the liberty of booking some flights...'

'Ryan... no...' I was allowing myself to be *bought*. If I kept accepting, I would have no voice, no comeback.

'Why not?' he smiled. 'You need to take time off work. I need a break. We could go to some nice restaurants, do a bit of shopping. Go and see *Les Miserables*...'

'Oh, good God, no...'

'Mum and Roger are going next month and we could go too...'

No way. 'I can't possibly...'

'I will pay for everything,' he said. 'Flights, hotel... Mum and Roger are staying in the Plaza and we could too. Mum says it's the best place in the city. They know them there, always look after them... Roger went to school with the manager.'

'I won't be able to take time off work,' I said, firmly. 'Catriona needs me more than ever. And there's my Mrs Murphy case...'

'Your what?' I'd forgotten I hadn't told Ryan anything about Mrs Murphy. He was never that interested.

'I want to stay in Dublin,' I said. 'I don't want to go.'

'But it's the *Plaza*. And Broadway. And Tiffany's. How can Dublin compete with New York? I mean, *hello!* It's New York.'

'I can't take the time off,' I said. 'I really can't. And I've got Mum to worry about, and Sarah and... well, everything.' I tried to smize at him and change the subject. 'Anyway, I thought *tonight* we could go to the wine bar I mentioned?' Whatever was rational and sensible, didn't matter. I had to do this for Siobhán. At least one of us could have passion and excitement and *fun*. And as her friend, I was going to do what she wanted.

Ryan groaned. 'You would prefer to go to some crappy wine bar than New York? What on earth is so good about that stupid wine bar? What do they serve? Something you can't find in any other bar? I bet they serve bowls of olives and have crappy breadsticks.'

'No, it's just run by a friend of mine. He moved to Italy and...' I was still smizing. Now, more than anything, I wanted to go to Teolaí. I didn't want New York, I loved Dublin, I loved this city, and I loved my friends.

'Oh God, and now this friend is back, full of *la dolce vita*, am I right? Wanting to bring a little bit of Italy to depressing old Dublin.'

'Siobhán is going too...'

'Oh God.' He rolled his eyes and I felt that familiar gnawing in my stomach, the whispery breath of the Black Terror creeping its way up my spine, my skin crawling and itching, making me feel as though I had to get out of it, like a snake, then I would be okay. I kept my head down, trying to get my breathing and my thoughts in order. Not a panic attack, I thought, not here, not now. 'Why aren't you wearing the necklace?' he said. 'The *diamond* one.'

'It's too much,' I said. 'I can't wear anything that expensive.'

'Of course you can,' he said. 'The best for the best, or don't you see yourself as the best.'

I decided to be honest. 'I don't really believe in the best,' I said.

'Oh, don't be ridiculous,' he said, dismissing me. 'I buy you the best and you don't wear them. I've never seen you use the bag, the earrings you've worn once... the perfume is...'

'I'm saving it for best,' I said.

'I might have got you all wrong.'

'I'm sorry.' He was right, and finally he realised it, and this quest for the perfect half-hearted relationship was finally over. I waited for the sword to fall.

'Oh Milly,' he said.

'It's okay,' I said. 'I understand.'

'Yes,' he said.

'Yes what?'

'Yes, we'll go to Toilet or whatever it's called.'

'Teolaí?'

'We'll go. I do love you, you know,' said Ryan. 'I know I don't say it very often, but I do.' He leaned over to me, smiling. 'You just keep getting it wrong.' I thought he was going to kiss me, but instead his hand reached for my head and tousled my hair. 'You're a work in progress,' he said. 'But you're *my* work in progress.'

33

The sound of laughter and talking coiled in the air like smoke on the early-summer evening above Teolaí. It was glittering like some kind of vision. The long awning dipped over the crowd, fairy lights sparkled in the gloaming, tea lights flickered in the breeze. The world transformed, like Brigadoon, a magical place which had just appeared. It was beautiful. Maybe Teolaí would work its magic on Ryan and he and I would find some kind of whole hearted and wonderful relationship. Or not. He had said he loved me and I wished I could love him back. Maybe I would... I wasn't quite sure yet.

Ryan was looking horrified. 'When you said *wine bar*,' he said, 'I imagined something a little more sophisticated. This looks like something you'd get on the continent, you know, wines out of barrels, they probably have hams hanging from the ceiling and candles stuck in chianti bottles...'

'They don't,' I said, 'it's much nicer. It's—'

'It's not what Dublin needs, that's what. People here either like an old pub or a smart bar. This is neither. It's a mess,' Ryan was saying. 'Good God! Is this the future of socialising in Dublin? Who wants to sit on a rickety chair on a wobbly pavement? I mean, it's the kind of place which would sell you a vino locale for five times what you'd pay in Italy, piss for pounds, that kind of thing. The cheese rancid, the toilets a cesspool. Teolaí? What the hell does that even mean?'

'Let's just enjoy ourselves,' I said.

His mouth dropped open. 'Milly, you accept my gifts, you accept my family's hospitality, you allow me to pay for meals, and yet you are quite sulky at times.'

Out of the corner of my eye, I could see Siobhán over by the windows, under the awning, sitting with George.

'Are you having your...' He stopped. 'Well, something is making you behave like this. I don't have to be here, you know. Mum says that women are difficult... and she is one, which is how she can speak with authority. Right, we're not staying for long. Say our hellos, chat to the ever-so-lovely Siobhán, and then go.'

This evening was unravelling so fast I didn't have a chance to work out why or whose fault it was or if there was anything I could do to fix it. But there was Siobhán waving us over. She stood up excitedly to welcome us, hugging me and going to hug Ryan but he held out his hand and she shook it.

Siobhán looked straight at Ryan, smiling, her eyes twinkling. Ah, so this was expert smizing. 'How are you both? How lovely to see you, Ryan. Beautiful suit. This is George, my boyfriend.'

Ryan nodded curtly. 'Siobhán,' he said, 'a delight, as ever.' He shook George's hand.

Siobhán twinkled back at him, not picking up on his slightly cold tone. 'Likewise! Prosecco everyone?'

Did he not *like* her? Who wouldn't like Siobhán?

'Oh God, prosecco, yes,' I said, gratefully.

Ryan turned to George. 'This your kind of place?' he said. 'A wine bar? You look like a pub kind of man, pints and lots of them.'

'I have been known to partake in the odd glass of wine from time to time,' said George with a shrug. 'I have broad tastes when it comes to alcohol.'

We all fell into silence for a moment.

'Well,' Ryan said, stiffly, 'this is *nice*. So...' He let the word hang in the air as though he couldn't think of a thing to say, amplifying the awkwardness.

'Darragh!' Siobhán shouted out, with relief. 'How's it going? Come over and say hello!'

Darragh looked effortlessly handsome, smiling at us, happy in his skin, as he walked over. Even Ryan, who had his arm around me, as though he owned me, was staring at him. Only George was staring into the middle distance, yawning widely.

'Good evening,' Darragh said. 'Good to see you all.' He smiled generally at us, not quite making eye contact with me. And I suddenly longed for him to look only at me, but now I was just another person in his bar. Darragh was looking at Ryan, checking him out. I supposed he was curious about what kind of man his ex-girlfriend was marrying.

'How's the dog bite?' said Siobhán. 'Started foaming at the mouth yet?'

Darragh turned to her and laughed. 'Maybe,' he said, 'but not because of rabies. Just my usual fulminating at politics.'

'It was a full moon that day,' went on Siobhán. 'I was worried.'

'What? About werewolves?'

Ryan gave me a look of utter bewilderment.

'She's going on about the stars again,' said George, waking up.

'I thought you were talking about the moon.'

'I was, it's just that on a full moon things happen. Not necessarily bad things. But *things*.'

'Being bitten by a dog is a bad thing.' I was starting to feel trapped and suffocated beside Ryan.

'Yes, but there is a chain of events,' insisted Siobhán. 'With Mars and Mercury in free fall *and* a full moon... well...' She shook her head. 'You were lucky to escape with just a bite.'

Darragh's eyes flicked over to me and looked away.

'Will someone tell me what the hell you are all going on about?' said Ryan, trying to be jocular but actually on the brink of anger.

'On our walk,' I said. 'There was an altercation between Betty and another dog. Darragh stepped in and was bitten.'

'And who is Betty?'

'My family's dog,' I reminded him. He had met Betty once but hadn't paid her any attention. If someone doesn't bother to remember you have a dog, then surely that was a pretty big red flag.

'Ah! Thank you for enlightening me.'

Darragh squinted at Ryan as though he was trying to place him.

'Ryan Kingston? Darragh O'Toole.' He held out his hand. 'Long time no see!'

Ryan stared back, shaking his head. 'Sorry, no idea.'

'We were on the rowing team in first year? We all went to Henley for that trip? Remember?'

Ryan then let out a snort. 'Oh yes! But you forgot to say Darragh *O'Fool*!' Dublin was really a village and it was not unusual for anyone to meet someone they knew, but I was surprised by how Ryan immediately had launched into the schoolboy nicknames. Siobhán caught my eye, looking shocked.

'It's a long time since anyone has called me that,' smiled Darragh. 'But I don't blame you for not remembering me. I was only in the rowing club for a year. It was a very competitive atmosphere. I became quite serious about hillwalking then.' Darragh glanced at me for a moment, but I looked away.

'Sorry, sorry,' said Ryan, laughing. 'It just came back to me. You know nicknames never go away. I bumped into Worzel the other day. And I met Gormless a couple of years ago – he's heading up a massive estate agents in London. And remember Shortarse? Selling cars in Brooklyn.'

Darragh tried to look interested. 'Great, great...' Again, he glanced at me, his face giving nothing away. 'Anyway,' he said to Ryan, 'good seeing you again.'

A few tables away, Lorenzo flicked back his mane, his ripped T-shirt revealing half his chest, he looked over and smiled at us. 'Ciao! *Uno momento*! I'll be over, yes?'

Next to me, Siobhán wriggled out of her scarf. 'Jesus,' she said. 'It's so hot tonight.'

'I'm tired,' yawned George. 'Can we go home?'

'No!' Siobhán squealed. 'We've only just arrived!'

'I have to go,' said George. 'I'm knackered.'

Ryan turned to Darragh. 'Good to see you again, O'Fool.' He laughed. 'We were always messing around, remember?'

'Yeah, I remember.' Darragh's smile matched his. 'Have a good evening, okay?' He walked away from us, without looking back.

I need to end this, I thought. *I need to end this with Ryan now.* I felt like Siobhán, suddenly possessed with the thought of getting away from him. I wasn't sure how I had got into this thing with someone so obviously wrong for me.

'Meely! The dog? How is the dog?' Lorenzo had joined us, popping open a new bottle of prosecco and refilling our glasses. 'I've been so worried about that little dog? He is all right? No shock or anything?' He turned to Siobhán, kissing her on both cheeks and then slapping George on the back. 'I teach you to make proper bread, remember? It's all in the muscles. You need muscles to make bread, no? And the best olive oil.'

Ryan slipped his arm around me, pulling me close to him, as though claiming me. 'Thank you for making me come this evening,' he said in my ear. 'It's been good for me to do something different.'

'That's great.'

'I can't tell you how grateful I am that you have shown such patience and kindness with me. I know I have been an arsehole. Will you forgive me?' He looked into my eyes. 'You know I'd do anything for you,' he said. 'And if it means me trying to be a better person, then I'll do it. I know I am too attached to my mother. It's always been the same. One day, I would like to set up on my own. Make my own way in the world, and I would love to have someone like you at my side.' He smiled at me. 'Would you?'

I was stuck. I'd got myself into this relationship and now didn't have the bottle or the confidence to get myself out of it. I really wanted to get it back. But I wasn't sure how.

Behind us, George was now asleep in his chair, while Siobhán and Lorenzo were deep in conversation. We drank our prosecco and I listened while Ryan filled me on his week, his new training schedule and how we should go to Cannes for the weekend. 'Aperol Spritzers are so over,' he was saying. 'Aperol Martinis are the next big thing...'

'Really?' I tried to focus on what he was saying, but I felt very strongly that I was having the wrong conversation with the wrong person.

'Yeah, we should go to Cannes, drink Aperol Martinis at Kontiki – it's the best beach bar in the whole of the Riviera. Drinks are thirty euros a pop but it's so worth it. Mum and Roger have a place there... we could stay there and maybe they would join us...'

Eventually, we'd finished the bottle and we could either order another one or call it a night.

'Let's just go home,' I said to Ryan. 'I've got a family brunch tomorrow so I can't stay out late.'

'At last,' he said. 'It was such a dive! It was kind of you to support enterprises by friends, but really that O'Fool is not going to make any money... people want class. The prosecco was only twelve euros a bottle. And tasted it as well.' He put his arm around me and we walked away.

I glanced back, and Darragh was staring right at me. The old Milly would have known what she wanted. And now, not only did I not know how I got into this relationship with Ryan, I didn't even know how to get out of it. At least, I thought, Siobhán looked happy, still laughing with Lorenzo, having the time of her life.

34

Auntie Angela picked up one of the huge menus. 'I do love this place,' she said. 'Delicious food. Not like restaurants we used to have when we were young, is it, Kitty?'

It was Sunday brunch and we were waiting for Harold and his two children to arrive.

'Everyone okay?' said Mum. 'All ready?'

'We're delighted to be meeting Harold's children,' said Angela, speaking for all of us. 'Isn't this what they call a blended family?'

'Not yet we're not,'said Sarah. 'They could be psychos.'

Mum laughed. 'They seem...' she tried to find the word. 'From what I can tell, they are still a little... well, they seem nice enough. We just have to get to know them better. Life is nothing if not interesting.'

'I find life is interesting in all the wrong ways,' said Sarah. She'd taken off her sunglasses and was drinking her tea. 'I wouldn't mind boring for a bit.'

'Why?' I said, sitting forward eagerly. 'What's going on?'

'Jesus, Milly,' she said. 'Nothing you need to know about.' She stopped. 'And nothing worth getting excited about.' She picked up her phone to check something and quickly put it face down again.

But then they were suddenly upon us and we all scrabbled to our feet to greet them.

'Salve! Salve!' said Harold, grasping my hand, and then Sarah's and then Angela's, and then, shyly kissed Mum on the cheek. 'Kitty,' he said, his whole face flushing pink. She was smiling back, radiant, glowing, it was only a moment but Sarah caught my eye, and we both knew Mum was happy.

Angela was standing beside us, glowing more than anyone, a tear in her eye, her hands clasped in front of her.

But behind Harold were two scowling adults, looking as sulky as teenagers.

'May I present,' Harold said, like a ringmaster, 'the lights of my life, my two children, Horace and Hadriana.'

The man, who was wearing a fleece and walking boots, shook our hands in turn without making eye contact.

'I'm Hadriana,' said the woman. 'Or Hades for short.'

'What interesting names you have,' said Angela, as we all sat down, Horace and Hadriana sat together beside Sarah, then me at the top of the table, and then Angela, Mum and Harold next to Horace at the other end.

'Dad's fault,' said Hadriana to us. 'His obsession with Latin even extended to naming his children.' She took out her phone and began looking through it.

'My mother was obsessed with angels,' said Angela. 'I'm Angela and my lovely sister is Kitty.'

Hadriana didn't even feign interest but turned to Sarah. 'Well, what do you do for a living?' She asked.

'I'm a nurse.'

Hadriana sniggered. 'It's not exactly a glamorous job, is it?'

'Not remotely,' agreed Sarah, who was annoyingly very hard to insult. And she loved obnoxious people. 'And you're in a band,' she said. 'What kind?'

'Oh, it's experimental, ambient music. We don't release music on a label, we make music for other media. It's not something ordinary people know about.'

Sarah winked at me. 'Brilliant,' she said.

'Thank you,' said Hadriana, giving her a second glance.

'Well, this is nice,' said Harold. 'Shall we order? I like soup and a scone, if such a thing exists.'

Horace rolled his eyes. 'Such an outlandish request.' He turned to Hadriana, 'Dad wants a soup and a scone but doesn't know if such a thing exists.'

She laughed. 'Dad always acts as though he is confused by the modern world. But he's the one with the massive high-definition TV.'

Harold was smiling patiently at her, as though he heard that kind of thing a great deal.

'I think the soup of the day is sweet potato,' said Mum, quietly. 'I asked earlier. I do like soup myself, so filling and not too rich.'

A waitress came over and took our orders.

'Yes, I like a soup,' continued Angela. 'Especially a tin of Heinz tomato. Do you like soup, Milly?'

'Mushroom? Or a stew. Does that count?'

'She likes a goulash,' said Sarah, who obviously had perked up and was determined to enjoy herself by keeping the inanities going. 'Do you like a goulash, Hadriana?'

Hadriana gave her a confused look. 'I've never tried it,' she admitted.

'Well you should, it's delicious.'

'What do you do?' Hadriana asked me.

'I am a corporate lawyer.'

She laughed. 'That's funny,' she hooted. 'No, really, what do you do?'

'I'm a corporate lawyer.' I looked to Sarah for support.

'She really is,' nodded Sarah.

Hadriana was shaking her head, as though she couldn't believe it. 'My God, you're the first corporate lawyer I've ever met. I thought they were herded out of the country after the financial crash, like St Patrick and the snakes. I didn't think any of you were left!' She tugged on Horace's fleece sleeve. 'This one's a corporate lawyer,' she said.

'What?' His glasses streamed up in shock. 'Are you having a laugh?'

'No, no, I'm not.' I kept smiling, even though I was quite sure I hated both of them. 'And you are a geologist, is that right?' And then I felt it again, the whispery breath, the skin-prickling rash of anxiety, the hands closing over my throat making it difficult to breathe.

'Geo*physicist*,' he said. 'It's quite, *quite*, different. I specialise in paleo-magnetism. I have just returned from six months in the Tenere desert.'

'Of course you have,' said Sarah.

At the other end of the table, Harold was raising his glass. 'To new friends,' he was saying. 'And new adventures. Dum vivimus vivamus, let us live while we live. And here's to South Africa!'

'I hadn't actually told the girls yet,' said Mum. 'But now is as good a time as any. Harold and I are going on holiday. Ten day tour of the botanic gardens around Kirstenbosch. Harold was going anyway and a spare place came up.'

I felt Sarah's foot kick mine, hard. She was looking up at someone behind me. 'Oh, hi!' she said. 'Darragh!'

'Darragh!' Mum was now standing up.

'Well, if it isn't the wanderer! Returned!' Angela was on her feet.

I turned to see Darragh clamped in the arms of Auntie Angela and next being hugged by Mum. He glanced at me, a brief nod.

'This is quite a gathering,' he said, looking around the table, taking everyone in. 'Celebrating?'

Mum looked a little embarrassed all of a sudden, as though she didn't know how to explain who we all were.

Hadriana and Horace looked bored and disinterested to the point where I thought they would both be playing Snake on their phones like teenagers. But Harold was standing up, his hand outstretched.

'Harold Hawkins,' he said. 'I have the great honour of escorting Kitty these days.'

'Great!' Darragh shook his hand.

'And these are the fruit of my loins,' Harold went on, his hand flinging out to present Horace and Hadriana. They slunk in their seats, cringing with embarrassment. Hadriana even managed an 'oh, Daaa-ad', but they vaguely and weakly acknowledged Darragh.

'What brings you here?' said Angela. 'Indulging in a little *bruncheon* like us?' She giggled. 'See what I did there?'

Darragh grinned at her.

'I'm with Dad and Shirley,' he said. 'They'll be along in a moment to say hello.' And then he looked straight at me and I looked straight at him and for the first time in five years, we saw each other. *I love you*, I thought. *I shouldn't. But I do.* And this time I wasn't confused, it wasn't complicated, it was simple: I didn't hate him, or despise him for what he had done. I loved him. Sometimes hating someone was so much easier. Oh God. I wished I didn't. I had tried so hard to imagine we could be friends, I had avoided him, gone hillwalking with him, chatted to his new girlfriend, spent money in his business, I had tried to commit more readily to my relationship but none of it was working. I was back where I was when we first met and what was more, I hadn't shifted along the dial. Over the last five years I'd tried to react properly – by disliking him, but I loved him – full-on, deeply, truly and wonderfully. He'd dumped me, he'd left me the week my father died, he had arrived back in Dublin without warning and had turned up with the most beautiful woman in the world on his arm. I should detest him. And yet... and yet...

I loved him.

And I knew I had to get out of there because I was beginning to drown in the air, to choke and to struggle for breath. I felt like my whole body was being crushed in the hand of a huge, evil, invisible giant, squeezing every good thing out of me. I had to get out of there, and I began to run for the door, knocking over chairs, the light of the door just ahead. And then I threw myself down on the pavement, prepared for it all to end. Anxiety and grief – a malevolent cocoon.

I doubled over in full panic, desperately trying to suck in enough air, just enough to get the next one in and the next, but each too shallow and too small to actually breathe and ease the pain in my chest, which felt as though there was a metal cage around it. I was drowning, but my own body, my own mind, was the thing that was stopping me from breathing. Angry at myself for letting myself down, furious that this was happening to me after everything I had put in place to ensure the days of panic attacks were long over. Nothing had worked. I was back at square one, just as grief-stricken, just as vulnerable, just as much a failure as ever.

I was vaguely aware of passers-by stopping to look, a couple of people asking if I was okay, but then Sarah's hand was stroking my back. She was giving orders, telling people to stand back, asking for water. 'Give her space,' she said. 'Nothing to see here.' And her voice in my ear, 'It's okay, Milly. You're doing so well. You're okay.'

I was aware of Mum and Auntie Angela behind her, their voices saying things I couldn't quite make out. And there was Darragh looking... I wasn't sure what.

Sarah's voice again, 'That's it, breathe... and again.' Her voice, calm, insistent, strong. My sister saving my life. 'Come on. Another breath, and another... keep going. You are amazing...'

My eyes closed, my breath slightly deeper and each time, each inhalation, an infinitesimally bit bigger, and then the relief of the one breakthrough breath, the one you've been searching for, that gasp that fills your whole body up with life. And I'm back. And it's over. And I'm crying.

35

'If we end up being related to *them*, I think I might have to find a new family,' said Sarah, driving me home. Mum and Angela had gone together, which was a relief as I didn't need any more worried faces or fuss. All I wanted was Sarah's cool and calm, her brilliance in a crisis. I could still hear her in my ear telling me I was okay. Isn't that what we need more often, not just when you are huddled on a pavement, someone telling you you're okay?

'They're not too bad,' I said, looking out of the window at the normal life that was going on. It was early May and the trees were at their billowy blossomy bridesmaid whitest, there was a spring in the step of the world, and here was Sarah doing her very best to be normal with me, to bring me back to earth.

'We're going to have to stop the wedding,' she went on, giving me a wink. 'I mean we can't have Horace and Hadriana our new step-siblings.'

I nearly laughed, deeply and newly appreciative of Sarah's skills in making me feel so much better, despite the clawing mortification and embarrassment. My chest hurt as though I'd been in a car accident, I was wrung out and exhausted. God knows what I looked like, but I remember Hadriana's hand over her mouth in shock. 'Horace and Hadriana must think I'm mad.' I didn't say anything about Darragh, but I dreaded to think how I must have seemed, deranged and damaged.

'Well, I think *they're* mad,' Sarah went on. 'Harold's a sweetheart, but his children are horrible!' She grinned at me. 'How did a nice man have such truly awful offspring? And I'm glad you had that panic attack, totally brightened up the whole proceedings. We were going to have to endure another two hours of *that* and you got us out of there.' She looked over again and smiled. 'Nice move.'

'Thanks.'

'And it meant that we didn't have to have that awkward conversation with Darragh. I mean, who does he think he is? Coming in like that, as though nothing had happened and Mum and Auntie Angela all over him.'

'You were the same in the hospital,' I reminded her.

She shrugged. 'Yeah. I had to be. Professional, I am. But they could have cold-shouldered him. Mum could have had a go, *EastEnders* style, threatened him with a glass bottle and Angela could have shouted names at him.'

I laughed. But even thinking about Darragh was painful. Was emigration to Australia my only option to escape ridicule and humiliation?

'Seriously, though,' she said. 'What brought it on? Was it *him*?'

'I don't know,' I said truthfully. 'I've been feeling more and more panicky lately, but I don't know why exactly. Him, yes... but also... I think I haven't quite sorted out my feelings about Dad...'

She didn't say anything, her eyes on the road ahead.

'They say time heals everything, but that makes it seem like a forward trajectory...' I paused. 'But it's not. It's all over the place.'

There was silence in the car. And then she said, 'I wish it was just one, neat journey. You go through all the seven stages, or however many there are, and then you're okay again. I mean, sometimes I don't even think about him. I'm getting on with things, or even sad about someone like Ollie dying, and then I remember my dad died, and I should be sad about him, not Ollie, who I barely knew.' She paused. 'Such a lovely man, though. A real gentleman.' She cleared her throat.

'All the things he's missed. The birthdays, the Christmases, Angela's pavlova...'

Sarah gave a laugh. 'Yeah,' she said. 'We're going through all these things, and he's not here to enjoy them. All these family things are happening because he's not here... meeting Harold, his horrible children... it's all because Dad *died*...'

'I just want to see him again,' I said. 'Just as he was, exactly how we remember him...'

Sarah was smiling now. 'I used to think he looked like an off-duty Santa. I had this fantasy that he really was Santa and during the year he was our dad, but then on Christmas Eve, he would have to disappear and do what Santa always does, but he couldn't tell anyone, but he guessed that I guessed, but, of course, he couldn't talk to me about it and it was like this secret between us. I was the only person who knew he really was Santa. And it made me feel like the luckiest child in the world. My dad was Santa!'

'Maybe he was,' I said.

'Maybe he was,' she repeated. She stopped the car at the lights and we fell silent again.

'Do you remember what Dad used to call us?' I said.

Her faced softened, and she looked over at me and smiled, that beautiful Sarah smile. 'Of course.'

'His sparkling drops of joy.'

'It's kind of nice,' she said. 'Don't you think? To be someone's sparkling drop of joy.'

I smiled back. 'Yeah, it's kind of nice.'

'God, I miss him,' she said. 'Hugh tried to buy me loads of books on grief and recovery and everything... but there is nothing you can do, just let the days pass. I don't get panic attacks like you... I've just become impossible.' She gave me a half-smile. 'Ask Hugh.' She was silent again and then, 'He called me overwrought. Described me perfectly.' She rolled her eyes. 'I'm officially a nightmare.'

We were driving down the main street, past Teolaí, which was busy and full of light, and towards my flat. I wondered if Darragh was back at work, or was he with his dad, or Francisca, telling them about his crazy ex-girlfriend?

'Hugh and I... we love each other,' said Sarah, 'always will. But it got to a point where external forces became too much.' She stopped. 'Work was, is, will forever be shit. Hard, stressful, demanding...' She shook her head. 'It's so *hard* to try and be normal when you are not working, and then spending your working life on edge because at any moment someone could die, and it might be your fault, or you are surrounded by the unrelenting pace of the job, everyone needing you, your call going off... you can't relax for a moment, you feel like your heart is permanently on edge and that it's going to explode.' She looked at me, and shrugged. 'Relationships, even with someone you love, are impossible...'

'I had no idea that was how you felt about work.'

She shook her head, looking at me as though I was mad. 'I'm a *nurse*. Remember? It's what it's like for all of us. We don't complain, not until we're at breaking point, because it's a vocation... you've spent all those years wanting to help people, and then the training... and then how can you leave because if you don't do it, who will?'

'I'm sorry.'

'Yeah, well, so am I. And Hugh was stressed with work, both of us bringing it all home. He was working so hard and so... well... sometimes you can't make love work. Or love *becomes* work and you can't do it *and* actual work...'

We sat in silence again.

'Do you think you will work it out? Find your way back to each other?'

'Who knows?' And then she said, 'what about you? What's going on with your love life? Is Ryan *the One*?'

I shook my head. '*The One* left me five years ago...' I looked at Sarah and she reached across and took my hand and held it, an uncharacteristically soppy expression of affection from Sarah, but it felt exactly right. 'So, that's what I am trying to deal with, transferring all the love I have for him onto someone else. But it doesn't work that way, does it?'

She took her hand back, and looked out of the window. 'No,' she said softly, 'it doesn't.'

We'd pulled up outside the flat and I suddenly felt exhausted. I didn't know how I was going to get myself from the car, up all those stairs, put my key in the door and get into my bed. How on earth had Mrs Murphy done it for all those years?

'Do you want me to come in?' she said.

'No, I'm fine,' I smiled, hoping to reassure her that I was. I didn't want my little sister worrying any more about me. 'I just want to go straight to bed. I'll see you soon.'

'You sure? Well,' she said, 'if you don't mind me giving you my opinion, I think you should finish with Ryan.'

'I will,' I said.

'You shouldn't worry about being alone. Or being lonely. It's just part of being human.'

I got out of the car and hovered on the pavement while she put it into gear and indicated she was pulling out, and then, just as she was moving away, Sarah opened the passenger window and leaned towards me.

'You don't need to settle for half-heartedness,' she said. 'You have plenty of love in your life. You see... I love you.' The window went up again, and she drove away before she could hear my answer.

'I love you too,' I managed, and cried all the way upstairs.

36

Renewed and rejuvenated, by the next morning, I was in deep concentration at my desk, trying to work out how to respond to another letter from Alpha Holdings and Mr Hessling.

I searched for an image of him online, but nothing came up. I searched for more information about the company and the co-director R De Vere, but the company had only been formed two years ago, and there was very little to go on. There was the completion of the sale of the building to the rear of Number One, Merrion Square, and the submission of the architect's plans. If all went well for them, the buildings would take in the rear gardens and coach houses to create quite an unusual residence. There were other applications in from Alpha Holdings for similar developments around the city. Whoever Mr Hessling and Mr DeVere were, they were ambitious.

Something made me look up from my computer. Jarleth was standing at my desk, staring, his head at an angle. I nearly screamed.

'Just marvelling,' he said. 'That's okay, isn't it? Not breaking any of the codes... I mean, I'm not being invasive, am I? Or maybe I am? Because if I have inadvertently crossed the invisible line into not-okay behaviour, then let me know. I wouldn't want one of those complaints about me. Hashtag Me Too.'

'What is it?' I asked.

'Have you ever thought about smiling a bit more? You should get more involved in the craicathon. We're doing the three-legged race around the offices later.'

'I'm busy,' I said. 'A few things to do...'

'Of course! You're so busy, the busiest person in the entire organisation!' He laughed. 'The one propping up McCoyMcAvoy all on her own. Without whom the place would implode...'

'Jarleth...'

'I'm teasing, right? God, can't you take a joke? So uptight! And all I'm doing is injecting a much needed dose of fun into this office, lubricating the social wheels, making people *happy*, that's all. Nothing sinister. God, you women are so touchy these days! What's your problem? Anyone would think you didn't like working in Dublin's most prestigious law firm? Are we not at the top of our game? Working hard and playing harder?'

The Mrs Murphy case was highlighting just how much I realised I actually hated being a corporate lawyer. I'd stopped remembering how transformative being a lawyer could be. You could actually empower people, help them gain amazing things like freedom or personal security. You could keep them safe from people, you could ensure they didn't lose their homes...

'Talking of which,' he said. 'If you would like to have a bit more fun in your life, but outside of work, we could go for a drink on Friday night. Of course, it wouldn't have to be one drink, we could make it six or seven. And I am quite the disco dancer after a few shots of tequila.'

I gazed at him with mounting disbelief, segueing into horror. 'Jarleth...'

'I know you're very busy and very important,' he smirked, confidently. 'But even the busiest people have to take time out. Now, I don't mind being your guide for the evening... it would be just the two of us... a glass of vino, a nip of Teelings, a round of sambucas... or should that be sambu*cae*?' His smile was annoying smug.

'I don't think so,' I said, firmly.

'But I would be giving up my Friday night,' he reminded me. 'To take *you* out.'

'I know,' I said, 'and it's very kind of you...'

'But what else would you be doing? You give the impression that you don't have much on.'

'I have a *lot* on,' I said. 'I really can't.'

He stood there for a moment, mouth moving as though he was speaking without words. 'But I don't do this very often,' he said. 'I didn't think you would say no... but, of course...' He was recovering, I was relieved to see. 'Well, I was only asking because I felt sorry for you...'

'Milly!' Catriona was calling me from her office. 'Can you come in here a moment.'

'Her master's voice,' sniggered Jarleth. 'Quick, run along. She's probably got some dry cleaning you need to collect. Or a letter to type or a present to choose for her husband's birthday. See you for the three-legged race. McCoyMcAvoy is taking on the other law firms, it's going to be a race to the death. Or are you too busy and important for *that*?'

I didn't wait to answer because Catriona had called me again. She looked up from her desk as I went in. 'I'd like you to take the lead on the Gregory Group,' she smiled somewhat awkwardly. 'If you don't mind.'

'Of course,' I said, trying to look enthusiastic but feeling that everything was piling up on top of me. 'But is everything all right?'

'I am delegating,' she said. 'Previously a word which had yet to be introduced to my vocabulary, but after extensive middle-of-the-night personal crises and long talks with Noel, I have decided that it should be. So I am del-e-ga-ting.' She pronounced every syllable, as though trying out the word in her mouth to see if it fitted. 'Milly,' she went on, 'you're highly talented and experienced and this step-up is long overdue. In fact, I think my inability or reluctance to delegate has held you back. My own selfishness,' she admitted.

'I don't mind!' I said, desperately. 'I really don't mind being held back.'

She smiled. 'That's sweet of you to say, but we both know I've been unfair.'

Of course, I *could* take the lead with the Gregory Group, it wasn't impossible. I was a trained and experienced lawyer and I knew I was good. Except, along the way, I'd lost all confidence. Enthusiasm and passion and verve for law had leached out and my lack of ambition was embarrassing, and unheard of for a lawyer. If it got out, I'd be disbarred.

'I have faith in you, Milly,' Catriona was saying. 'But I find I am just too tired to work with the same gusto as I used to. The only thing that is keeping me going is sugar. Would you like one of these?' She dug around in her bag, produced a bag of toffees and held it out. 'Maternity leave may be a statutory right, but here it's a sign of weakness. And please, this is in confidence.' I took a toffee, I needed the sugar as well.

'Don't worry,' I promised, unwrapping the sweet. 'I won't say a word.'

'As the only woman partner in this whole stupid building,' she went on, putting two toffees in her mouth which made it difficult for her to talk. 'I can't share the joys of parenthood in the same way. I am desperate to talk about Lydia, but she will have to remain invisible.'

'I know.' All the male partners ostentatiously accessorised their desks with pictures of their exceptionally photogenic children, usually blond and smiling and curiously, always on some kind of boat.

'I'm tired, Milly,' she went on. 'I am so bloody tired and all I want for Lydia is for her to go to sleep, but as soon as she does, I miss her. *Dreadfully.* Her little body, her beautiful face, the feeling of her little body on my lap or lying beside me.' She smiled. 'She's got this funny little way of reaching out for me with her tiny hand. And the other day, I could feel someone looking at me, and it was her, staring at me, right into my eyes, deep into my soul. It was almost unsettling. She wants to know me and she loves me, as much as I love her!' She stopped to recover herself. 'It was quite a moment.' Catriona made a strange noise as though she was clearing her throat, but someone more observant than me might have thought she was trying not to cry. 'I never realised that naps were important...' Catriona went on.

'For Lydia?'

'For me,' she said. 'I used to be able to survive on four hours. I was the weirdo in college who'd be up at 6 a.m. to go for a run, or the person who would start an essay at midnight and hand it in at 9 a.m. and then go to a lecture. I never knew sleep was an actual thing.'

'It's definitely a thing,' I said.

'Well, my four hours a night isn't cutting it any more. I think it's mental and emotional overload. You can cope if you only have work, but add any other complications to the mix, then your body starts malfunctioning.' She unwrapped another toffee and popped it in her mouth. 'So, before I start snorting sugar straight from the packet, I think it might be sensible to share some of my workload and hopefully save my sanity. And my marriage.'

'Of course,' I said, because I *had* to. 'Whatever you need.'

'So, Milly, you'll take the lead with Peter Gregory and you can ask my advice when you wish, but otherwise I trust you. You'll have to be in court on Friday.'

Court? Jesus Christ. 'I don't know if I can do it,' I said, fear chasing over my skin like mist on a swamp.

'Nonsense,' she said, as though she'd made a decision and was done with it. 'It's time you stepped up. I've been keeping you back and now you have a golden opportunity to show that you should be made partner.' She gave me a nod. 'Get everything in order and let me know how you get on.'

37

In the ladies' loos of the Four Courts, I was attempting every trick I knew to keep myself calm.

You're an experienced, talented lawyer, I told my reflection, trying to remember what else Catriona had said. *You've got this. You can do this.*

I had stood up in court before, I knew I could do it, but having to be so publicly confident was taking a bit of a build-up. And hiding behind Catriona hadn't done me any favours, I was out of practice. How did other people do this so effortlessly?

I went over the case, thinking of the argument I had devised. My defence hinged on one word in the Housing Act that I felt could swing the case to our benefit. But I just had to be out there and channel someone far more confident and powerful than me. I had to find my inner Catriona.

The door opened and there was Susie. 'There you are!' she said. 'I've been looking for you everywhere. Catriona asked me to pop down. As part of my course, I need to get more experience.' She paused. 'Or maybe you don't want me to?'

'Of course I do,' I said. 'I'm just feeling nervous. I get... I get, you know, a bit anxious from time to time.'

'You?' For a moment she didn't know what to say. 'But you're so...'

'So what?'

She stepped towards me. 'Put it to one side, okay?' she said. 'Say to it, thanks, I see you, I feel you, but it's not convenient right now. You can come back and be all over me later. Okay?' Susie looked at me. 'Say that to it now.'

'What? Speak to my anxiety?'

She nodded. 'Try it. It works.'

'How do you know?'

'Told you, I've been around. Go on, do it. Speak to it, nicely. Say you understand that it needs to do its job, but right now you have to do yours. And later you will give it all the attention it needs.'

I stood for a moment, taking what she said in. 'Okay.'

I spoke inside my head. *Thank you for coming. I understand that you need to be heard, but it's not convenient right at this moment. I'll be ready for you tonight when I'm at home. Okay? I'm so sorry.*

I used my politest voice and everything.

'Out loud this time,' ordered Susie.

And then I said it again, out loud.

And we waited; Susie looking at me as though I was an Icelandic geyser about to blow.

'I think,' I said. 'I think I'm okay.'

'Told you!' She looked delighted. 'Now come on.'

Outside, my face arranged into neutral, I met Peter Gregory and his right-hand man.

'Ready?' said Peter.

I nodded. 'Yes,' I heard my voice say, 'let's go for it.'

It started quite badly, you might say. The only people who looked happy were the members from the council's planning department. I stumbled over my words, corrected myself and blinked in the ray of sunlight that shone through the high row of windows, full of dust and skin and particles of all the briefs that have been waved around in the courtroom. But there was Susie nodding gravely beside me, believing in me. And then, somehow, I began to believe in myself. I knew what I was saying, what I was doing. And the council's planning department began to shift in their seats.

'I would like for one moment to read from the Housing Miscellaneous Act of 1992,' I said, reading from my notes. 'Notwithstanding section 58 of the Principal Act and subject to such regulations as may be made by Dublin City Council, the developer may provide twenty per cent social housing for use by the council for its tenants...'

It was one word among hundreds of thousands of words. The word *may*, rather than *must*, meant that Peter Gregory was under no obligation to provide housing that would be rented out to those on low incomes.

'And therefore my client is under no legal imperative to make such accommodation...'

Maybe not legal imperative, I thought grimly. But definitely moral imperative. Again, I felt as though I was being bought. I was paid to defend and to win this case and yet it was wrong, so wrong.

But Peter Gregory was happy, giving me a thumbs up in his seat on the other side of Susie.

'It appears,' said the judge, 'that the counsel for the Gregory Group is right. And that the wording in the Housing Miscellaneous Act of 1992 is ambiguous.' He tossed his notebook down in front of him. 'And I think the lesson from today for Dublin City Council, Housing Department, is to ensure that its literature is watertight. Mr Peter Gregory has every right to continue to build his development.'

Susie flung her arms around Peter. Her flapping arms pulled me into this awkward hug sandwich, squashing Peter between us. 'I knew you would do it,' she said. 'You're a genius. The way you had everyone in the palm of your hand, leading us a merry dance and then, wallop, the sinker!'

Peter was smiling. 'Good girl,' he said. 'I knew you would pull it out of the bag.' He shook my hand. 'I'll be phoning Paddy McAvoy about you,' he said. 'I like to put in a good word where it's due.'

He looked so pleased with himself, his red face even redder as he thought about the millions he wouldn't be obliged to spend on social housing. We shook hands and I walked away. I should feel good, I had led a case, without Catriona's handholding – and won. Moments like this should be noticed. A job well done. I should feel proud and strong... but instead I felt empty as though there should be more. A win is only a win if you feel it in every fibre of your body. This wasn't a win. This was a job and I felt weirdly empty.

* * *

That evening, I met Ryan in the foyer of the Four Seasons hotel before we went to the bar, where Carole and Roger were waiting.

'Milly?' Ryan said. 'What's wrong *now*?'

'Nothing,' I said, remembering to smize. 'I'm fine.' Something was very wrong if you had to force yourself to smile at someone. A few weeks ago, I'd felt safe with Ryan, protected from the highs and the lows of relationship emotional rollercoasters... and I'd been willing to accept a lack of depth in exchange for the wonderful feeling of never being hurt.

'There *is* something wrong,' he said. 'I can tell by your face.'

'I'm okay,' I began, 'I just...' I was about to open my mouth. 'I'm just feeling...'

'It's not your *anxiety*, is it?'

'It's nothing,' I said, giving up. 'Come on, let's just have a nice evening.'

'I know what it is,' he said. 'It's because we are meeting Mum and Roger and you want us to meet your friends instead.'

'No, I...' I stopped, defeated. 'Sorry.'

'Milly, I bought you the necklace. And those earrings. And the handbag... I mean, you'd think you'd buck up a little!'

'I'm sorry... I...' I didn't know what to say exactly. Did you give presents to someone so they would behave perfectly. But if you accepted them, wasn't that, too, some kind of deal?

'Look, I'm sorry,' he said. 'I shouldn't have said that about the gifts. They are for you. I like being generous. One should not give to receive, should they? Look, I don't know what's wrong with you,' he went on. 'But I like what we have together. So, I want to make this work.' He took my hand. 'You're special to me, I try and show it. By giving you things. I *like* buying you things, and you could... I don't know... we're good together. And I appreciate you spending time with Mum. She is important to me. Roger, not so much.'

'You're welcome.'

'I really like you. More than anyone I've ever met. You're a good person, you're beautiful, intelligent, kind.' He smiled. 'I promise that if you want to talk about your *thing*, I will listen. Maybe it is real, who knows?'

I was officially out of words. I realised that it is better to feel hurt and bloody and bruised than feel nothing at all. Nothing at all was pointless and a waste of my life. And I had chosen all this. It served me right.

'Well, what are we waiting for? Let's go!'

Ryan had hold of my hand, rushing us through the hotel, to the bar, desperate not to be late to see his mother. Was it normal, I wondered, for a thirty-two year old man to want to hang out with his mother, or was it just nice? But going out with Ryan meant going out with Carole and it was all a bit too much.

From their seats at the bar, Roger waved us over. 'You'll have to speak up,' he shouted as we walked towards them. He had two huge wads of cotton wool sticking out of his ears. 'Had my ears syringed today and they are still oozing. There was a serious amount of gunk in there. My guy said he'd never seen the like, said he should have brought a snorkel.' He beamed delightedly at us.

'Roger,' said Carole. 'It's my birthday and ears aren't quite the kind of thing one likes to talk about on one's special day.'

'No, indeed,' he said, flattened.

'And take out the bits of cotton wool,' she said, 'You look ridiculous.'

'Sorry, dear,' he said, whipping them out. 'I am sure the oozing has stopped and if not I'll...'

'If not, you will remove yourself from our company.' Ryan and I watched as he visibly withered under her stare. It was clear she was in a bad mood.

Ryan kissed her hello and she held her cheek to me and I bent down to place a kiss on her. 'Happy birthday, Carole,' I said, as she gazed at me coolly.

'You look tired, Milly,' she said. 'It's so good of you to take time out of your exceptionally busy schedule. You must tell me how you're getting on. I am here to advise.' She patted the seat beside her for me to sit down. Her beady eyes met mine. Ryan practically pushed me down beside her, pleased that his mother and I were such good friends.

38

The next afternoon, I was sitting on the windowsill of Mum and Dad's room – *Mum's* room – watching her packing for South Africa. The flight was in four hours' time and she was busy folding jumpers and trousers and packing sandals and dresses.

On either side of the bed were two bedside tables. On Mum's side was her book, a lamp, a box of tissues, a water glass and a silver-framed photograph of the four of us. The other was completely empty, apart from a matching lamp. When Dad was alive, it was always a mess, strewn with half-read newspapers and a cold cup of tea from that morning and whatever Dickens he was ploughing through. It had remained like that for months and months after he died and then one day I passed their room and glanced in and realised that Mum had tidied everything away.

'Are you looking forward to the holiday?' I tried to sound happy and enthusiastic, but I couldn't take my eyes off the lifeless bedside table.

'I really am,' she said. 'It's going to be really interesting. And beautiful weather. And I couldn't have gone if Sarah hadn't moved back home. Who would have looked after Betty?'

I nodded. 'You deserve to have a good holiday,' I said, 'especially somewhere so exotic... and far away...'

Mum put down the shirts she was folding, sat down next to me and took my hand. 'How are you feeling?'

'Better.' I swallowed. 'Sorry about last week.'

'Please don't apologise.' She clutched my hand in both of hers.

'But I kind of ruined the whole thing. Embarrassed you.'

She shook her head. 'No you didn't,' she said, firmly. 'I couldn't be prouder of you two. You're human, like us all. After losing your dad, do you know how many times I just wished I could let it out, cry in public or shout in the street?'

I smiled. 'But you didn't though, did you?'

'I just wish I had helped more,' she said. 'Grief is a terrible thing. It is in charge, you have to submit to it. That's why gardening helped me, I was just out there, letting it flow, the thoughts come and go. I don't know what I would have done if I had to go to an office, or like Sarah, go to a hospital every day.' She still had my hand in hers. 'I'm so sorry, my beautiful Milly.'

'I'll survive.' I gave her a half-smile.

She hesitated for a moment. 'We're both worriers, you and I. Dad always used to say to leave the worrying to him, and I did... until something worth worrying about happened, didn't he?'

I nodded.

'Your dad was so adventurous,' she went on. 'He always found joy in the smallest thing, like he was wringing the last drop of life out of everything. Remember the camping in the back garden, the fires he would make and he'd cook sausages in a frying pan...?'

'And the sparks and embers would float into the sky,' I said. 'And Dad's face would be red from the fire. He looked so happy.'

Mum nodded. 'That's because he was. Every day was a potential adventure. Going for a walk with Betty on Killiney Hill was an adventure. When the mist came down and no one else was out walking, he would be soaking up the atmosphere...'

'And the rain.' I smiled.

'He used to say that it was like being in a Dickens novel. Every time he came home for a walk, do you know what he said?'

'Tell me.'

'He used to come back, and he was so energised, just from fresh air, just being outside, just being alive, and he would say, well, *that put years on my life.'*

We looked at each other.

'Except it didn't,' I said, stating the obvious.

'Except *it did,'* she said. 'Don't you see? While he was alive, he was *alive.* He enjoyed every single moment of his life. More than some people who live to be a hundred. He made the most of his sixty years. Whether it was being here with us, his family, or going on those camping holidays, or walking Betty, he was fully present. There are some people who live much longer lives but they haven't really been present. It's like eating without chewing, just swallowing your food. Never tasting.' We stayed silent for a moment and then she said, 'I'm worried about going to South Africa. Am I doing the right thing? Is it too far? Will something happen while we are over there? What would Charles think? Why am I going with Harold? Is Harold the right person for me? Am I being disloyal to the memory of the love of my life? That kind of thing. But I'm trying to take a few risks in my life... be braver.'

'You are brave,' I said.

'And so are you.' Her hand holding mine, mine holding hers.

'I'm going to try to be braver.'

For a moment, she didn't say anything. 'I felt very angry when Dad died,' she said. 'I felt he'd left me. After all the promises we'd made, the plans... and then he died. I wasn't angry with him, of course, but with the world. I felt it was so unfair, I couldn't get my head round it. I stopped going out and seeing friends. If it wasn't for you, my darling girls, and for Angela and my friends... I don't know what I would have done.'

'My point is,' she went on, 'that you can't control anything. You can just hope to keep being here. Being alive. We lost Dad. And we are all still really sad about it. Every day, I wish he was here with us. But life is precious. We're still here. We are lucky to be here, right now, *talking.'*

I nodded. 'I know.'

'Dad would want us to live life and be happy,' said Mum. 'I know it's time for us all to keep going, to move along in our lives, and feel good about what we do and where we go.' She stroked my hand. 'I'll miss the two of you, though. My lovely girls.'

I suddenly thought of Darragh. All my hurt and sorrow and disappointment was long gone, I realised, and all that was left was how I probably would always feel about him, love. I loved him. I hoped he and Francisca would be happy.

I stood up. 'Come on, let's get you packed. You'll need your silver sandals for the evenings when you go for all those nice dinners you're going to have.'

'Ooh, yes,' said Mum, excitedly. 'Angela says the food there is to die for.' She suddenly looked so thrilled about this imminent adventure that she had pushed through fear and wariness and that's why she was having this moment, this happiness. Fear, I realised, could be a good thing. But you did have to push your way forward, through that forest of trees and twigs and spikey things. You had to keep going, not hang around on the edges. It was fear which held us back, fear which stopped new growth and new adventures. My mother was fearless and brave and fabulous. I loved her for it. 'Pin this on for me,' she said. It was the little silver brooch Dad had given her for her fiftieth birthday, a little silver dog. 'I thought I'd bring him with me,' she said. 'Didn't want to leave him behind.'

I wasn't sure if she meant Dad or the brooch, but before I could ask, the doorbell rang.

'There's Harold now!'

'Come on then,' I said, 'let's get you to the airport.'

Harold's bow tie was a red beacon on the early-summer evening.

'Kitty,' he said, formally. 'Are you all set?' He put out his hand for her suitcase.

'Yes, yes, I've packed rather too well,' she said, passing it to him. 'I don't think we'll be running out of anything.'

'Ah, but have you packed the most important item of all? The humble tea bag?'

Mum laughed. 'No, Harold,' she said. 'I haven't packed a tea bag, I've packed a hundred and eighty of them! Do you think that's enough?'

Now he laughed in response. 'It might be enough to get us through the first couple of days, I suppose.'

Sarah waved us off, as we set off for the airport, Harold in the back of my car, Mum beside me at the front.

'We've plenty of time,' said Harold, rather submerged under the suit-cases and bags. 'I find that when one goes to the airport, it is best to leave as much time as possible, because *tempus* does have a habit of *fugit*.'

Mum turned round to him. 'Well, we can have a nice glass of something on the flight, and watch a film. I'm looking forward to the flight as much as the trip.'

I could see Harold's beaming smile from the rear view mirror. 'So am I, Kitty,' he said. 'So am I. And I've bought you the new Hilary Mantel you were talking about. I can't think of a single other thing.'

At Departures, among the swirl and swarm of travellers, I waved them off.

'See you in two weeks!' said Mum. 'Now, I expect texts and phone messages. And if you are feeling panicky or anything, please call me.'

'I'll be fine,' I promised, thinking that Susie's technique was surpris-ingly and reassuringly successful. It was as though you could take control of it, master it, rather than fighting it.

'Until we meet again,' said Harold to me. 'Vale!' He put his arm through Mum's. 'I'll look after her,' he said. 'Precious cargo, this one.'

'And I'll look after him,' said Mum. They smiled at each other again and all that was left for me to do was to hug them both and wave them off.

39

The following morning, before I'd even got to my desk, Daphne called.

'Mary doesn't want to go ahead,' she said. 'She's contacted Sunnyside Nursing Home and they have a place available next week. I drove past it last night, and it looks awful, torn blinds in the windows, the faces of elderly people looking out.' She sounded near to tears. 'And they don't accept cats!'

'But why? What's happened?'

'I found her on the floor of the living room. Frederick came into my kitchen, miaowing, and I knew something was wrong. I think it really upset her. She's been very quiet ever since and then last night she told me she'd been on the phone to Sunnyside.'

I went straight up to Merrion Square and met Daphne outside Number One. She had a roll of paper under her arm. 'I've come up with a plan,' she said. 'Just something to present to her before she books herself into Sunnyside.'

We waited for the click of the main door and we worked our way up to each floor, the empty flats and offices which were once ballrooms and billiards rooms and libraries, the old kitchen, the large bedrooms, to Mrs Murphy's at the top.

'This would have housed those poor servant girls,' said Daphne. 'I found the original plans to the house; I was in the library doing research on the family that lived here when it was first built.'

'So what's your plan?' I said.

'Just an idea. I'll show you once we're inside,' she said, just as Mrs Murphy opened the door with Frederick in her arms.

'My young saviours,' she said, smiling.

'Hello, Mrs Murphy,' I said. 'How are you?'

'Reconciled,' she said. 'I am reconciled.'

Daphne and I glanced at each other.

'Daphne said you didn't want to go through with the court case,' I said, following them through to the sitting room.

'That's right, dear,' she said. 'I was going to call you this morning.'

'But we can win this,' I insisted. 'We aren't going to give up.' I felt quite desperate all of a sudden. Here was the one case that I really cared about and now it was just going to go away, unheard in court, Mrs Murphy would move to Sunnyside Nursing Home and I would go back to defending people like Peter Gregory.

But no. I would not be going back. I knew now I was done with property developers and corporate law. I'd found what I wanted to do with my career and it involved a woman and a cat. Or people exactly like Mrs Murphy and Frederick. And yes, I was fully aware that I now considered Frederick to be Frederick. Madness comes in all forms, but I liked this kind the best.

'You're both very kind to an old lady like me,' Mrs Murphy was saying. 'And I don't want to let you down, but when I think of the time you have both given to me, and Daphne, my niece...'

'Fourth cousin,' corrected Daphne.

'Whatever it is, you coming in every day to look after me, and, Milly, you taking the case on and being so sure and so confident that I almost felt that I would win... but...' she sighed, stroking Frederick, 'I know it's probably a bit late with you facing the court on Thursday, but I thought it better to say this now. I don't want to put you through it, Milly. Defending me, and then we lose.'

'But we might not lose!' I said.

She shook her head. 'I have no doubt as to your abilities, dear. Mr McAvoy couldn't speak more highly of you, and you are full of enthusiasm and energy. Whereas... whereas I am not. I am just too tired for all this nonsense. If that crowd want it so much, then they can have it. It's a house. Only a house. And I'm old, too old, to climb those stairs, too old to feed myself. And all I need is a room and Frederick, and Sunnyside have a place for us.'

Daphne shot me a look. Mrs Murphy obviously didn't know they wouldn't take cats.

'My memories are up here...' Mrs Murphy went on, tapping her forehead. 'And all my stories and thoughts and feelings are in here.' She placed her right hand against her heart. 'Let them have it. Let this house go to its next adventure...'

'But—'

'I have had a wonderful life in this lovely flat,' she said. 'Nothing and no one can take away my memories; the voices and the music and everything that happened here within these four walls won't disappear. I have them right here, tucked within me.' She smiled at me. 'I'm so sorry, my dear, after all your hard work.'

'You want to just walk away?'

'It's just a building. We all hold on to things so much. I've held on for too long.' She looked defeated. For the first time, since I'd met her, she looked as though she was beaten.

Daphne was on her knees, unrolling sheets of paper onto the carpet. 'I've come up with an alternative plan,' she said. 'When you told me yesterday, Mrs Murphy, I stayed up all night and did a few very rough drawings.' She was trying to hold down the corners of her plans but they kept curling up.

'Use some of those ornaments, dear,' said Mrs Murphy. 'They'll do just the ticket. Use the brass monkey, and the little Japanese box. Eileen's thing.'

'Eileen as in Eileen Grey?' Daphne's eyebrows were at her hairline. 'You mean one of the finest designers of the twentieth century? *That* Eileen?'

'Oh, Eily was an old pal from school. Used to send me little things every now and again. The box was a wedding present. She put little liquorice sweets inside it, lovely shiny black things, much better than the ones you could buy here. She knew I liked liquorice because I'd always buy some on our way home from school. A wonderful woman.'

Daphne and I exchanged impressed glances.

Once we had secured the plans with these priceless objects, Daphne began explaining. 'I would like to put in a different proposal for the building,' she said. 'I am going to try and stop the planning by submitting an alternative proposal, and I think I can get people on board with me. If, for example, we try for a crèche in the basement, I can ask a business to come in with me. And...'

And on she talked. Every room, every floor had a distinct purpose. She spoke about a central lift shaft, a café on the first floor, a cultural centre and on the very top floor, she had plans for an Irish Women's Archive, something which would concentrate on the history of Irish women, their achievements. 'I have a friend at the National Museum,' she said. 'I called her last night, and she says it is very possible that we could be part of the Museum.' She looked up at Mrs Murphy. 'What do you think? We will apply for cultural grants, the museum and heritage building for public use.'

'But what about Mrs Murphy?' I said. 'Are you suggesting Sunnyside?'

'No! Of course not.' Daphne turned to Mrs Murphy. 'Sunnyside don't accept cats, but I was thinking that you could move into the basement of *our* house.' She unrolled her final sheet.

'They don't take cats?' Mrs Murphy held Frederick to her chest.

Daphne shook her head. 'But this is how I propose your living arrangements might look,' said Daphne. 'It's just a rough approximation...'

Mrs Murphy had a look, closely scrutinising the plans. 'And my kitchen would be here? And how will Frederick access the garden?'

Daphne pointed everything out. 'I am trying to recreate these rooms you are in now, downstairs. I will try and keep everything as close to this as possible.'

Mrs Murphy was silent.

'You don't like it?' said Daphne.

'I am still going to fight this case,' I interrupted. 'We haven't lost yet.'

When we said goodbye, with no assurance from Mrs Murphy about what she wanted to do, I crossed the street to the National Archives on Kildare Street, and began searching for any documents I could think of that might be relevant to Number One, Merrion Square.

It wasn't a building, it was a repository of memory and stories that belonged to the city. There was something in the stories Mrs Murphy had been telling me and something intangible about the way her quiet voice carried down the stairs to me. People don't disappear, I thought. They may not come back as cats, but something of them endures. And whether or not it was Dad who was cheering me on, I couldn't be sure. But I definitely felt his presence. He hadn't just disappeared – he lived on in Mum, Sarah and I. And for all those women and children, and for everyone who had ever loved that building, for whom it had been a place of safety and sanctity, I wanted to preserve it.

I was invigorated with a renewed sense of purpose and energy. This was not a normal case, and it did not deserve a normal response. I knew what I was looking for and what kind of case I was now creating. I loved law, and the good it did do and could do. But corporate law wasn't for me. Instead, I felt imbued with the power of possibility, of being in control, with a plan and a future. But first, the court case.

40

I'd avoided Teolaí for the last couple of weeks, taking the longer and more circuitous route home. It was a Wednesday evening and I was looking forward to getting home and into my pyjamas and watching some TV. It was now ten days since the panic attack, and more than two weeks since the hillwalking day. I wasn't quite sure what to do with all my feelings, but I knew I had to unknot them and untangle them before I could even begin to inspect them.

But as I crossed the road, I heard a voice.

'Meeeely! Meeely!' Lorenzo was waving to me from across the street, standing astride an old bike. 'How are you?' He was wearing his low-slung jeans and a wide necked T-shirt which showed more of his chest than the Irish weather could cope with. He cycled shakily towards me. Holding my shoulders, he kissed me on both cheeks. 'You come with me to the bar, I make you a nice drink. You have had a long day, no?'

'Yes... but I want to go home,' I said. 'I'm hungry.'

'You come. We make you food. You rest, recover, and then you go home.'

Somehow, he was persuasive enough so that I found myself walking alongside him and his bike to Teolaí. The untangling and unknotting would have to wait, I thought. I was going to have to push through the fear.

As we walked up to the bar, we met Francisca coming out of the front door, with a tray of small nightlights, ready to put one on each table.

'Ah! Beautiful Milly!' she said, kissing me on both cheeks, as Lorenzo locked his bike to the rack outside. 'How are you? Good? Yes?'

'I'm fine, and you?'

She shook her head. 'Me, not so good. Cold all the time. I like this country, the people are so nice, so friendly, but the buildings are not designed for this weather. Everywhere is damp and there is wind coming through every hole and every crack...'

'Draughts,' I said. 'Yes, it is draughty.'

Lorenzo came to stand with us, listening.

'But why?' Francisca exploded. 'Why! Tell me why! Why after millions of years, are the buildings so useless for the weather? I sleep in a jumper and socks and a hat every night. This is no way to live.'

'Frankie,' said Lorenzo, 'you need some of my nonna's grappa, yes? That will warm you up. And you, Milly, will have some wine, yes?'

At the bar, he set up a glass into which he poured a glossy red wine.

'Made by my friend's father,' he explained. 'The very best.' He laid out bread and cheese and a sliced fig. 'Food,' he said, 'for the gods.'

'Thank you.' I sipped the delicious wine.

Lorenzo topped up my glass. 'Good, no?'

I nodded. 'Amazing.'

'Will you take me away from the city?' he said, suddenly. 'I want to see the real Ireland... not this city life... but what I see in films... you know, donkeys, children with red hair, those things on faces...' He dotted his nose with his fingers.

'Freckles?'

'Yes! Freckles! I love freckles. I want to see them. And hear music, and get rain on my face and feel the wind in my soul.'

'I think you may have been watching the wrong kind of films,' I said.

'No! It's not true?' He winked at me. 'There are no Irish donkeys, or children with freckles? It's like saying that not all Romans like to bathe in the Trevi fountain... bathing in *la fontana* is our right of birth.'

'No, there are donkeys and children with red hair, but I would lower your expectations...'

'I disagree...' Darragh was suddenly standing beside me. 'Never, ever lower your expectations. We all deserve the best.' He was smiling, but I could see concern in his eyes. 'Good to see you, Milly,' he said. 'I was thinking of you. How are you?'

'I'm fine!' I said, a little too enthusiastically. 'Lorenzo is being very nice to me.'

'She's had a hard day,' said Lorenzo. 'Being a lawyer, fighting crime, and putting away criminals. She's a hero.'

If only he knew that I was doing quite the opposite. I wasn't that kind of lawyer.

'Siobhán!' said Lorenzo, suddenly. 'Ciao! Bellissima!'

'Just thought I'd drop in and see how the gang were getting on.' Siobhán looked at me and then back to Darragh and then back to me again, as though trying to work out what was going on. 'Everything all right?' she said.

I nodded. 'Of course! Everything's fine.'

'So, how is your boyfriend?' Lorenzo said. 'Your captain of the industry?' He and Siobhán glanced at each other.

'He's fine,' I said. 'Why?'

'Nothing, just interested.' Lorenzo began polishing some of the glasses, peering through them and wiping them with a cloth.

'Funny that you used to know each other,' said Siobhán, 'at the rowing club.'

'It's a small world,' said Darragh. 'Anyway, I didn't last very long. You had to be a particular type of male to get on the team. I fitted in much better with the hillwalkers.'

I needed to be alone, I decided. I may have still loved Darragh, but it was time to move on... alone. I wasn't the same person as I was five years before and it was time to find out who I was now and where I was going. I was going to end this thing with Ryan the next time I saw him, which was in two days time, on Friday.

'You will both come to my birthday party, next week?' said Lorenzo to me and Siobhán. 'I'm making pasta with ricotta and it will be delicious. Right? It's my special day, no? I will be an old man of twenty-eight. So, to drown my sadness, *aperitivi* at 7 p.m.. Yes? You come?'

'I'd love to,' said Siobhán, quickly. 'Milly and I would love to attend. We'd be honoured...'

I shook my head. 'I can't,' I said. 'Work's so busy...'

Siobhán nudged me.

Lorenzo flung an arm around my shoulder, and one around Darragh's. 'We cannot have a party without new *and* old friends. Darragh is my old friend, Meely is my new friend. And Meely and Darragh are old friends. And it is beautiful, is it not? Life is beautiful. Yes?'

But I could have sworn that he and Siobhán made eye contact as if they had been discussing something and we were but pawns in a plan.

41

The following day, Catriona swept out of her office. 'I have to go,' she said, her face utterly drained of colour. 'You do the contracts and send them across to Nesbitt's asap.'

'Is everything okay?'

'Lydia's in hospital.' She didn't stop walking. 'She had a seizure. Josephine has taken her in an ambulance.' She was standing at the lift pushing the buttons repeatedly. 'Noel's in New York. He's not due back until tomorrow morning. I've called him and he's trying to get a flight. Again!'

'I'll come with you.'

She stopped and turned round and for a moment, I thought she was going to cry. 'But you're too busy. I've already asked too much of you... I have to be able...'

We filled our life with work or work filled our life, but if I couldn't make room for what was really important, then things were very wrong. 'I'm not too busy,' I said, running for my coat and bag.

Outside, Mr McAvoy was about to step into a taxi when I called out, 'We need this, Mr McAvoy. We have an emergency.'

He stepped aside, allowing us to rush in front of him, and into the car.

'What sort of emergency?' I heard him say. 'Is there anything I can do? Is it a case?'

But his voice receded as Catriona and I scrambled aboard, her telling the driver to take us to Crumlin Children's Hospital, 'as fast as you can!' Catriona's hand was trembling as she gripped my hand all the way there.

Once we rushed into A&E, it didn't take us long to find Lydia. A blur of corridors and faces and signs and arrows on the ground, we zigzagged through the hospital. And then, standing beside a bed in a room just off A&E, I saw a woman waving. 'Catriona! Catriona!'

'Josephine!' Catriona raced towards her and to where Lydia lay, a tiny doll in a large metal cot, eyes tightly closed. She'd already been attached to a tube and a heart monitor and Catriona sank down beside her, placing her head close to Lydia's, 'Oh Lydia, my sweetheart,' she said. 'My little Lydia.'

'We're waiting for the neurologist now,' Josephine said, pale and worried. 'She was on the bed,' she went on, 'and I was changing her nappy and... she started shaking, convulsing, and I picked her up and...' She started to cry from delayed shock. 'I thought she was dying because she just fell back, like she is now... Oh God.'

'Dying...?' Catriona could barely get the word out. She had one hand on the top of Lydia's head, her other on her leg, holding as much of her as possible. 'Mummy's here, sweetheart,' she whispered, 'Mummy's here. And Daddy's on his way home and we love you, we love you so much. Because you're our angel, you know that. You're the best thing that has ever happened to us. And we love you with all our hearts. You are the most wonderful thing that has ever happened to me. I have been waiting for you all my life. And I didn't realise I was. I didn't realise quite how much I was until you came along... my Lydia. My perfect little Lydia...' Catriona wasn't crying; instead she was perfectly still and completely focused, as though she was willing, with every fibre of her being, that Lydia would be all right. Catriona gently kissed Lydia's head. 'My little girl,' she said. 'My special little girl.'

And I was sure that Lydia's breathing changed, her small body relaxed a tiny bit now her mother was here.

The three of us spent the next couple of hours watching the monitor of Lydia's brain activity as though it was the Moon Landings, as nurse after nurse took readings and filled in the chart at the end of the cot.

I opened my phone and looked through my texts and emails. Peter Gregory wrote:

Building to begin on Monday! Thanks again for your help. Saved me a ton. Case of champagne being delivered to you today.

One from Angela:

Are you free for a little meet-up/catch-up? Just missing my joint-favourite niece? Cuppa in that café across from your office. Let me know when free.

Another from Ryan:

Dinner with Mum and Roger on tomorrow? Bringing us to Guilbaud's. It's her birthday. Love you xxx.

I wouldn't be able to finish with him tomorrow, I realised. Not on Carole's birthday at the poshest restaurant in town. This was the veritable Hotel California of relationships. You couldn't ever leave.

I put my phone on silent, desperately hoping that Lydia's tiny chest, which was almost imperceptibly moving, wouldn't stop.

'What do you think caused the seizure?' Catriona's voice was quiet and low.

Josephine shook her head. 'Everything was normal, nothing was different.'

'I feel like I should have been there,' said Catriona. 'Do you think I should have been there?' She sounded so unsure of herself. 'I'm trying to work out if it was better or worse that I wasn't there. Because maybe I would have panicked if I had been. I've never panicked in my life before her,' she said. 'Once Noel dropped a glass bowl on the floor when we were on holiday in Granada and a massive shard severed an artery and he was screaming, but I had him upside down in a second, with a tourniquet on, blood draining towards his head, and an ambulance on its way. I can't even speak Spanish. But Lydia makes me panic... sometimes I don't think I deserve her.'

'Shush now,' said Josephine. 'Don't talk like that.'

'Babies redefine the word precious. I've never loved anything like I love Lydia.'

'And she loves you,' said Josephine. 'She knows I'm not you. She is different with you because she can be, because you're going to be there forever. Because you're hers and she's yours. It's a special bond.'

Catriona nodded, tears in her eyes.

Finally Dr Mukherjee joined us. He nodded gravely at us, read Lydia's notes and checked her charts. Eventually, he focused on Catriona.

'We don't have a prognosis yet,' he said, 'it could be epilepsy, it could be meningitis. We'll keep her here, monitor her for the next twenty-four hours and see what the problem is.'

Catriona nodded, taking it all in. 'Will she be all right? Will she live?'

'We'll have to wait and see,' he said. 'We'll do all we can.' He gave Catriona a sympathetic smile. 'It's harder when they are so tiny, isn't it?'

She nodded, tears in her eyes, as the doctor turned and left. At the door was a woman. 'Cat?' Dressed in yoga clothes with blonde hair and full make-up, she was rushing towards us. 'Cat, oh Cat...'

'Louise...' Catriona and the woman embraced. 'Thank you for coming...'

'Now, don't worry,' Louise was saying. 'Okay? Everything is going to be all right. Hamilton had the same thing. Do you remember? When he was two. And it turned out to be a peanut allergy. The girls will be here all night, with you, okay? Sorcha is going to bring in coffee for us and we are going to sit here until you want us to go.'

'Thank you,' said Catriona, turning to introduce us. 'You know Josephine, and this is Milly.'

'Ah, Milly!' Louise smiled. 'Catriona's work rock.'

'Work rock?'

'That's what she calls you. Says she couldn't do any of it without you. Now...' Louise was taking control. 'How is she? What has the doctor said? Do I need to make any phone calls, get a second opinion? All you have to do is sit there and mind Lydia, I'll look after everything else.'

And I watched as Catriona succumbed to the power of friendship. We all need a Louise in our lives... and it was heartening to think that Catriona saw me as empowered and effective. It was exactly the opposite to how I'd thought of myself. I'd spent so long worrying about having lost Dad, and it was time to find some way of living with the loss. And I prayed with all my heart that Catriona wasn't going to experience that.

42

When I arrived at the hospital the next day, Lydia had been moved to a large, silent ward, each cot holding a tiny figure, and each with a stricken-looking parent beside it, some slumped half-asleep, others –the ones who'd been there for days – were stretching or drinking vending-machine coffee. Catriona had Lydia in her arms and behind her was Louise, looking impeccable, along with two other, equally impressive, women.

Catriona looked up. 'She's going to be absolutely fine,' she said. 'It isn't meningitis or anything like that. It was just a fever... nothing serious.'

'Nothing that paracetamol wouldn't cure,' added Louise. 'Sorcha and Becca, this is the famous Milly.'

They both shook my hand.

'Good of you to come in,' said one of them. 'I'm Becca.'

'We're the cavalry,' said the other. 'Sorcha, lovely to meet you! We've been here all night, talking. Turns out that our Catriona thought we were all perfect parents and she was getting it wrong. My twins once both ate my David's malaria tablets when he was on a Peru cycling holiday. Cat seemed to have forgotten that massive parental balls-up. And Louise's Hammy had appendicitis and no one knew for a whole week.'

'I kept telling him he was eating too many sweets,' said Louise.

'And my Aurora once fell down the stairs because I was too lazy to keep locking the stair gate,' said Becca. 'So, parenting has its lows. As well as its highs.'

They all smiled fondly at each other and at Cat.

'We boss each other around,' said Louise. 'We all went to boarding school together so we've been friends since we were eleven. Now,' she turned back to Cat, 'no more Mrs Perfect, okay?'

Catriona nodded.

'There's no joy in the pursuit of perfection,' said Sorcha, 'and when this is all over, we're going to Paris. And yes, Lydia is invited, she'll be the star of the show.'

There were footsteps behind us as Noel arrived, his arms open wide, scooping up Catriona and Lydia. 'My beautiful girl,' he said, as she laid her head on his shoulder. 'My *two* beautiful girls.' His voice broke and he looked as though he was about to cry. 'I thought we were going to lose her. Now we've found her, now we've fallen in love with her...'

Catriona nodded. 'She's been a whirlwind,' she said. 'How can something so small mean so much?' The two of them gazed at Lydia, Noel was smiling.

'If I'd known she was going to make us this happy, I would have suggested it years ago. And I've even been thinking about going part-time...'

Catriona smiled. 'Steady on, Noel,' said Louise. 'Don't make promises you're not going to keep.'

'We know you love her,' said Becca, 'but you two are the last great workaholics. Don't change too much.'

Noel shrugged. 'I don't know. I fancy staying at home and making the house all nice for when Catriona comes home. Dinner on the table, Lydia and I covered in paint and food...'

'We'll talk about it,' said Catriona, and kissed him on the cheek.

* * *

It was Friday evening and Ryan had called earlier to say he'd be picking me up on his way to Guilbaud's. It is an eye-wateringly expensive restaurant, the kind of place for lottery winners and the more-money-than-sense brigade. The kind of place that you had to dress up for. And so I pulled out an old black dress which I hadn't worn for years and took my hair out of its perma-ponytail, before having a long bath and beautifying, and tried to make myself look less corporate-office-dweller and the kind of person who does see the outside world occasionally. I wasn't going to end things tonight but for some reason I packed up the presents he'd bought me and put them in my bag.

'Woah!' Siobhán said. 'Who let the fox out?!'

'Shut up,' I said. 'It's like you never see me in make-up.'

'I *never* see you in make-up,' she dead-panned. 'But, seriously, you look gorgeous! I like that dress and those earrings.' I was wearing a cheap ten euro pair I'd bought in Accessorize last summer. 'You look like a sexy Audrey Hepburn.'

'That sounds so wrong.'

'Wrong in a good way,' she said.

'And so do you,' I said. 'Dressing up for Lorenzo?' She was wearing her maxi-dress and had tied her hair up in a loose, tousled bun.

'Maybe,' she said in a small voice, and then let out a sigh of angst. 'Oh God, I don't know what to do,' she said. 'I don't know what I am doing. It's like I've been hypnotised... and George... I am awful, even thinking of Lorenzo... poor George. I told him I wasn't feeling well.' She held up a hand. 'Please don't judge me. I'm not proud of myself. I know I'm being cowardly. I just haven't worked out how to do it. I mean, how do you end something with someone who you've been with since you were nineteen?'

'I don't know,' I said. 'It should be a lot easier with someone you've only been with for four months.'

'You and Ryan?' She made a throat slitting gesture complete with sound effect.

'Not tonight, though,' I said. 'It's Carole's birthday, but asap, I want to be along.'

'So more Garbo than Hepburn?'

'I want to do it,' I said. 'I want to focus on me.'

'What are you going to say to Ryan,' she said, 'you know, when you...' Again the throat slitting.

'I am going to be really nice,' I said, 'tell him how great he is and what a nice time we've had together and to thank him for his friendship and to wish him well...'

'Wow. That sounds civilized!' she said.

'Yeah, well, it's the only way.' For a moment, I really felt that it would be civilised and dignified. I would wish him well, and I am sure he would wish me well. It would be the perfect ending.

She hugged me tightly. 'Good luck,' she said. 'Good luck to both of us.'

And she was gone, down the stairs, while I stood at the hall mirror, trying to remember how to put on lipstick.

43

I was all ready when the doorbell rang. I took a deep breath and opened the door. 'Rya...' I began.

But it was Darragh. He stood for a moment, not saying anything. 'You look... beautiful,' he said eventually.

'I'm just going out,' I said.

'Yes, of course, of course...'

'Do you want to come in?'

'Just for a bit, if that's okay. I won't keep you.'

He followed me into the kitchen.

'I saw Sarah,' he said. 'Earlier, in town.'

'Sarah?'

He nodded. 'She was with Hugh. I thought you said they'd split up.'

Hugh and Darragh had always got on well. They'd endured many Christmases and our family do's. I'd always thought that we'd all be like that forever.

'They *have* split up,' I said. 'Maybe they were just hanging out?'

'They were holding hands.'

My eyebrows shot up. 'Are you sure?'

'Unless one of them was having trouble walking, and the other was assisting,' he said. 'But, to my untrained eye, they looked very happy.'

'Okay...' Why was Sarah so secretive, what exactly was going on with her? 'Well, that's nice.'

'Sorry for just coming like this but...' He stopped.

'But what?'

'I can't stop thinking...'

'About what?'

'You.' He looked at me. 'I can't stop thinking about you... it's like it's all I want to do, think about you, worry about you... just hold you in my head.'

'Darragh...' I wanted him to stop. He didn't need to say anything else. He'd said he was sorry. I hoped he wasn't here from an idea that he needed to make me feel better. I was fine. I would be fine. I would finish with Ryan, and then I was going to be happily on my own.

'Don't worry about it,' I said. 'You don't need to be concerned about me.' I tried to smile. 'You really don't.'

'I know,' he said. 'I just want to talk, that's all. Just explain something.'

We stood on opposite sides of the kitchen, facing each other, and then he began.

'First of all. I want to say sorry for bothering you. I know you've moved on with Ryan and everything else and I am sorry I keep dragging you back into the past. It's unfair of me.'

'That's okay.'

I still loved him, but it was okay. I would survive. Life was precious and it was time to start living.

Darragh's head had dropped. 'I went to see Mum's grave today.' He paused and looked up at me, his eyes meeting mine, and I realised his were full of pain, far deeper and greater than anything I had. 'You know?' he said. 'I've never actually been before. I feel ashamed, I mean, why haven't I gone? Isn't that awful?' He looked at me, confused and upset. 'How could I be so selfish? How could I have let *her* down like that? I... I just don't know... except, it felt meaningless. Why would I go and stand in a place where I was meant to connect with my mother... my *mother*.' He let the word hang in the air. 'Dad kept asking me to go with him... for all those years after she died, through university and later, and I just would not go. He eventually gave up.'

I realised something that I hadn't before, that for all those years that I knew him, Darragh had been going through so much anguish and turmoil.

'Why did you go now?'

He let out a sigh of a lifetime. 'Coming back to Dublin has made me face it all. I'd run away, you see. And finally, I was ready to accept she's gone, and I wanted to tell her I missed her and I loved her. And I wanted to say that I wasn't angry.'

'Angry?'

'Yeah. I was angry at her. I didn't acknowledge it to myself, because who in their right mind would be angry at a woman who didn't want to die? Someone who didn't want to leave her only child behind. She didn't want to go, and yet I was angry with her. I felt ashamed of myself, as though I was picking on someone who didn't deserve it, as though I was bullying my own mother.'

It was like the whole world had gone quiet. Neither of us moved or spoke for a moment.

'So, what made you go today?' I said, gently.

'I don't know. But something did. I've been thinking and thinking about her ever since I got back. And...' He looked at me. 'I wish I could do it all differently.'

'What?'

'Everything.' He looked at me. 'I'm sorry for running away.'

'It doesn't matter any more.'

'It does.' His hands pushed against the counter as though to keep him upright. 'I can't tell you how much I needed to leave Dublin.' His voice was quiet, flat. 'Every day, I felt the weight of all of it... Mum... memories... grief...' He looked at me, embarrassed. 'God, I sound so sorry for myself. Everyone loses someone. I'm not the only one. You did... and I left at the worst possible time.'

'It's fine,' I said. 'I'm okay.'

'I suppose I want to try and explain. I didn't really know then why I did what I did, why I left you. All I knew was that I couldn't stay. I was embarrassed and ashamed. I didn't want to feel sorry for myself. I didn't want my friends – you – to feel sorry for me, so I just pretended for years and years that I was okay. When I wasn't. And it all... it all kind of pushed down on me until... until it was too much.'

'I'm sorry.'

'You lost your dad, and I wasn't there for you.'

'I got through it.' Now I understood him better, I felt nothing but sadness and sympathy and empathy... And also love. But that had always been there.

'Yeah, but if I had been a better person, I could have supported you.'

'You could have told me how you were feeling,' I said. 'I could have helped.'

He shook his head. 'I didn't know where to begin. My priority was just surviving. And when I was with you, I was happy. I could forget about it. But it got worse. You can only push things away for so long. They start to overwhelm you. And I thought I was going mad... I mean, I was really worried about what would happen to me.' He gave an embarrassed laugh. 'That would have been all you needed at the time, a crazy boyfriend. I just knew I needed to run away.'

Silence. 'I'm sorry,' I said. 'I wish I'd known.'

He shrugged. 'I know it's too late to ask for forgiveness, but I wanted to at least give an explanation. I know you have your new life and you're happy with Ryan... but I just wanted to tell you what happened. That's all.'

I didn't know what to say. 'Thank you.'

'I went to the right place,' he said, 'if that's relevant. Running away to Italy was a good idea. It scooped me up, made me better and made me strong enough to come home.' He paused and looked up. 'I thought of you... all the time... wondering how you were and if you were okay. You see...' He paused. 'I didn't want to leave, but I had to learn to deal with *things*, things I'd refused to face or sort out or even talk about much. I knew I had to spend time just letting them settle. They were like wasps in my head always buzzing around, I couldn't get it to stop. It was driving me mad. And I knew if I didn't, I wouldn't be good for anyone.' He stopped again and looked straight at me. 'I wouldn't be good for you.' He pulled a face. 'Sorry, bit heavy there.'

There wasn't much to say.

He held out his hand and found mine. 'I'm sorry.'

'It's all right.' And it *was* all right. I forgave him but nothing mattered. There was nothing to forgive. I loved all of him... even more than ever. I didn't want Darragh to go. I wanted him to stay for ever. I wanted everything to be as it was. But there was Francisca and there was all that time between us. We weren't the same as we were once. Too much had happened, but he had had the guts to come and try and explain. I loved him even more for that.

He brought my hand to his lips for a moment. I realised that I'd never really known him before, because there was so much of him he didn't reveal. And here, standing in front of me, was all of him, the full Darragh O'Toole, stripped back and rebuilt. I forgave him with my whole heart. But I realised, much as I loved him, it was time to say goodbye, and to let him go and do whatever he needed to do with his life, and I had to do the same. We'd been over for a long time, but I hadn't managed to move on properly until now.

'Oh, Milly...' he said, 'I wish...'

The doorbell rang. 'Ryan,' I explained.

'Of course, of course...' said Darragh, standing straighter, pulling himself together, clearing his throat. 'Well, thank you for letting me ramble.' He pulled a face. 'And if you both would like to come to the party next week... I think Lorenzo has had more of that grappa sent over.'

The doorbell rang again.

'I'd better get it. Thank you for coming,' I said. 'Thank you for explaining.'

The doorbell rang again.

'It's okay...' He didn't move.

Neither did I.

'I've missed talking to you.'

'Me too.'

The doorbell again. This time, I went to the hall to open the door.

Ryan was standing there with a bouquet. 'I come with flowers!' he said. 'Appassionata made them especially. Roses, lilies, the green flowers... I went a bit mad.'

'They're beautiful.'

'I know. Not that I am an expert, but the woman in the shop said that I knew how to treat a lady. Well, *two* ladies. This one is for you and I bought a rather massive one for Mum. Well, it is her birthday...'

'Thank you,' I said, not really listening, aware Darragh was right behind me.

Ryan stepped inside and spotted Darragh. 'Hey, O'Fool,' he said. 'Only joking. I mean, *Darren*.'

'How's it going?' Darragh said, smiling. 'Have a good evening. See you, Milly.'

'See you, Darragh.'

Ryan stood slightly aside as Darragh had to squeeze between the flowers and the door to get out. At the top of the stairs, he turned again and gave me a wave. 'Thank you, Milly,' he said. And he was gone.

44

Back inside the flat, Ryan was itching to leave.

'You ready? We've got to be quick, because the dinner reservation is at 8 p.m..'

'Ryan, I'm not sure if...' But one last meal, I thought. One last hernia-infused conversation with Roger, a few more passive-aggressive comments from Carole, I could smize away all night and then be done with it. Later, when Roger and Carole were gone, I would tell Ryan that it was over, that it was me not him, and that I wished him well on his life journey. And then I would be done.

'Mum and Roger are waiting... come on, get your coat. And what did O'Fool want?'

'Oh, nothing...' I couldn't think of what to say.

'Right. Come on, chop-chop. We can't keep Mum waiting.' He turned back. 'Come *on*, Milly.'

I took a deep breath. I just need to get through one more evening and then get on with my new life – my new, single, life. How bad could one more evening with Carole and Roger be?

* * *

Carole and Roger were already seated at the window table at Guilbaud's, sipping champagne when we arrived. Carole waved just the tips of her glass-holding fingers while also whispering to Roger behind her other hand.

'Welcome, welcome!' he said, standing up. 'So good of you to join us.'

Ryan shook his hand and then kissed Carole, while she kissed me on both cheeks, European-style.

'Happy birthday!' he said. 'Have you had a nice day?' I noticed for the first time, for someone so supremely confident (some might say arrogant, *obnoxious* even), that he was awkward around his mother. He wanted to please her, yes, but he was scared of her, as though he didn't feel safe. I didn't blame him. The only person on whom she didn't have that effect was Roger; he was so laid back that he was immune to her supersonic powers of intimidation. Ryan handed Carole the bouquet. 'I thought you might like these. Roses and freesia. They were flown in from Kenya this morning.'

'Kenya, you say?' said Roger. 'I knew a chap from Kenya once. Nice enough but was taken out by the humble mosquito. You'd think us humans would be more than a match, but you'd be wrong...'

Everyone ignored him.

'They are beautiful,' gushed Carole, with a quick crowing glance at me. 'But have the roses been dethorned? You know my phobia. Thorns,' she explained. 'They bring back terrible memories.'

'Some might call it a Jesus complex,' said Roger.

'Well, I wouldn't be so immodest,' said Carole. 'I wouldn't like to think of myself like that, but I do agree, it is strange to have such a visceral reaction to thorns.' She smiled at Ryan. 'Darling, thank you. And I've had a simply lovely day. Roger surprised me with this little thing...' On her wrist was what looked like the koh-i-noor, the sparkles turned the room into a disco while she flashed the bracelet. 'And now you two are here. So blessed. Aren't we?' She smiled, no teeth, just a scrunch of the bottom half of her face.

'What's that?' said Roger.

'We're so blessed!' she said, the scrunch fading, and patted the chair beside her for Ryan.

Roger pulled out the chair beside him for me.

A waiter materialised.

'Anozzer boddle of Bollinger,' Roger told him. 'And we're still waiting on those two dozzzen oysters. My darling wife needs her fix...'

'Yes, certainly, Mr De Vere,' said the waiter.

De Vere? Where had I heard that name before? Beside me, Ryan was sitting extra-upright, solicitously listening to Carole talk about business as the waiter placed a platter of oysters in front of us, the grey shimmering bodies looked like a dozen mini hernias removed in some mass surgery. I felt my stomach lurch.

'You'll have one of these,' said Carole, 'won't you?' She thrust the plate at my face. 'I'll be terribly hurt if you don't. They're my favourite. Go on, slide one down.'

She looked at me as I held the mollusc to my lips. Her sharky, beady eyes watched me as I tipped it down, feeling it slide and slither in my mouth and then gagged as it peristaltically inched its way down.

'I like the squirming sensation, like drinking a sea monster,' said Carole. 'You know, they don't die until a whole twenty minutes after they've been in your stomach. They stay alive as long as they can.'

'Like us all,' said Roger, as the waiter passed us all a glass of champagne.

Ryan held his up. 'To my mother, Carole,' he said. 'On her birthday.'

'To Carole,' I found myself saying, holding my glass. Ryan handed around the oysters again. 'Another morsel?' he said.

'I don't mind if I do,' said Carole, taking one and popping it in her mouth. 'Milly? Another little sea monster? They are fascinating things, oysters. They can change sex, did you know that? They can do it at will, like most teenagers these days.' She let out a laugh. 'And they eat plankton? So if they eat plankton, then we eat plankton.' Carole rolled her eyes and turned back to Ryan. 'Well, we had a very productive meeting today,' she said. 'Didn't we, Ryan?'

'Yeah,' he said. 'Yeah, good meeting. A lot done.'

'So, everything is going well?' Roger said. 'That building is bought...?'

'Well, not *bought*,' said Carole. 'Leased. Milly should know the difference, her being a corporate lawyer and everything. Or maybe you don't know everything, do you?' Her laugh had a tinge of donkey bray, a kind of equine cackle.

I thought of Darragh laying his heart and soul out to me in my kitchen... I could have helped him at the time or let him go, set us both free with the hope he could mend himself and maybe one day have come back to me. If only I'd known, I thought, if only he had told me what he was going through, I would have let him go.

And then I realised. De Vere was the co-director of Alpha Holdings. Carole and Ryan ran Dublin Investments, but could they also own Alpha Holdings? Could Roger be some kind of stooge director? I stared at Roger. It wasn't as if De Vere was a common name, like Murphy or Doyle or Byrne, even. It was too much of a coincidence. Surely...

But beside me Ryan had suddenly slipped to the floor. My first thought was that he had had a stroke. But then I heard his voice from somewhere at tablecloth level. 'I dropped it!' he shouted, before pushing through the folds in the tablecloth so it looked like Mother Theresa was lunging from the depths.

And there was something in his hand. A little box, opening and proffering it. Inside was a glittering diamond ring. Oh God. No!

All eyes turned to me. Carole's stare had a venomous tinge to it, Roger perked up momentarily.

'Milly,' said Ryan. 'I wonder, would you do me the honour of marrying me?'

'Ryan... I can't believe it,' I said.

'You've meant so much to me over the last year,' went on Ryan. 'And I would like to share a future with you.'

I gaped at him. What was going on? Did he really want to marry me?

'*Yes*, is what is needed here,' said Carole, irritated. 'Just say *yes*. My God, we choose the biggest bloody ring in the country and she doesn't have the manners to say yes straight away!'

Would it be unethical to fake a panic attack? I wondered. Would that be doing a great disservice to my fellow anxiety sufferers? But Roger came to my rescue.

'I think she might be a bit overwhelmed,' he said. 'I remember when I proposed to Carole, and I must say, I didn't think much of my chances, but I think it was the fact she liked the ring...' He turned to me. 'I had it made in Zurich, based on a ring that Onassis once had made for Maria Callas... quite the sparkler...'

'The oysters,' I said. 'I'm terribly sorry but...' I stood up. 'I'm just going to go to the bathroom.' I began to run.

45

I locked myself in a cubicle and sat on the seat, trying to focus on everything that had happened. Carole set me and Ryan up, maybe thinking that a corporate lawyer might suit their needs, but how had they known I would be asked to work on the Mrs Murphy case? Was that luck for them? Did they then think that I would help them get the building, if I was on-side?

I could feel the oysters squirm inside me, the whispery breath was making my whole body creep and crawl. I was covered in a film of sweat. I thought I was going to be sick, and I leaned my forehead against the cool of the wall, trying to make sense of this. Maybe I was wrong about Roger being the De Vere of Alpha Holdings. Maybe it was just a coincidence? It was feasible that there were two people of that name in this city. I'd overreacted. I should just go back out there and get through the evening.

Eventually, I opened the door. Carole was standing right outside. 'I just wanted to make sure you were all right. It wasn't the oysters, was it? I don't think you want to say yes, do you?' she said, in a low voice and speaking through a rictus grin which didn't reach her cold, dead eyes. 'I don't think you want to join my family. And that's the right response. I don't know what he's thinking. He didn't need to go that far. And I can see you don't care for him. You never have. And we don't much care for you.' She bared her teeth at me. For a moment, it looked as though she had a double set, like a shark. 'We're a very close-knit family,' she said. 'You may be used to getting your own way, and that's all very well in your little world. But I'm in charge in this family, I get to say what's what. And do you know why? Because I've earned it.'

'Okay,' I said, thinking she was bonkers, far worse than I actually had even imagined. 'Well, thanks for telling me.'

And I suddenly understood Ryan, no wonder he was the way he was. He was scared of his own mother and probably never felt good enough for her. By buying me, he was at least trying to have some kind of relationship where he felt powerful. Maybe asking me to marry him was the bravest thing he'd ever done? My heart went out to him.

But being trapped in this small space was really triggering. The whispery breath and churning stomach were gearing up for a full-on panic attack, the Black Terror was arming himself. *Not now*, I told myself. *You can come back later. Now, I'm too busy telling this absolute nightmare where to go.*

'I'm going home,' I said.

'Oh no you're not,' Carole said, grabbing my wrist. 'You're not going to ruin my birthday? And you're not going to hurt my son's feelings. What kind of sociopath does that? You're staying.' She gave me a nudge with her exceedingly sharp elbow – for a tiny woman, she had remarkable power – and I had no choice but to go back to the table.

Ryan pulled out my chair, and then hers. 'Well, not quite the proposal I had planned,' he said. 'But maybe...' I suddenly admired his perseverance. Poor Ryan. I hoped one day he'd get away.

'It's oysters,' said Roger. 'Some people don't have the stomach.'

'Especially when they begin to eat your insides,' said Carole. 'Before they die, their last act is to eat away at your stomach lining. Sometimes they can cause real damage.'

'How are you feeling?' Ryan said to me.

'I'm not sure,' I said.

'Is it your...?' He began.

'No!' I squealed, a little too loudly, making people at the next table look up. I drank some of my champagne and felt a little better. Another sip and even better.

'She's *fine*,' said Carole. 'Just some people haven't got sophisticated palates, and oysters don't agree with them.' She smiled at us all. 'Ryan, you can continue with your proposal,' she ordered.

'I'll do it later,' he said. 'I don't think it's appropriate to propose when someone is feeling sick.'

The waiter materialised again to take our food orders.

'Why don't we let Roger order for us,' suggested Carole. 'He's good at that.' She lowered her voice. 'It's nice to keep him busy. Doesn't do much else.'

Roger looked up affably. 'What's that, Carole?'

'Nothing, nothing...' Even her wink was terrifying.

'Anyway,' she went on. 'I just want to raise a glass...' She smiled at the two of us, 'to business! And to our companies, Dublin Investments and Alpha Holdings.'

I froze. *Alpha* Holdings. Alpha *Holdings*?

Carole was looking right at me, as though she'd been waiting for the penny to drop. Roger was *the* De Vere. Alpha Holdings was the company forcing through the buy-out of Number One, Merrion Square. *They* were the property developers. They *were* the people I had been writing to, sending my cease and desist letters. And, of course, Carole knew it was me. But I had been writing to a Mr Hessling.

'Isn't that right, Milly?' urged Carole. 'To Alpha Holdings!'

'To Dublin Investments,' said Ryan. 'And to Alpha Holdings.'

'You know,' she said, eyeing me, 'there's a very annoying firm of lawyers who are trying to stop us from buying the building. Bernard keeps being sent rather irritating letters from them. He says they won't know what has hit them when he finishes with them.' She picked up her glass, her long fingernails painted bright red, with a single diamanté nail. 'He can get pretty nasty when he needs to.'

Ryan laughed, delighted. 'Well, maybe we will need to. Can't let anyone stand in our way.'

I sat there, matching Carole's stare. Stupefaction became anger became utter determination, and then perfect calm. All panic, all upset was gone. I wanted to go straight to my office and begin my litigation with renewed verve and zeal. I stood up.

'Ryan,' I said, 'it's over. I don't want to see you again.'

Even Roger looked surprised as I grabbed my bag and left. Behind me, I heard Carole say, 'She's got a nerve, that girl. After everything... those oysters cost thirty euros a plate...'

Damn. I hadn't given Ryan all his presents back. I couldn't go back in there now.

But Ryan caught up with me outside, at the top of the steps. 'What's wrong?' he hissed, grabbing my arm. 'This is embarrassing. It's Mum's birthday and you not only walk out but you *finish* with me?' He pulled at me, trying to get me to turn round.

I looked at him, and for the first time, I felt something for him. We had been half-hearted, but I now felt whole-hearted empathy.

'Milly!' His voice cracked. 'I knew I should have listened to Mum. But I stuck my neck out for you. You would have thought you'd be more grateful! What's wrong with you?' Teeth gritted, he seethed. 'It's your fecking anxiety again, isn't it? The rudeness! To walk out of a restaurant on my *mother's* birthday. And I'd proposed! I wanted to marry you. I must be mad. You're *mad*, more like.'

'Ryan, I'm sorry,' I said again, feeling not remotely mad, but utterly delighted. Especially because I knew my enemy. I understood Carole, I knew her game. And when you know exactly what you're dealing with, and you know who they are, the battle is easier. I was now looking forward to our moment in court.

'You don't know what you've done!' he blustered. 'You've made a massive mistake...!'

I held up my hand to silence him, all traces of anxiety, all whispery breaths, all crawling, creeping icy fingers along my spine gone. It was like I had been dipped in holy water, I was free from it all, that skin was shed and I felt calmer than ever in my life, the way a Samurai must feel before swinging his sword. Everything was suddenly uncomplicated and there was nothing to understand or to work out or to ponder. Ryan wasn't for me and I wasn't for him. And that was fine. I liked me enough to be able to do life on my own.

The people I really cared about were Mum, Angela, Sarah and Siobhán. And I loved Catriona and Susie. And... I loved Darragh for everything we had been together and everything we would be separately. And I was okay, I was *really* okay. Anxiety didn't define me. I was someone who experienced it from time to time, the way we feel anything. I was free.

I delved in my bag and pulled out all of Ryan's gifts. 'You should return these,' I said. 'Hopefully you will be able to get your money back.'

Ryan's mouth was moving, words frothing and fulminating as he remonstrated as he took them all back, and then, behind him, the ferret face of Carole, nose twitching, teeth bared.

'I had no idea that you were Alpha Holdings,' I said, 'and I'm representing Mary Murphy. The woman in the top floor flat, Number One, Merrion Square.'

I watched his face while the cogs whirred and then his mouth dropped open. 'You didn't say. Why didn't you say?'

'It was part of my job, I didn't see it as particularly relevant to you. I don't tell you about all my work...'

Carole stepped forward. 'I hope you don't mind,' she said, all sweetness. 'But I couldn't help overhearing. I didn't realise that you were the lawyer representing that woman... I mean... did you say her name was Mrs Murphy? Bernard looks after all our correspondence, he didn't mention *your* name or *hers*.'

I shrugged. 'Really, Carole? *Really?* You think I'm that stupid. You *knew* it was me.'

'You knew exactly who was behind it, and don't say you didn't. And anyway, she *should* sell. She can't get up and down those stairs. She'll fall down and then that will be on your conscience. And...'

'Goodbye, Carole,' I said. 'Goodbye, Ryan. Give my regards to Roger, tell him I was sorry I couldn't say goodbye in person and that I hope his ears are better soon.'

I stalked off, feeling invincible, Chaka Khan in my head.

'Does this mean...' shouted Ryan. 'Does this mean you're not going to marry me?' Several passers-by stopped as though they were suddenly in the middle of a Richard Curtis film, all excited and delighted to witness a special moment, a few fumbled for their mobile phones and pressed record. I felt bad for them that I was going to disappoint.

'I'm so sorry!' I shouted. 'There's no happy ending. Not a chance!' I could see a couple of faces frowning as they tried to work out what was going on.

'You're making a fool of yourself!' yelled Carole. 'Knew you would. No class, you.'

'Milly! Please!'

I had wanted a half-hearted relationship and I had got one. But one thing was clear, it was better to have nothing than half of something. And so nothing it would be.

'Good luck, Ryan!' I felt like singing. 'Bye, Carole!' I broke into a run, the crowd parted to let me through.

'We'll see you in court!' Carole was now screeching. She wobbled on one of her heels and grabbed onto Ryan to steady herself. 'And thanks for ruining my birthday!'

There was a gasp from the crowd. I could tell they were disappointed in me.

'She's mad,' I heard Carole say to them. 'We tried to love her like our own daughter... but...'

I didn't hear the rest because I was already running down the street, away from them, looking for a taxi to take me home.

My triumph made me feel invincible and ridiculously happy. And I don't know if it really happened, or if I just imagined it, but there was the very strong feeling that Dad was with me. I can't explain it, but I sensed the warmth of his approving smile spreading through my body as if it were litmus paper. He was everywhere, in the air, in the ether, a warm blanket of love enveloping me, cheering me on. And then I did start singing. *I'm every woman... it's all in meeeeee.*

46

'There you are!' Angela said, giving me a wave from the window seat in the café. 'My lovely niece,' she said to the woman behind the counter. 'She and her sister are apples in their mother's and my eye. Eyes, I suppose.' She turned back to me and smiled, her hair a cascading froth of rolls and curls.

'Nice hair,' I said.

'Oh, do you like it?' She didn't sound quite her normal ebullient self. Usually, she would be the first person to lap up a compliment.

'Yes, it's lovely.' I sat down across the table from her.

'Well, you look lovely. A little peaky, I suppose, but that's only because you work so hard. Your mother asked me to keep an eye on you both and I've been a little lax on that.' She smiled at me, but it seemed a little forced, as though she was trying too hard to seem herself. 'Now, tell me, how is everything in the world of corporate law? Have you had a shouting match with a colleague, has one of you gone to the loos to cry about losing a case? Do you have an overbearing boss who is struggling with either a drinking problem or feelings of inadequacy based on childhood neglect?'

'None of the above,' I said. 'You've been watching *Ally McBeal* again.'

Angela laughed. 'Well, enough about me,' she said. 'How are you? Any news in Milly-ville?'

'Well, if you must know, I've finished with Ryan,' I said. He'd already left six messages that morning, and they ranged from angry to apology and back to angry again.

'Oh thank God for that!' said Angela. 'He was obnoxious with a capital O. Never trust a man with prominent cheekbones. They'll cut you quicker than a knife.'

'I had no idea you didn't like him.'

'Well, we only met him that once, but I think he liked himself rather too much. I'm glad you are now single again, and able to concentrate on being nice to yourself.' She smiled at me.

'Mum is having a good time, isn't she?' I'd been getting daily photos, mainly of cacti, food and glasses of wine.

'Yes, I had a text last night,' said Angela. 'And a photograph of her and Harold with some kind of plant. It looked like the kind of thing you could buy in any good garden shop. Not something worth swapping hemispheres for, but there you go. Weather beautiful, food delicious, company delightful. Everything a holiday requires.' She smiled at me again, but this time it faded on her face. 'So...'

'Angela?'

She took a drink of her tea.

'I have something to say.' She stopped, trying to compose herself. 'Well...' She tried again. 'Right.' She threw her head up and focused on a point on the wall opposite, either steadying or readying herself. And when she looked at me again, her eyes were glistening. 'A few months ago, I was given a little bit of bad news.' She held up a hand. 'Now, I do not want sympathy or kindness or anything. That is exactly why I told no one... only lately... in the early hours of the morning, while I am binge watching *LA Law*, I've been feeling a little guilty. More than a little guilty. If Kitty found out, without me telling her, then she would be very annoyed.

I stopped, and looked at her. Her face was twisted into a kind of smile, but her eyes looked so sad and scared... and lonely.

'Angela... what kind of bad news?'

'Well...' She swallowed and then looked me straight in the eye. 'I fear I've been rather a coward! Me! Who won the Courage, Confidence, Character badge in Girl Guides when I was eight which was unheard of; everyone else was eleven.'

'Go on.'

'I meant to tell you, of course. When I went for treatment, everyone else had someone with them. But I didn't mind being on my own...'

'Treatment?'

She nodded and then tugged at a strand of hair. 'This isn't real,' she said. 'I haven't had real hair for eight months. But I've struck up a rather nice friendship with a girl at No Hair Don't Care. She's been giving me a few to try.'

'Angela, what are you saying? You don't mean...?'

She nodded, her eyes filling with tears. 'Cancer. You see,' she said, dabbing at her eyes with the paper napkin. 'This is why I didn't tell Kitty or you girls. When I think about it, I feel rather sorry for myself and it's the last thing any of you need. You see, it turns out I'm not as confident or courageous as I thought I was. I should hand back my badge. Serving tea and biscuits for Brown Owl and speaking on a subject of my choosing for five minutes does not perhaps prove one's fortitude quite as definitively as I had thought.'

I put my hand over hers. She was bone-cold. 'Oh Angela...'

She nodded. 'I've been thinking the same thing. Oh Angela, what has happened? How will you get through this? You have so much to live for – Kitty and the girls, all my friends... everything I want to do in life. I had signed up for a tango course in Seville and then there was Sexy Sixties Singletons... I wasn't ready to die.'

My eyes filled with tears and Angela handed me one of the paper napkins. 'What kind of cancer?'

With a glance to make sure no one was watching, she pointed in the direction of her breasts.

'Oh, Angela,' I said again.

She nodded. 'I've had a few long nights of the soul. I didn't want to worry Kitty, not after she's been through so much, losing Charles, and not now she's so happy with lovely Harold... but the guilt at keeping this secret has been gnawing away. Imagine if something happened, and I hadn't told her? She'd be angry, wouldn't she? I didn't want to die and her not to know.'

I tried to take in all she had told me. 'Have you been going through treatment all on your *own*?'

'I didn't want to worry anyone,' she said. 'The consultant said it would be all over by the summer. And everything is ticking along nicely. Okay, so the hair's gone. But then it was never my crowning glory. Always a little on the wispy side. But... well, it's been a little lonely.' She dabbed at her eyes again. 'Look at me, I knew this would happen, feeling sorry for myself. But the thing is, Milly, I didn't realise I had the capacity to feel sorry for myself. I have prided myself all my life on being self-sufficient. Obviously, I have enjoyed being a peripheral member of your family, to be tolerated on occasion...'

'Tolerated? Peripheral? Don't be silly...'

'Oh, you know what I mean. But I thought that it was time to come clean. I was going to wait for your mother to come back... but being the coward I now find myself to be, I was wondering if you could tell her? I think I might cry and I don't feel quite able to cope with all the emotion.' Angela's eyes filled with tears and I realised that I had never seen her anything but upbeat and enthusiastic.

'I wish you'd asked us to come with you to the hospital,' I said.

'But you are so busy,' she said. '*You* can't get time off work.'

'I would have,' I said. Work was increasingly dropping in my priorities.

'I should have told you all. But I have chickened out of telling your mother. But I do want you all to know. I was thinking and thinking, and I woke up last night... not that I sleep much any more, but I thought, what is a proper relationship if you are not your whole self, if I am not honest. I have been lying to you all and I feel just awful about it.'

'I'll tell her,' I said. 'Don't worry.' I placed both of my hands on hers, hoping all my warmth would flood into her body. I had taken her for granted all my life. She'd been just my aunt, who had always been around, but now I saw her for who she was; my family.

* * *

Sarah arrived at Angela's straight from her shift and soon as I opened the door to her, she flung her arms around Angela and hugged her. When they eventually pulled away, I saw Sarah had been crying.

'Well, you're not going to die,' she said. 'As a medical professional, I think that you are going to be absolutely fine.'

Angela nodded at her, smiling. 'Time will tell.'

'You're my favourite auntie,' said Sarah, wiping her eyes.

'I'm your *only* auntie.' Angela laughed, but she seemed very pleased, shy almost, at this display of affection.

'Yeah,' Sarah grinned, 'but also my favourite.'

The three of us sat in Angela's small living room and watched television all evening, everything from Nationwide and its stories of quirky folk doing quirky things, to a home improvement show, to a cooking show, to the late news and more news. Until we noticed that Angela had nodded off. Her head was back, her mouth slightly open, her arm hung lifeless off the side of the sofa.

'Oh God,' I said. 'She's not...?'

Sarah took one step closer to Angela, bending down to see if she was breathing. 'Angela?' she said. 'Auntie Angela?'

Nothing.

'Angela?' I tried this time.

Sarah and I looked at each other. Oh no...

'Whassit?' Angela's mouth twitched. 'Whassgoinon...'

'Angela!' She had risen from the dead! We both screamed with fright and delight, clutching at each other.

Angela opened her eyes, wide awake now. Beadily watching us. 'What are you two up to?'

'Nothing!' We glanced at each other guiltily, both secretly blaming the other for the histrionics.

'You should go home and get a good night's sleep,' Angela said.

'But...' I didn't want to leave her.

'Don't worry about me,' she said. 'You just do as I ask.'

We both hugged her on the doorstep, first Sarah and then me.

'We love you, Angela,' I said. 'This family doesn't work without you.'

'And I love you,' she said. 'It's the only thing, love. Makes the world go round and everything tick. You girls and Kitty are what I love most in the world and, when the chips are down, it's all that matters.'

I nodded, agreeing. It was all that mattered. When you loved someone and if you were loved in return then life was worth living. I thought of Angela and how much we loved her, and I thought of Noel and Catriona and Lydia. And I thought of Darragh. If you had love, then you couldn't let it slip through your fingers.

Back at the flat, I dug out the letter which he'd left me all those years ago. I'd read it a million times that first year, trying to work out why he'd done what he did and what could it all mean, and each time I had, I was none the wiser.

And here it was now...

My dear Milly,

I can't believe what I am about to do and I wish I could explain why. But the truth is, I am not exactly sure why I am about to hurt the very last person I want to hurt.

When I met you, I was in shock that I could meet someone with whom I could be myself, the answer to everything. You made me so very happy, as though we were carved from the same piece of stone, reunited again, two people just made to be together.

But it's not how it works, I've discovered, and if I don't leave, I don't know what will happen to me. And I like being alive, I want to find the joy again but I feel utterly stuck, and afraid and lonely. None of which has anything to do with you. This is my own doing, and it's something I've run away from for too long. Being with you helped me ignore all the things I should have been focusing on and taking care of. And so, it's time to go. I am sorry.

I wish I was a better person, more mature and able to deal with problems. I aim to be. More than anything I would like to be someone I am proud of. And I would like to think that one day you will understand and be proud of me. You probably won't, and I don't blame you because now, at this moment, I couldn't be less proud of me for walking away from us. I don't think I am doing very well and I just know that I need to go. I can only live in hope that one day you will forgive me. I just hope that I will forgive myself.

I love you.

Your Darragh.

I read it again, and where once I didn't understand a single thought, a single word, now it all made total sense to me. He sounded so lonely, so tortured. Was it a breakdown? I wish he'd talked to me at the time and that I'd been a more understanding girlfriend, but while he was having his breakdown, I was dealing with a dying father. Maybe he did the only thing he could have done? And maybe it was exactly the right thing to do?

I forgave him utterly. I hoped he would forgive me too. It was too late for us, of course. But I would have liked to have had the chance to tell him I was proud of him. And wherever he went in life, whatever he did, he would have my love and my support. At least, I thought, life had worked out for him. But it made me feel sad, what we'd lost and would never recapture. I wished I could go back in time and have that conversation with him and tell him it was all right, and that if he needed to go, then I understood.

Before I went to sleep I texted Auntie Angela:

Sleep well. See you in the morning.

But then my phone rang and it was Sarah.

47

Sarah was babbling and uncharacteristically hysterical when I arrived at Mom's house.

'She's dead,' she said. 'She's dead!'

'Already? What? But I thought she was going to be okay!' My blood went cold. Oh, Angela. We couldn't lose Angela, not now she'd just told us. 'She's too young to die. She's only sixty.' I began to cry.

'Not Angela! Betty!' Sarah sobbed. 'She's sixteen... that's about one hundred in dog years.'

Sarah headed inside and crouched over Betty's bed. 'I thought she was sleeping,' she said. 'And I went over and she felt different. Even before I touched her, I knew she was dead.'

I kneeled down beside her, wrapping my arms around Betty.

'She was the best dog in the world,' said Sarah.

I nodded, too choked to speak, as the two of us sat by her bed, our hands on her cold, lifeless body, the body which we had seen grow from a tiny puppy with fluffy fur, a tiny little thing who pranced around like a miniature pony, a magnificent specimen of the canine world. And the last living remnant of our father.

'Do you think it was what happened to her on the mountain?' I sobbed. 'Do you think that I killed her?'

Sarah shook her head. 'It's old age,' she said. 'It's no one's fault. You can't blame yourself.'

I hoped she was right and not just trying to be nice to me. I took a moment to try and get myself under control. 'We just have to make her comfortable. Be here for her, like she's been here for us,' I said, fetching the velvet throw from the sofa, which normally Betty was banned from lying on.

'Betty would be furious if she knew she had to die to get on that velvet throw,' said Sarah, making me laugh.

We sat on the floor, our backs against the kitchen cupboards, Betty between us. 'Do you remember when we first got her and she chewed my brand new pixie boots?' said Sarah. 'I was so annoyed!'

'And when it snowed and we forced her onto the toboggan and she fell off?'

She nodded. 'Betty was a good dog.'

'The best.'

'She'll be missed at the park,' she said. 'Everyone knows Betty.'

For hours, we remained there, talking a little, crying a little, remembering the life of the world's best dog.

She looked like she was sleeping. 'Goodbye, Betty,' I said. 'Thanks for everything.'

'What an evening,' Sarah said.

'I know. Poor Angela, poor Betty. Do you think Angela will be okay?'

'I hope so,' she said. 'She's been under the best care, her consultant trained at John Hopkins.'

I nodded. 'I wish she'd told us.'

Sarah nodded. 'I can't believe she did it all on her own.'

'Do you sometimes think that we haven't been like a family. Since Dad died, we've all been separate, as though we didn't know how to join up again.'

She nodded. 'I suppose so.'

'What do you think Mum will say? It's not the best welcome home, is it?'

'Understatement of the century.' She leaned down to kiss Betty. 'It's a shame she's dead,' said Sarah. 'She would have liked to have known she was finally allowed on that velvet throw.'

'She'd be beside herself,' I agreed.

We sat beside Betty, each with a hand on her body.

'It's been quite a year,' Sarah said.

I nodded. 'Quite the decade.'

'I should call Hugh. He would want to know.'

'Of course.' I paused. 'Darragh said he saw you and Hugh holding hands.'

'Did he now?' She gazed at me. 'And you want to know what's going on, do you?'

I nodded.

'Well,' she said, looking away. 'I was trying to get pregnant, you see.'

'Pregnant?'

She ignored me, and carried on, 'We thought it was the right time and that it would be easy. And... well, it turned out not to be easy. Nothing ever is when you expect it to be. And... I had a miscarriage. Well, several actually.'

'Sar... I'm so sorry.' My little sister, my lovely sister. I felt my heart break for her.

'Yeah, well... it happens. Hugh was working hard and I was trying to nurse on top of that and I was hard to live with...' She wiped a tear away. 'I blamed myself, thinking it was my fault I couldn't stay pregnant. What baby would want to grow inside someone full of so much sadness and depression? I mean, I wouldn't! Who would want to have a mother who was all miserable and a complete bitch to boot? Poor Hugh was doing his best, being nice and supportive, but he was knackered and confused.' She stopped again, her voice mangled with emotion. 'Each time, at six weeks, ten weeks... I got to thirteen weeks once... each time, it didn't work... It took its toll. In the end, I didn't want to inflict crazy old me on him any longer and so I ended it. Happiness, I decided, and nice things and babies and love and normal life were for other people and it was better if I just did my own thing in the little misery bubble I created. I never thought I wouldn't be a mother,' she said. 'It was the one thing I thought would definitely happen to me. Once I'd given up on marrying Kurt Cobain. But it's the one thing you take for granted and then it doesn't happen. It's so cruel... But then...' She was looking up, and she was smiling...

'What?'

'Well,' she said, 'for some reason my body decided to work properly again.'

'What do you mean?'

'Now, you have to promise me to remain calm.' She paused and drew a breath. 'I'm pregnant.'

'What?!'

'Five months, twenty weeks!'

'Jesus Christ!'

She was crying, but her smile was growing bigger by the second.

I couldn't quite take it in. 'You're not serious?'

'It's not something I would joke about,' she said.

'Oh my God! That's wonderful! Sarah!' I was crying as well now. My beautiful little sister looked exactly as she did when we were small, the constellation of freckles across her nose, that cheeky smile that lit up the world. 'I'm going to hug you,' I said. 'Just a warning.'

She rolled her eyes but held out her arms, as though surrendering. 'If you must.'

And as I wrapped my arms around her, I could feel her squeezing me as much as I was squeezing her. We just stood there for a moment, but when we pulled away, she quickly wiped away a tear.

'Wait a minute!' I said. 'I'm just going to get something.' I raced to the larder, where in the back were six bottles, dusty and nearly forgotten about, of Dad's non-alcoholic elderflower wine. I brought one back to Sarah with two glasses. 'We should raise a glass to Betty and to you and to the baby and to Dad,' I said.

'Yes, we should.' She smiled at me, and I sat back down on the floor next to her, and eased the cork from the bottle and poured us both a glass.

'To Dad,' she said.

'To the baby,' I added.

'To Betty.'

'To you and Hugh.'

'To Angela.'

'To Mum and Harold,' I said.

'To us,' she said. 'To Milly and Sarah.'

'To us.' We clinked, and sat back and sipped our non-alcoholic wine. Was it possible to feel such sadness and such happiness at exactly the same time? Obviously it was, and maybe that was what it was to be human, happiness and sadness in perfect co-existence.

'You know you said that you thought Betty was your connection with Dad?' I said.

'Yes?'

'Well, it's not. You've got me.'

She smiled at me. 'We've got... each other.'

'And the baby...'

She smiled. 'The baby... oh my God, the baby! A baby...' She shook her head as though she couldn't believe it.

'It's got all of us... Mum, Angela, me...'

She nodded. 'A family.'

'And a grandfather... She may not meet him in real life, but maybe she met him on her way...'

'Now you're getting weird.'

'Well... maybe.'

She grinned at me. 'Weird or not, I like it.'

'Me too.'

'Thanks.'

'It's my job, isn't it. Looking after you. And now I've got another to look out for... my niece or nephew.'

'*Godchild.*'

'Godchild.' We smiled at each other. And it was enough. More than enough. Better than anything. My sister, her baby... our family.

48

A week later and Sarah and I were waiting in Arrivals for Mum and Harold, in the midst of excited families and friends and relatives, bouquets and banners and bored drivers holding names of arrivees... and us clutching a jar with the ashes of freshly cremated Betty inside.

'It feels still warm,' said Sarah, her hands around the urn.

'Put it back in the bag!' I looked around nervously. 'People will think we're weirdos bringing an urn to meet someone at an airport.'

We'd picked it up on our way, not wanting to leave it standing around all day. It was the kind of situation where you didn't know what best practice was. There's no book on what to do with a cancer diagnosis, a dead beloved pet and – most wonderfully – a pregnancy. And I was getting on with my life, avoiding Teolaí and Darragh. It was time to forget the past and focus on my future and work out exactly what I wanted.

Standing beside me, Sarah was looking back to her usual self – leather biker jacket, skinny jeans and trainers. Actually, she looked better than usual. Less tired. She was *glowing*.

'How are you feeling?' I said.

'Normal.' She shot me a look. 'Well, normal for someone who is holding an urn with the ashes of a dog in. It won't take us long to scatter those. The ceremony will be pretty short.'

'One sneeze and she'll be gone.'

We half-smiled at each other.

'It's the best and the worst homecoming, don't you think?' I said. 'On the one hand, she's going to be a grandmother, on the other hand her sister is recovering – hopefully – from cancer and her dog has died.'

Sarah grimaced. 'I'm actually glad I'm pregnant just to mitigate the bad news.'

'Girls!' Mum was standing behind a huge trolley, tanned and wearing a rather beautiful African kaftan dress. Beaming, her whole face was alight with the adventure she had just had. Oh God, how were we going to tell her? 'Hello, my darling girls,' she said. 'I've missed you both so much.' She looked at us. 'I have decided,' she said, 'I like going away, but I like coming home so much more.'

Harold came up behind her, pushing a trolley. '*Ubi bene obi patria*,' he said. 'Home is where it is good.' He smiled at us, but his glasses seemed a little fogged up and his bow tie looked wilted. 'It's so good to be home,' he said again. 'Now, that was a long flight. Much as I like to meet new people, I was seated next to a man who needed to get a few things off his chest. There was the ex-wife who ran off with his best friend, the business that went bust and the daughter who stole and sold his car. I was hoping to watch a film with Kitty. But she watched it on her own.'

Mum laughed. 'You're too nice,' she said. 'That's your problem.'

Sarah glanced at me. 'The car's outside,' she said. 'Harold? Shall we drop you... are you coming...?'

'No, no,' Harold said, 'very kind of you, but I think Horace said he'd collect me.' He stood to attention and saluted us. 'Thank you, Kitty, for your company,' he said, formally. He waggled his arms a bit and then darted towards her, in a shy and very sweet hug. Afterwards, they stood apart, both smiling. 'Ah!' said Harold. 'And thus walketh Horace. Oh, and Hadriana! What a lovely surprise.'

There, skulking moodily, were Horace and Hadriana, looking like over-sized, over-hormonal teenagers. Hadriana whispered something behind her hand to Horace and he laughed. They walked towards us.

'Horace,' said Mum, shaking their hands. 'Hadriana. So lovely to see you! How are things? All well?'

'Grand,' said Hadriana, shrugging. 'I suppose. How was the trip?'

'Wonderful,' said Harold, enthusiastically. '*Bene*.'

'Yes, wonderful,' said Mum, equally enthused.

'Going all the way to South Africa to see cacti is a little over the top, don't you think?' said Horace.

Harold ignored him. 'Well, Kitty,' he said, shyly. 'Thank you for a lovely holiday.'

Mum smiled back. 'Thank you, Harold.' They grinned at each other for a moment, like teenagers. Harold bobbed towards her and planted a small kiss on her lips.

'Well, I look forward to seeing you soon,' he said politely.

'And I look forward to seeing you soon,' said Mum.

'Very much,' he said.

'Me too,' she said.

They hovered for a moment, and then he reached into the inside pocket of his jacket. 'I almost forgot,' he said. 'I bought you some Werther's Originals in the shop for the flight and we didn't have them!'

'You were too busy talking!' she smiled.

'You take them.'

'Are you sure?'

He nodded. 'They're for you.' He pressed the sweets into her hand.

'Thank you.' She looked as delighted as I'd ever seen her. 'I'll have to share them with the girls in the car,' she said.

'Well, then, I shall have to buy more for next time,' he said.

'What about tomorrow? Breakfast and a wander around the garden,' she said. 'The girls have been watering it for me.'

Had we? I hoped Sarah had, because I hadn't been near it for weeks.

Mum noticed our worried looks. 'How are my tomatoes?'

Sarah and I looked at each other and suddenly both burst into tears.

49

'What's wrong?' Mum said. 'What's happened? The tomatoes...?'

'It's Angela,' I said. 'The tomatoes are fine.' I hoped.

'What about her?'

'She's been going through treatment for cancer,' I blurted. 'She's going to be fine, but she felt guilty not to have told us. She's been wearing wigs.'

Mum was silent as she took it all in. 'I knew there was something,' she said. 'I asked her over and over again, but she said nothing.'

'She didn't want to burden you after everything you'd been through.'

Mum shook her head, annoyed. 'She's impossible.'

We told her the details of the treatment, the positive prognosis, the next round of tests and check-ups in three months, and three months after that... and so on. All we had to do was hope that each time we would be getting the all-clear.

'Will you drop me to Angela's now?' she asked.

'Of course.' I took out the urn from the bag. We may as well get everything out in the open.

'Have you two been pickling onions?' said Hadriana. Horace sniggered. 'What's in the jar?'

'It's Betty, she died!' said Sarah, beginning to cry again.

Mum's hands flew to her face. 'No!'

'We're sorry Mum,' I said. 'We didn't know how to tell you.'

'Who is Betty?' insisted Hadriana. 'Is she a close friend?'

'She's our dog,' I explained.

'The best dog,' said Sarah, who suddenly let out a huge heaving sob. 'She was sixteen and had been through so much.' She tried to regain some self-control, by gasping in air, while Mum hugged her and the urn tightly. 'Sorry,' Sarah managed, once she could breathe and speak again, 'it's just my hormones.'

'Hormones?' Mum pulled away and was studying her, working something out.

Sarah nodded, looking straight back at Mum.

And then Mum began to smile. 'You're serious?'

Sarah nodded again, smiling back. 'I'm serious.'

Mum flung her arms around her neck. 'No!' She pulled me into the hug and we huddled together until we could huddle no more. Even Mum was crying. When we had said our goodbyes and it was just the three of us – and the urn – Mum put an arm through ours and pulled us closer.

'I love you two,' she said, 'I'm so glad to see you. Now, let's go and find Angela.'

We drove straight there, Sarah and I hovering in the kitchen, making tea while Mum and Angela had a good cry.

'I'm going to be just fine,' I heard Angela say. 'And anyway, the big news is the baby! I'm going to be a great great-aunt! And you, Kitty, are going to be the world's best grandmother.'

Sarah's phone rang. 'Hello you,' she answered, her face softening and breaking into a smile as she walked away. 'Feeling fine. Not so sick any more... yes... I don't know. She's just upset...' When she came back into the kitchen, she said, 'Hugh's coming to pick me up. He's just down the road, he'll be here in five minutes. Wants to make me lunch. Says I need some food.'

'He's right,' I said, following her back into the hall.

'And just so you know,' she said casually, in a low voice, 'Hugh and I are getting married. Now!' She held up a hand, 'no fuss, no squealing, no jumping around... Hugh thinks we should. And I find myself without a reason why we shouldn't. But don't tell anyone quite yet. Now is not the time.' She was slipping on her leather biker jacket but looked up, a big grin on her face. 'I don't want to do life without Hugh,' she said. 'Everything is better with him. I've now realised that. And this little thing...' She nodded towards her stomach, 'hopefully will have its father's temperament.' She called out to Mum and Angela. 'See you later!' and then turned back to me. 'Will you be all right?

I nodded.

'By the way,' she said, 'I always thought you and Darragh were good together.'

I rolled my eyes. 'And I thought you said that he had treated me badly?'

She shrugged. 'He's a good guy.'

We heard the crunch of the gravel on the front path.

'Hugh! My betrothed!' Sarah grinned. 'Come and say hello.'

At the front door, I watched as they embraced, Hugh burying his head in her neck and Sarah wrapping her arms around him.

'Hello, Little Bird.' He kissed her on her lips so gently, and lovingly.

'I've missed you,' she said. '*We've* missed you.'

And his face as he realised what she meant was priceless, a rising sun of happiness. 'Little Bird and Littler Bird.'

She laughed.

'Milly's here,' she said, turning round. 'Remember this stranger?'

'It's only been a few months,' I said.

Sarah giggled with glee. 'Finally,' she said.

'Finally.' Their fingers were entwined, their bodies close. They'd always looked good together.

'It's wonderful news,' I said. 'Congratulations.'

'I'm the luckiest man in the world,' he said. 'All you need is love, isn't that right?' And he pulled her closer, the two of them – the three of them – a perfect family.

50

On Thursday morning, I was first to arrive at court number five, a large and draughty space which had seen better days, where a hundred years of damp wood, stale sweat and the scent of defeat lingered in the nostrils. The wooden benches were sunken under the weight of all those who had come before us and a tiny row of safety glass windows ran across the top of one side, the only sense that there was a world outside the yellow painted walls.

The night before, I had stayed up until the early hours ensuring every detail, every receipt, every payment, every contract relating to Number One, Merrion Square was in place. There was the 5,000 word document I had written about Mrs Murphy and her life in the building, the history of it before her and the future we envisaged for it. Mrs Murphy was right, staying there wasn't practical, but we could make it work for her, and for Number One, Merrion Square. She and it deserved better. Buildings reverberated with the lives of those who had lived and loved there. This one had homed and housed generations of women, their stories, their lives, keeping them warm and safe. A place of greater safety. We all need one, somewhere to return to when life gets hard. I'd still been working at 2 a.m., when Siobhán had woken up to get a glass of water and found me at the kitchen table, typing furiously. She made me a cup of tea and let me fill her in at rapid speed about what had happened, and what my next move was going to be.

'You're going to kick their arses,' she'd said, confidently. 'Couldn't happen to a nicer mother and son.' And then I remembered I hadn't told her about Sarah and the baby and she hugged me, sleepily, 'Super auntie,' she'd said. 'And super lawyer.' before drifting back to bed.

Now, here, in court, I let the fear thrum in my body, settling it down, soothing it, calming. If anxiety was part of me, I should be nicer to it and maybe try to work with it rather than against it. Grief and anxiety were the same, you had to let them take you where they were going to, and you couldn't be scared.

And for the first time, I was truly unafraid. I'd survived the worst and could face anything to come.

'Good morning!' The door behind us opened. 'Are we too late?' A walking stick had been thrust inside the door as it opened. Mrs Murphy, dressed in a long red winter coat – despite the fact it was now late May – and carrying a large carpet bag made her way in, followed closely by Daphne, Mr McAvoy and Susie.

'Morning, Milly,' Mr McAvoy boomed. 'I thought I'd pop down and see how you're doing. Susie's here for more work experience. Don't mind us, we'll be quiet here on this bench, won't we, Mary?' he said. 'It's all in your capable hands, Milly.'

Daphne gave me a double-thumbs up of support.

Susie slipped in beside me. 'How are you doing?'

'Pretty good,' I said. 'Keeping everything happy.'

She nodded her approval. 'Well done. Now, if there's anything I can do?'

'Just moral support,' I said.

'Got it.'

The door opened again and a man with an unfortunate and uncanny likeness to Boris Karloff, all forehead and bushy brows, entered. He studiedly ignored us as he made his way to the bench opposite, holding a single folder. He looked like the kind of man who never saw daylight, the kind of person who liked the taste of human blood.

Behind me, Mrs Murphy was talking into her carpet bag. 'Can you breathe all right?' she said. 'Do you have enough air?'

'Frederick?' I said, as she nodded.

'Who?' said Mr McAvoy.

'Frederick,' I said. 'Her husband.'

'But he's dead,' said Mr McAvoy, looking confused.

'He's the cat, or he's *in* the cat,' I explained, as Mr McAvoy looked increasingly bewildered. 'Or the cat is in him... anyway...'

There was a sound behind us as the judge arrived.

'All rise,' said the clerk, and we quickly scrambled to our feet.

'Court, to order,' said Mr Justice Joyce. And then, just as Mr Justice Joyce lifted his gavel, about to begin, there was a late arrival. Carole and Ryan. Her eyes darted laser-like until she found me and then, as they walked in front of us to take their seats, she kept them directed on me.

Mr McAvoy tapped me on the shoulder. 'Do your worst,' he said, giving my back a slap.

'Shall we start?' said the judge.

And so it began.

Bernard Hessling was the first to take the stand, and spoke for three hours detailing the amount of work needed to do up the building, how it wasn't fit for human habitation and how only a company like Alpha Holdings, aka Dublin Investments, would be able to bring it back to its former glory. There was dry rot, rising damp, a rodent infestation, subsidence. There was woodworm in the rafters, asbestos in every wall. It would take millions to put it right. Alpha Holdings, said Bernard Hessling, were willing to spend that money to ensure that one of Dublin's greatest buildings on Dublin's greatest square would be restored lovingly for future generations, especially the residents of Georgian Splendour.

Mrs Murphy poked me with her walking stick. 'If there's rising damp and dry rot in the house, I will eat my hat,' she said, when I leaned in to hear her. 'I've lived there for more than fifty years and it's dry as ginger ale.'

Mr Justice Joyce hit the gavel. 'Court adjourned for lunch.'

In the café, we sat around a table eating desultory sandwiches and sipping watery coffee, only enlivened by Mrs Murphy handing around a small leather hip flask. 'Brandy,' she said. 'I think it's just what we need.'

Mr McAvoy liberally topped up his coffee with it and took a sip. 'Improves it no end,' he agreed.

'Well, well, well...' Carole was standing beside us, Ryan in her shadow. 'And how do you think it is going? Think you're doing well? Isn't Bernard Hessling a formidable attorney?'

'Carole,' I said, 'you can't talk to us while the case is being heard.'

She smiled. 'Am I breaking the law?' she said in a sweet voice. 'Am I doing something wrong?'

'Yes you are,' said Mr McAvoy. 'And I would suggest that you—'

Carole smiled at him. 'We all liked Milly so much at the beginning. But looks can be deceptive, can't they? How we trusted you as a family, how we took you in! I felt sorry for you! Yes, sorry for you, with your awful hair and no make-up.' She shook her head sadly. 'Ryan felt *sorry* for you as well... we all did. Roger too...'

'I think you should go,' I said. 'This is against the rules of the court.'

'Oh, we're going all right,' she said. 'When we *win*. And I hope you get the medical help you need. I'll say a prayer for you.'

'Mum...' Ryan tugged on the sleeves of her Chanel jacket like a toddler. 'If they throw us out, then we lose the case.'

Carole swivelled on her heels and left. Everyone around the table was silent, they all looked at each other in shock. But I felt something else. Dad had returned, I could feel him. Invisible, obviously, but very definitely there. And his voice was distinctly him. *'You can do this, Milly, my sparkling drop of joy. I'm right here.'*

That was all I needed, all I had been looking for. *I love you, Dad*, I said in my head. *I love you and I miss you. Thank you for everything.*

I smiled to myself and Mr McAvoy looked up. 'All right?'

I nodded. 'Very much so.'

51

'My Lord,' I said when we were back in court, 'on behalf of my client, we propose the building is zoned for cultural, social and community use. Under the Local Government Act 1988, clause 15b, any building which has historical and or special significance cannot be developed into something which does not reflect its historical and or special significance. I would like to say a few words on the aforementioned historical and special significance of the building as outlined. If my Lord permits—'

'Objection!' Across the way, the fuming eyebrows of Bernard Hessling bristled. Beneath them, his eyes glared at me. If eyebrows could be intimidating, then Bernard Hessling's were the scariest on the planet. It was the way they twitched and bristled menacingly, and then there were the hooded eyes and the thin lips which snarled and curled.

'And what is the detail of your objection, Mr Hessling?'

'Irrelevant! We are here to discuss the application to change the designation of the building and to reduce its heritage status so development can take place...'

'Objection overruled,' said the judge, who seemed somewhat on autopilot, as though he'd seen it all before, which, of course, he probably had.

I continued. 'My Lord, I would like to take the opportunity to talk about the building and explain that it is not just a building and therefore should not be turned into an exclusive development.'

Carole didn't take her eyes off me. It was as though she was casting some kind of voodoo spell. I could see Ryan crossing and uncrossing his legs, fiddling with his cuffs, and then the pleat on his trouser leg, and then pleating his tie between his fingers.

I took a deep breath.

'I would like to take a moment to tell a story,' I said. 'It's the story of a building which began life as a home. Built in 1762, the rock was taken from Dalkey quarry and over three years, a row of fifteen houses were built. And over six years, the whole square was finished.

'It wasn't just a home for the Worthington family, it was also the home of fifteen other people. There was a cook and two kitchen maids, two ladies' maids, a housekeeper, a butler, a footman, a head gardener and gardener's number two and one other. A scullery boy by the name of Arthur Joyce, a young lad of thirteen, who had come up to Dublin, all the way from Athenry in Galway...'

Mr Hessling's eyebrows twitched with irritation. What is she on about? They seemed to say. 'Objection,' he said, bouncing up. 'Irrelevant. Inconsequential and wasting the court's time. May I—'

Mr Justice Joyce held up his hand. 'Let Ms Byrne continue.'

In my research into the history of the house, I had found a small book in the National Archives: *Memoirs of a Scullery Boy* by Arthur Joyce. It was quite the find.

'Mr Arthur Joyce,' I went on, 'slept on a mattress on the pantry floor, which he rolled up at the start of the day and unrolled at the end of the day. He was the first up and last to bed.'

'My Lord,' said Mr Hessling, 'we really must stick to the point in hand—'

'Ms Byrne, continue.'

'Mr Joyce went on to become Attorney General,' I said. 'And his is just one remarkable story in the life of this house. The point of my speech is that the house tells stories. After Home Rule, the Worthingtons left for England, and the house was used, not as tenement housing, but as a home for the Salvation Army. It was they who fed the poor and the starving during the famines. I found another interesting piece of archive which showed that the house fed more than 120,000 hungry people in 1889 alone, many of those on their way to England in the footsteps of the Worthingtons, but also to the States. There was a newspaper cutting which referred to a certain Thomas Fitzgerald from Bruff County, Limerick—'

'Please, my Lord,' said Mr Hessling. 'No more of this pointless waffle. My clients would like the court to remain focused on the case.'

'I won't be much longer, my Lord,' I said. 'It's just that the Thomas Fitzgerald of Bruff County, Limerick, went to make a life in Boston. He had a son, John Francis Fitzgerald, who had a daughter, Rose Fitzgerald. Who...' I smiled at the court, leaving my most charming smile for Carole, '... went on to have a son, John Fitzgerald Kennedy.'

Even Ryan was looking quite interested.

'My point is, my Lord, that a building is more than just bricks and mortar. Every floorboard, every wall, has a story to tell. The place became offices for the Women's Suffrage movement. Then it became a centre for Cumman na mBan – the women's political movement. Mrs Mary Murphy was a member of that organisation. And it is Mrs Mary Murphy, now ninety years old, who is being forced from her home. She lived there with her husband, Frederick Murphy, who worked across the road at the Department of Finance. He would wave to her from his office every day at 12 p.m.. She set her clock by it.'

'Please, my Lord...' Mr Hessling blustered.

'Just one last point. My client's associate, Daphne Kelly, is an architect. Her plans, which I will now distribute to the court, take into consideration the history and cultural significance of the building.' I cleared my throat. 'May I present Mrs Mary Murphy. The woman who has lived in the top floor flat of Number One, Merrion Square for more than sixty years and will be forced to go into a home, by the order of Alpha Holdings and its parent company Dublin Investments.'

Mrs Murphy got to her feet, leaning heavily on Mr McAvoy. 'My husband and I were very happy in that flat,' she said, her voice clear and strong. 'I am old, as you can see, and there might be an argument for sending me out to pasture... but I would say there is a little thing called principle... it's not something I see much of these days. But it's what made this country great. We fought and died for principle. We were colonised, but we prevailed. I feel that Alpha Holdings are trying to take – with their letters and sending people to my door – something which doesn't belong to them. They are colonising something to which they have no earthly reason to have.' She smiled at the judge. 'And that's all we have to say.' And she reached into her carpet bag and pulled out Frederick, who for a moment looked undignified as his long body uncoiled and then with a flick, he was his normal dapper self, sitting upright in Mrs Murphy's arms.

The judge looked unperturbed by proceedings and we all sat back down again, waiting in silence while he shuffled his papers, made notes, scratched his head, looked up at the last of the afternoon sunlight which tried to creep through the high windows, and finally delivered his verdict.

'I rule that Alpha Holdings should desist from having anything to do with the property. It is ordered to stay away from Mrs Murphy, not to send any further correspondence and in fact I will be augmenting the preservation order of the building. Any development will be sensitive. It will not be rezoned for commercial use but must be in line with the very strict heritage and cultural designation. And any attempt to change its status will be looked upon as a dereliction of the Planning and Property Laws 1999. And I accept the plan submitted by Ms Daphne Dupont, but only – and I mean *only* – if it has the full approval of Mrs Murphy.' He slammed the gavel down. 'Case dismissed.'

We won! I was shocked, Daphne was in tears, Mr McAvoy gripped all of us in turn and the five of us swept out into the central foyer, where, just under the central dome, we danced an impromptu jig around Mrs Murphy and the carpet bag.

Mr Justice Joyce called me over. 'Ms Byrne,' he said. 'That was impressive. Well done. Now, how did you know that it was my great-grandfather who was the scullery boy?'

'It's Dublin, Mr Joyce,' I said. 'Everyone knows everything about everybody.'

He smiled at me. 'Well, a job well done. McCoyMcAvoy are lucky to have you.'

'Thank you,' I said.

I returned to my triumphant team as Mrs Murphy opened up the carpet bag. We all peered in, a feline face looked out at us, two unblinking yellow eyes. 'He's very happy at the outcome and he looks forward to moving to Number Two, Merrion Square,' said Mrs Murphy. 'I have thought about it and, yes, Daphne, I will take you up on the very kind offer. And that Number One will be developed into all that Milly outlined. I think Mrs Hackett would approve, I really do.'

'And I will have all the contracts and papers drawn up in the morning. You don't need to worry.' Mrs Murphy and Daphne were beaming with delight, their arms interlinked. Frederick was buckled back in again, the rest of us basking in our victory.

Carole marched over to me. 'What was that about?' she said. 'What kind of display was that? I am going to sue you for... for...' She struggled to find a word. 'For contempt! Or... or...!'

Ryan stepped in front of her. 'Congratulations, Milly,' he said. 'You were very convincing. And it was well deserved.' He held out his hand. 'Best of luck with everything.'

'You too.'

Ryan turned and marched Carole away, but she shook him off and shrieked as though he was a wasp with a mission to sting. 'Take your hands off me!' The sound of her scream echoed through the building as they headed straight for the front door. 'And it's all your fault...' she hissed at him. 'You are pathetic... always have been...'

'Milly,' said Mr McAvoy, 'you were magnificent! Wasn't she?' He beamed at everyone. 'I'd forgotten how much fun it could be. Mother will be pleased,' he said. 'Let's celebrate in the Wig And Gown. Drinks are on me. Or at least on the expense account of McCoyMcAvoy.'

And then I remembered it was Lorenzo's birthday. There was absolutely nothing stopping me from joining the party. I wanted to be there. I wanted to be with my friends – Siobhán *and* Darragh. I loved him, always had, always would. But it was time to show him that I was okay, and anything he had done was forgotten. And forgiven.

'I'd love to,' I said to Mr McAvoy. 'But I'm heading to a party.'

'On a Thursday?' he said, looking impressed. 'Reminds me of being a young lawyer. We liked to burn the candle at both ends. Those were the days. No sleep, just work and play, on a loop.'

He sighed happily. 'What I'd give for a blast of some of the old energy but... there's something to be said for a nightcap by seven and into the old pyjamas by 8 p.m..

Luckily I still had some of the old energy. Enough to power me across town and to Teolaí.

52

'Buona sera!' said Francisca, unlocking the door of Teolaí. 'Come in, you are just in time for the food!' She looked her usual, staggeringly beautiful, self. 'Lolo and I show you a real Italian feast. We've been cooking all day.' Several tables had been pushed together to make one long one, covered in a huge white cloth. 'Lolo takes his birthday very seriously,' she said. 'He likes a huge... fuss... is that the right word?'

I nodded. 'I think he has the right idea. Everyone should have a fuss once a year.'

The room was full of people – some of whom I recognised from previous nights in Teolaí, mainly Italian friends of Lorenzo and Francisca, and there was Darragh behind the bar, pouring bottles into tall glass jugs.

'Darragh is on *aperitivi* duty,' said Francisca. 'He's made something with prosecco and campari. But I am so glad you are here, I go back to Italy tomorrow... to see my boyfriend...'

'Your boyfriend?' What did she mean?

'Milly!' Siobhán came over and squeezed me. 'You're here!' She looked delighted. 'How was the case? Did you win?'

I nodded and she hugged me again, shaking me like a bottle of pop. 'Yay! I knew you would!'

'It was luck,' I said. 'The right case, at the right time.'

'And Ryan and Carole?'

'Disappointed,' I said. 'Which is putting it mildly.' But I was distracted by the realisation that Darragh and Francisca weren't a couple. Both Siobhán and I had assumed they were.

'Hello!' It was Darragh, carrying a tray of glass jugs filled with a concoction the colour of a Tuscan sunset.

Siobhán took two glasses off the tray and handed one to me. 'We are celebrating! This clever clogs won her case. Against Ryan and Carole!'

Darragh looked at me. 'Which Ryan?'

'*Her* Ryan,' said Siobhán. 'Turned out he was the one Milly was up against in a housing issue.'

'It's a long story,' I said.

'Are you all right?' Darragh looked concerned.

'Very,' I said. 'I'm *very* all right.'

'And Hugh and Sarah are having a baby!' said Siobhán to him.

He looked at me, smiling. 'I knew something was up!'

'Yeah...' I smiled back. 'It's amazing. I can't believe it.'

'What the hell is this drink, Darragh?' said Siobhán. 'It looks like something from a kid's party. Hope there are cocktail sausages as well.'

Darragh laughed. 'It's lethal, that's what it is. I shouldn't be allowed to create my own cocktail.'

Lorenzo joined us, an apron tied around his waist, his long hair tied up in a man-bun, his chest all too visible through his low-cut T-shirt.

'I am so glad you are here,' he said, as he hugged me. 'It's my birthday so everyone is nice to me, no?'

'We're happy to be nice to you, Lolo,' said Siobhán. 'If that's what you want.'

He smiled winningly at her, and then, 'I need to check on everything in the kitchen,' he said. 'The pasta cannot be overcooked. Will you come with me?'

'Absolutely!' beamed Siobhán and ran after him.

'Come everyone, sit down!' Francisca beckoned everyone towards the long table. 'I think dinner is nearly ready.'

The lethal cocktail was downed far too quickly and Darragh was required to make another few jugs of it. But then he sat down beside me. Siobhán and Lorenzo were at the other end.

'I'm glad you're here,' he said.

'I'm glad I'm here, too,' I said.

'I'm glad we're friends,' he went on. 'I couldn't bear it if we weren't.' He laid his hand over mine for a moment and then there was the sound of the Italians chanting something.

'*Discorso, discorso!*'

'A speech!' Lorenzo said, standing up on a chair. 'I have to make a birthday speech.' He was grinning as he held both arms aloft like a triumphant gladiator. Darragh had moved beside Francisca who had her arm around Darragh's shoulders. 'I will speak in English for the sake of my new Irish friends,' Lorenzo began. 'But I must thank Darragh O'Toole, the Irish man who turned up at our vineyard with no Italian, no knowledge of wine. He believed that beans from a tin was a proper meal...'

Darragh held up his hands in surrender. 'It is!' he said. 'You lot just haven't tried it.'

Lorenzo laughed. 'But, Darragh... well, he learned. He worked hard. He enjoyed Italian life, the weather, our food, our wine, I would like to say our women, but no... I think his heart is taken long ago...'

I didn't dare look Darragh's way. I wanted to believe Lorenzo was talking about me but I couldn't bear to be wrong.

'And one day, after we had taught him everything we knew, after he could tell a *Sangiovese* from a *Primitivo*, he came to me and he said, it is time for me to go home. He said that although he had loved being in Italy, he felt as though he was in exile, like the great *Napoleone*. He had unfinished business in his country. And he needed to go. He told me about his dream to open an Italian wine bar in Dublin, he said he wanted to go back. It can't be the weather... yes, Francisca?'

She made a face and everyone cheered. Her dislike of the Irish frontal systems was obviously well broadcast.

'So, on this, my twenty-eighth birthday, I want to thank my friends – *gli italiani* – and my new Irish friends. But most of all Darragh, thank you for sharing this with me.' Siobhán's eyes were fixed on Lorenzo. 'Darragh,' he said, 'you told us that we would love Ireland, you told us it was a beautiful country, you told us that we would be happy here, and we are... my Irish birthday is a very happy birthday.' He held up his glass. 'To Darragh, to you, and to me!'

And we all cheered and threw back our drinks.

There was Italian pop playing and we drank and ate. Siobhán came over and wrapped her arms around me.

'Are you having a good time?' she said. I couldn't remember when I'd last seen her so happy.

'Yeah,' I said, 'I really am.'

'I ended it with George,' she went on. 'I went over earlier to his with his stuff and told him how sorry I was. Am. Will always be.'

'Was he okay?'

'He took it quite well,' she said. 'But said was there anything he could do to change my mind. Which there isn't.'

'Poor George,' I said, thinking of how sweet he was, a lovely guy who just wasn't right for Siobhan. He needed to find a fellow baker, someone who kept the same hours as him.

'I know.' Siobhan's face darkened and her eyes filled with tears. 'I feel awful. Poor lovely George. Not about Lorenzo. I feel bad about that, obviously. And I'm a terrible person. But I wish more than anything that he had someone who loved him. He deserves it. Everyone deserves it. Oh God.' She clung to me and had a good cry.

Five minutes later, she wiped her eyes.

'I'm okay now,' she said. 'Much better.' And I watched as she danced up to Lorenzo and he grabbed her and they swayed and twirled around the floor.

Later, when all of Nonna's grappa was gone, and we had drunk the place dry of Campari and when most of the guests had gone home, the floor swept, everything washed up and the bar made ready for the next day, I was ready to go home and sleep for a week.

Francisca was sitting having a cigarette with her feet up on another chair. 'I'm allowed,' she said to me. 'Once customers are gone? Am I not right, Darragh?'

He shrugged. 'No one is going to tell on you,' he said.

'Would you like one?' She offered me her packet.

When I said no, she tutted and threw back her head. 'Sometimes I feel like a criminal in this country,' she pouted. 'No one smokes. No one drinks...'

'We definitely do that!' laughed Darragh.

'But not *properly*,' she insisted. 'You all drink too much and fall over and make fools of yourselves, and then say you are never drinking again... until the next time.' She rolled her eyes, a ring of smoke floated to the ceiling. 'You don't drink properly, that means regularly, and tasting the wine... as though it is a part of life, *aqua vitae*... you all think it is alcohol, something to get drunk on... you are all *filistei*... philistines.'

Darragh caught my eye and gave me an amused look. 'We're still learning, Francisca,' he said.

Lorenzo carried the crates of bottles to the back of the building for recycling.

'You've forgotten these!' said Siobhán, running to follow him. Last time she looked that happy was when she got a selfie with Geri Halliwell.

Darragh came over to me at the bar. 'Why don't I make us all a coffee and we can have some more of that almond cake?'

I sat on the same stool where I'd been the very first time I'd come into Teolaí, the night Lorenzo had given me the red wine and the olives, the night I had seen Darragh after so long.

There was fizzing in the atmosphere, a charge, as though something had shifted. From the evening he'd come to my flat to say sorry, something had been building and building. And now I realised that he was not with Francisca, it had been released into the air. He knew it and I knew it. We couldn't stop smiling at each other. Maybe, there was a chance.

53

'So...' Darragh laid out two cups on the counter between us.

'So.'

'Did you enjoy yourself?' He smiled.

'Yes, the pleasures of Italian pop are much underrated. I feel like I have been at a disco in Rimini, and I think I will be singing that one song... what was it, something about a Bambina Impertinente – what's that, a rude baby? That one's going to go round and round my head for the rest of my life.'

He laughed. 'It's Lorenzo's favourite. He always puts it on.' For a moment he opened his mouth to say something and then closed it again.

'Go on,' I said. 'What were you about to say?'

'Just that I'm glad you're here. I like it when you're here. When I moved back, I didn't dare to imagine that we would even see each other, never mind go hillwalking, spend three hours in A&E and even go to an Italian disco together.'

I laughed. 'God, life has suddenly got fun. Nights in A&E and drinking grappa. Who'd have thought it?'

'I know how to show people a good time.' We smiled at each other. The music was still playing and there was enough noise from the other conversations that were still going on in the room, and the rattle of wine and beer bottles from the kitchen to create a sense of privacy.

'So, Francisca is leaving?' I said. Across the room, Francisca was chatting with a group of her friends, her long legs stretched out onto a chair, looking fabulous.

He nodded. 'She's going back to her politician – Giacomo – a crazy socialist who was too busy to be a proper boyfriend, which is why she decided to come to Dublin, to make him jealous. And it worked.' He looked at me. 'So, Siobhán was joking about *you* being engaged.'

I nodded. 'She was, yes.'

'Why?'

'Because she didn't want me to seem lonely and pathetic.'

'Really? You? Lonely and pathetic?' He raised an eyebrow. 'How could you be?'

'Because I am... was... you saw me having that panic attack. You saw how low I had become...'

He shook his head. 'Oh God, it was awful,' he said, anguished. 'I wanted so much to help you. When you felt anxious at college, we would talk, go for one of our walks... remember?'

'I remember.'

His hand touched mine as he passed the coffee. 'So, tell me about Ryan. What happened?'

'Oh God.' And I told Darragh the whole story, all about Mrs Murphy and Alpha Holdings and then about Carole and the oysters and Roger and his incessant hernia talk and how I was settling for something that wasn't at all what I wanted. And about the proposal.

'No!'

I nodded. 'It was all a bit strange. I think that maybe he was hoping I might be a way out but, obviously, I wasn't. I hope he finds another escape tunnel.'

'He was an absolute and total prat at college,' said Darragh. 'I couldn't believe it when I knew that your new boyfriend – your *fiancé* – was Ryan Kingston. So...'

His hand reached for mine and this time he held it, across the bar, the warmth of him on me and something else. Desire. Love. Lust. Happiness.

Excitement. *Possibility.* I had fallen right back in love with him. Of course I had never fallen out of love with him. It was as though nothing had come between us, that we had time-travelled to a happier time, that we were the same as we always had been, and that there was no leaving, no goodbye letter.

I loved him. And I was proud of him.

Except...

Except, *everything* was different. He *had* left. We couldn't go back and *I had* spent five years fixing and mending myself. I wasn't the same. We hadn't time-travelled. I was facing forward.

'Milly,' he said, 'I can't bear...'

He looked up at Francisca's voice. 'Darragh!'

She joined us, rattling the keys. 'It's midnight, we can't be open any longer. Our licence?'

Whatever he was going to say wasn't what I needed to hear. He couldn't bear what? That he'd hurt me? Or couldn't bear the guilt?

'Goodbye, Darragh,' I said. 'Thank you for a lovely evening.' I wouldn't see him again, I thought. I *couldn't* see him again, not if I was going to do anything with my life, not if I was going to live *whole*heartedly. I was not going to go backwards. 'I'd better get my coat,' I said. 'It's in the kitchen, I think.' I thought my heart would break again. But I was sure I was right. I knew where I was going and I needed all my physical and emotional energy to keep me on the right path.

The slurping sound was audible before I saw anything, like a dog licking an ice cream. And behind the fridge were Siobhán's feet and... Lorenzo's feet... facing each other.

I stopped for a moment, not knowing what to do. With one hand, I lifted my coat off the rack and silently turned round and walked back into the bar.

Siobhán was suddenly beside me, grabbing my arm. 'Ready to go, Milly?' she said. 'Thanks everyone! See you!'

We didn't stop to say anything else but sprinted out into the night.

'I think I'm in love,' Siobhan shouted, as we jogged home. 'Or I'm in lust! Or whatever it is. I am a woman obsessed!' She began dancing in the street, jumping like a gazelle over pavements, spinning around a lamp post, tap dancing across a junction. 'I had no idea! No idea at all. That men could be so... so... *desirable*.' she shouted. 'Milly... oh my God, Milly...' Her eyes were shining. 'Kissing Lolo was better than sex. Kissing. Just *kissing*.' She looked as though she'd found God. 'I would happily take just kissing him over anything else ever in my life. I would give everything to do that again... Oh my God! I think I will never be the same again.'

She put her arm through mine again.

'So, exactly how good was he?'

She thought for a while. 'Remember Augustus Gloop in *Charlie and the Chocolate Factory*? Remember when he starts drinking from the chocolate river... and how he can't stop...'

I laughed.

'That's what kissing Lorenzo is like...' She grinned at me. 'I will never wash my mouth again. Or rather, the inside of my mouth. I will never brush my teeth again!'

'You're disgusting.'

'I am sorry to flaunt my amazing good fortune on you. I can't help it. It was just so incredible.' She flung her arms outstretched, Hollywood musical style. 'It's the most amazing thing that has ever happened to my body. To me! To the world. Lorenzo should be available on the health service. We're going to meet tomorrow and spend the night together. He promised. Oh my God. And he's Aries. An air sign! Isn't that perfect?'

'Is it?' I could still feel Darragh's hand touching mine.

54

When I arrived in the office the next morning (rather hungover), Catriona was packing up her desk.

'I've just handed in my notice,' she said. 'And I have been put on gardening leave, so I'm going today. I'm moving to Goldhouse&Water. They are very much more family friendly than this antediluvian place. There's a crèche downstairs, so I can pop down and see Lydia. You can work the school year and take the summer off, there are fifty-five per cent women lawyers there... I think it might suit me better.'

For a moment I watched as she put her diary, her textbooks, the framed picture of Noel and Lydia into the cardboard box. 'I'll really miss you,' I said.

She nodded. 'Me too. And congratulations on yesterday. Patrick McAvoy said you were most impressive.'

'I learned it all from you.'

'Nonsense!' She smiled. 'I've really enjoyed working with you. You've been a really wonderful colleague. And an even better friend.'

'You too...'

'Will you come and see Lydia soon? Even at three months old, she knows who she likes.'

I laughed. 'I'd love to.'

'And Noel and I were wondering if you would be her godmother?'

A week ago, I didn't have a single godchild and now I had two.

'I'd be honoured.'

She slipped on her beautiful cream cashmere coat and picked up her box and her briefcase. She stood at the door. 'Well, goodbye, Milly.'

'Goodbye, Catriona.'

She held out her arms and clutched me to her. 'And Mr McAvoy wants a word. He told me to send you up. And, Milly? If you don't decide to take it, you can always follow me to Goldhouse&Water.'

'Take what?' I couldn't work out what she was hinting at.

She smiled and shrugged.

On the sixth floor, Susie waved me through to Mr McAvoy's office.

'Ah, Ms Byrne,' he said, pressing a button on his desk. 'Susie, bring in the sherry.'

Sherry? It wasn't even nine o'clock in the morning. My stomach lurched at the thought of more alcohol.

'I like to toast a new appointment,' he said. 'Promotions are something to celebrate, don't you think?'

'Promotion?'

He nodded. 'Partner. A vacancy has occurred. You may have heard that our esteemed colleague is leaving. She will be a great loss, but we'd be very pleased if you accepted. Now, it's more work, and longer hours, but I think you will find that the salary more than recompenses... and...'

Susie backed into the room, carrying a tray with a decanter and two tiny Waterford crystal glasses on it.

'Mr McAvoy,' I said, quickly, before he went any further. 'It's very kind of you, and I am deeply honoured, but...' I paused. 'I don't want it.'

Mr McAvoy's mouth dropped open. Susie froze.

Time was running away with me and there had been hours and hours and years and years I'd already wasted. I thought of Angela and what she'd gone through. The time I had spent not living life as fully as I should. This great gift. I wanted my own house, my own sanctuary, and I wanted to spend more time there, even work from home.

'I want to thank you for this opportunity and for thinking of me,' I went on, as Mr McAvoy and Susie both gazed at me, not in horror but with something that looked more like curiosity, 'but I don't think I am able to give the company the commitment it needs.'

Mr McAvoy didn't say anything for a moment. 'Let me be very clear, you are turning down the offer of a partnership?'

I nodded. 'I'm sorry. But I am leaving corporate law.' The words were out of my mouth before I knew quite what I was saying. 'I want to represent more Mrs Murphys, to be in charge and to choose my own cases and my own hours.'

He didn't laugh, thankfully, just nodded, thoughtfully, taking it all in.

'And... and...' What else? And then it came to me... there *was* something else. A dog. I really wanted a dog. 'I want a dog.'

'A dog?' *Now*, his mouth twitched. 'I think this still calls for a glass of sherry.' He waved Susie forward. 'We'll *all* have one. Susie, go and get a glass for yourself. Congratulations, Milly. To courage!'

And I thought of Mum watching Dad die and still getting up in the morning and being brave enough to move on. And Angela and her Courage, Confidence and Character badge and facing all that bad news and treatment alone. And Sarah turning up every day to nurse people who were at the end of life, while going through her own losses month after month. And Mrs Murphy, who faced those stairs every day, and even to Catriona for doing it all. I had been mentored by some seriously impressive women.

'To courage!' And the three of us clinked glasses.

As I walked back downstairs – with something of a spring in my step – I heard a scream from the open-plan offices. 'NOOOOOOOO! No! No! No!'

At the end of the corridor, Jarleth was standing with an envelope in his hand, some of the others, including Nora, standing awkwardly around him.

'What's happened?'

Jarleth had dropped to his knees, his arms cradling his head, he said something muffled.

'What was that?' Everyone edged forward. 'What did you say?'

'We didn't win!' Jarleth looked up at them. His eyes red-rimmed. 'We didn't win the Best Craic Office! Bank of bloody Ireland did! BASTARDS!'

55

Siobhán and I were still in our dressing gowns, drinking milky coffee and catching up on each other's news – my events at work, her feelings for Lorenzo.

There was a knock on the door.

George.

'I thought you were working,' I said.

'It's Saturday morning,' he said. 'It's only half a day. Where's Siobhán? She's not answering any of my texts.'

'She's...'

Behind me, I heard Siobhán come into the hall. 'George!' she exclaimed. But George had dropped to one knee.

'Siobhán...'

'Please don't,' she said.

'No, I have to...'

'You really don't and I'd rather you didn't...'

'Didn't what?'

'What you were going to do.'

'But I love you...'

'You don't. Not really. And I don't. Not really. I mean, I love you...'

'And I love you.'

'But like a brother. Or a friend. Like I really care about you. Too much for this.'

George was still on one knee. He wobbled. 'I can't...' he said, arms flailing. 'I can't stand up. My back.' He grabbed onto my arm as I pulled him up. 'Jesus Christ,' he said.

'Sorry,' said Siobhán.

'You should have told me before I kneeled down.'

'I know.'

'How long have you felt like this?'

'Forever.'

'Sorry.' He looked stunned. 'Run that by me again. I've been your *brother*? *Forever*?'

She gave me an agonised look, and then back to George. 'No! I mean, yes... Oh God. Yes. I do mean that. But it's not as horrible as it sounds. Being a brother is a good thing, a lovely thing. If I was to have a brother then it would be you. Sorry.'

'*Please* can we talk.'

'Do we need to?'

'I was thinking about my mother and how much you like her. You'd miss her,' said George, eagerly. 'You *love* my mother.'

Siobhán considered this fact. 'Yes, yes I do,' she said. 'I really love your mother. But I can't marry you just to have your mother. Yes, she's nicer than my own, but you deserve better than just someone who is pals with your mum.'

'Yes, you do,' I said. 'You're a lovely man, any woman would love to go out with you.'

'Someone better than me,' said Siobhán. 'Someone *actually* nice.'

Eventually George left, after a few tears (from him) and protestations as to him being the catch of the century (from us). And then it was just me and Siobhán.

'It's like the old days,' she said, putting the kettle on. 'Both of us single, drinking coffee and eating biscuits in our dressing gowns.'

'I thought everything was terrible,' I said. 'But it isn't. Everything isn't terrible.'

She nodded. 'You see?'

And I did see. And more than anything, I knew when it did go terrible again, I could handle it. Fear was what made things terrible and I had spent too long being afraid. Someone, after all, had thought of me as a sparkling drop of joy. And drops of joy didn't get scared. They were too busy sparkling.

'And anyway, I am meeting Lolo later,' said Siobhán. 'And I need to get myself ready.'

'Siobhán, it's still the morning.'

'I know...' She was already in the bathroom. 'But this might take time. I'm not only overgrown and neglected, I'm practically derelict. It'll take some serious maintenance to bring me back to mint condition.' She winked as she swanned off to the bathroom, not to be seen for another few hours.

56

It was one of those perfect days on Killiney Hill where the sky is blue and the clouds skid across it, the leaves the acid green of early summer and the world full of birdsong. Below, the land falls away as you make the steep climb along the paths, through the woods and up up up towards heaven, if you're quiet, you can hear the sea crashing far below you.

We'd argued over where to scatter Betty's ashes, I had thought the garden, Sarah had suggested the pier in Dun Laoghaire she used to trot along, but it was Mum who decided on Killiney Hill. 'It was where she and Dad used to love,' she said. 'They'll be together again, walking along the paths, sniffing out squirrels.'

Killiney Hill was where he and Betty used to come every day. They'd start at the car park, and walk the long incline through the old forest, up and up, meeting other dog owners (Dad), chasing squirrels (Betty), until they reached the very top where you could see north, south, east and west of Dublin, the sky bigger than you ever thought possible, the sea to one side stretching far away towards Wales and the mountains on the other side undulating towards Wicklow.

In the car park, I met Mum and Angela and Sarah, we hugged.

'All right, my lovely girl?' said Mum, her hand on my face.

I could tell she'd had a bit of a cry.

Mum had her arm through Angela's the whole way up, and we walked at a stately pace.

And then at the top, just beside the oak trees where the squirrels – who made Betty's life a daily torment – lived, Mum took a handful, then me, and then Sarah. 'One, two, three!' she shouted, and we released Betty into the air. And then we did it again, and again, until there was nothing left of Betty. She was gone.

'Goodbye Betty!' shouted Sarah. 'Best dog in the world!'

'I'll miss those brown eyes,' Angela said.

'Whose?'

'Betty's,' she said.

'I thought you meant Dad's,' said Sarah, giving me a wink.

'Both then,' said Angela. 'And I'm not even a dog person. It was as though she could see into my soul. She always gave me a special lick on my hand. And the day I came home from Dubai, things with Stephen having gone kerplunk, she sat against my legs all day, do you remember? She wouldn't leave.'

'She was a good dog,' said Mum.

We sat on the bench and looked out to sea. Angela took out a flask from her bag. 'Hot chocolate,' she said. 'Thought we deserved it. But we'll have to share the cup. I should have made more.'

'Do you think Dad misses us as much as we miss him?' said Sarah, taking the first sip. We were all giving her preferential treatment these days.

Mum nodded. 'I would say so. If it was me, I'd miss us.' She smiled at Sarah. 'It doesn't get easier, does it?'

Sarah shook her head. 'Life goes on, whether you want it to or not,' she said. 'It goes on too quickly sometimes, and I don't feel ready. I want to slow it down, take things in. I'm thinking of going to pregnancy yoga. Someone said that it's the only way you can get any control of time. That and meditation. But I don't think I'd be any good at meditating. But yoga I could do.' She passed the cup to me for my turn of the hot chocolate.

'Do you think Betty was the most spoilt dog in Ireland?' I said. 'Can you think of another dog that had chicken breast and had a Dubarry wax jacket?'

'Well, if you don't spoil your dog,' said Sarah, 'then there's something wrong with you. Dad was the worst,' she went on. 'Do you remember?'

'He wouldn't leave the house if Betty didn't have her jacket on? He'd look up to the sky and say, "There's a drop of rain up there, she'll need her coat on."'

'And he was the one who decided Betty should be allowed on the sofa,' Mum said, 'Charles said that she was also a member of the household, and therefore should be allowed. And it was him who hoovered it every day.' She smiled at the memory. 'He was a good man. I was lucky to have met him.'

'If you hadn't, you wouldn't have had us,' said Sarah.

Mum nodded. 'A stroke of luck indeed.'

'More hot chocolate anyone?' Angela took the flask and refilled the cup.

'I am going to make a toast,' said Sarah, 'Here's to Betty. And to our beloved auntie, Angela. The glue in this family, you have kept us all going when we didn't think we could.'

Angela looked very pleased. 'We're each other's glue,' she said.

'And to my grandchild,' said Mum.

'My grand-niece,' said Angela. 'Now, *she'll* be the most spoilt child in Ireland.'

'Or he,' said Mum. 'I don't mind what we get. Harold is already making a new kind of succulent... he's doing some kind of selective breeding. He's hoping it will produce a little flower.'

'Tell him, *it* is honoured,' said Sarah.

Mum smiled and screwed up the flask and put it back in the bag.

'Do you feel lucky to have met Harold?' I said. 'Does he... I don't know... do you feel differently about him than Dad... or...?'

'Very differently.' Mum took my hand in hers, and reached for Sarah's. 'It's not the same. At all. But who would want the same? Life moves on. But I can still remember Dad. I spent thirty years with him. I've spent only a few months with Harold. But...' I could feel her squeeze my hand. 'Sometimes different is good. You can leave the past locked away, the memories in a kind of box, that you can take out and examine whenever you want to, while you get on with whatever is happening right now.'

'Isn't the Latin getting to you a bit?' asked Sarah. 'Go on, you can tell us.'

Mum laughed. 'No, I like it. It's quirky. Better than some boring man who doesn't have an original thought in his head.'

'What about something in the café?' suggested Angela. 'We need more than a tiny sip of hot chocolate.'

The four of us walked back down the hill, Sarah had slipped her arm into mine. 'Do you feel anything?' she said.

'Yes, your arm.'

'Apart from that. Do you feel Dad?' She was smiling. 'He's here,' she said. 'I know he is.'

I nodded. 'I've felt him a few times now. He came back to me.'

'I think,' she said, 'he's been with us all the time.' She clutched me closer. 'You don't think it's creepy or weird?'

'Not really, I think it's nice. It makes me happy.'

'Me too.'

In the café, we sat with coffees for Mum and Angela, tea for me and a hot chocolate with cream for Sarah. 'I'm keeping my strength up,' she explained, eating the cream off her spoon. 'The baby needs nice things.'

'Now, just to let you know,' said Angela. 'I have decided to whisk your Mum off on a little holiday. Well, more of a long overdue odyssey.'

'It's a bit of fun, that's all,' said Mum. 'We're going to take the trip your dad and I never got to take,' said Mum. 'Campervan, same route, same stop-offs.'

'It's in honour of your dad,' said Angela.

'He'll be with you in spirit,' said Sarah, confidently.

'I hope so,' said Mum. 'I saved some of his ashes. Just a tiny bit. It was on the bookshelf in his study with all his Dickens... and... well... I always hoped I'd find the courage to take him to Bilbao.' she gave us both a small smile.

'Thank God you didn't mix them up with Betty's,' said Sarah.

'It's a brilliant idea,' I said. 'I hope you have a wonderful time.'

'You two could come with us,' said Mum.

'We could go in convoy,' said Angela. 'I once travelled to Dingle in the sidecar of a motorbike. And I once hitchhiked to Germany. It took us a month to get as far as Brussels.' She sighed happily.

'We're only going for three weeks,' said Mum. 'Angela's making it sound like we are Lawrence of Arabia.'

'No way,' said Sarah. 'Not like this.' She nodded at her belly. 'I don't want to give birth at a service station in France.'

'We could fly and meet you there,' I said.

'Would you?' Mum looked relieved, a proper smile spread across her face. 'That would be perfect. Sarah?'

She slowly nodded. 'Hugh will probably insist on coming too.'

'Well, Harold wants to meet us in Bilbao, so it's turning out to be a bit of a gathering.'

'Carpe diem,' said Sarah, 'as Harold would say. And anyway, Dad would want you to be happy.'

'And he'd really like him,' I said. 'He'd think Harold was worthy of you.'

'And I really like him too,' said Mum, blushing slightly.

'Oh! I nearly forgot!' said Sarah. 'I have a present for Milly.' She reached into her handbag and took out a small black box tied with gold thread.

I hesitated for a moment.

'Open it!' she said. 'I didn't just buy you a box, there's something inside it. I bought one for me as well. A matching set. It was so cheap, only a fiver, so you don't have to be *too* grateful. Just a *little bit* grateful.' But she was smiling as I opened it. I didn't care what it was, I was already full to the brim with happiness. I lifted the lid. Inside was a necklace with a small teardrop shaped crystal. When I held it up, a million lights danced around the room.

'It's beautiful,' I gasped.

'It's a sparkling drop of joy,' said Sarah, pulling a twin from under the neckline of her top.

'Charles' sparkling drops of joy,' said Mum, tearing up. 'Weren't we all so lucky?'

'We *are* so lucky,' said Angela.

'Dad would be so proud of you,' said Mum, and then corrected herself. '*Is* so proud of you. And I am so very and completely and totally proud of you both. My lovely girls.'

Sarah and I smiled at each other. This was real luck, I thought, to be surrounded by people I loved. You were doing well if you liked your family. You were winning if you *loved* them.

'Thank you,' I said to Sarah.

She smiled. 'I suppose it's just to say thank you for being not a bad sister over the last thirty years.'

Me and Sarah, Sarah and me, sisters together eternally.

And then before I started crying again, Angela insisted on asking the man behind the counter to take a picture of the four of us. I would get it framed and put it on my desk, next to the last photograph we ever took of Dad from the hospice and the one of him and Mum on their wedding day. My altar of love.

57

It was June the first, Irish summer at last. But when I went into the kitchen, I found Siobhán sobbing at the table, her eyes puffy, her cheeks red, her dressing gown sleeves on emergency tissue duties.

'Lorenzo is going back home.' She paused. 'We had the most amazing time together, but I asked if he wanted to meet up again and he said he couldn't... because he's got a *girlfriend*. Back *home!*'

'I'm so sorry.'

'*I'm* so sorry!' she sobbed. 'I'm so sorry for myself! I will never have this ever again. He was incredible. Even the *kissing* was incredible. But it's over before it even started. And that is my tragedy.' Her racking sobs made the tea cups on the table rattle. 'It was one night of lust and love and... well, everything in between... and now it's over.'

'Siobhán...'

'It's my own fault,' she said, bravely. 'I brought this on myself.'

'Will you get back with George?'

She looked horrified. 'Hell no! Once you have had Lolo you can't go back!' Suddenly, she was all clear-eyed focus. 'I would prefer to enter a nunnery than not have passion in my life. Once bitten – literally – there's no return. My mercury has risen, I can feel it! I am Siobhán, hear me roar!' Her clenched fist punched the air in triumph, but I watched as her mouth wobbled, and her face slowly crumpled, and tears began to roll down her face. She tried to speak. 'I am so glad, so, so glad...' she managed in an urgent whisper. 'So glad that I had what I had. It was all in the stars. I am changed. I have been reborn.' She looked like Jeanne D'Arc, a woman who has seen the light. And then she grabbed me, hugging me hard. 'I have bathed in the river,' she said in my ear. 'I am no longer Siobhán. I am Siobhán redux.' Finally, she let me go, gazing at me as though she had been touched by God. Or rather, Lorenzo. 'Mercury retrograde was quite the rollercoaster,' she whispered, deadly serious. 'How was it for you?'

I laughed. 'I survived,' I said. 'Actually, more than survived. I rather enjoyed it.'

'I've been thinking about something for a while,' she said. 'And it's just come to me that I should do it.' She looked at me. 'If I left Dublin, will you be all right?'

'Of course I will,' I said, 'but where will you go?'

'If I can't have Lolo, I was thinking about New York. I've been dreaming about it for a while. But now Lolo has released me from that. He forced me to make a decision. My aunt knows someone who knows someone who has a magazine there. They need an office dogsbody. It's a magazine about dogs. It's not quite the feminist dream, but I feel that this could be my path.' She paused. 'I'll miss you though.'

'Me too.' We both smiled at each other, tears in our eyes. 'But I'm glad you're going to have an adventure.'

She nodded. 'If it goes wrong, I'll let you know. But this morning my forecast said that the choices I make today will not be ones I regret.'

'Good.' We hugged again. 'I'll come and visit.'

'You'd better,' she said. 'Or you could just come with me. We could find a grotty little apartment somewhere. Hang out. Be best friends with Lena Dunham.'

'I'm tempted, except there's the baby, and Angela and getting Milly Byrne, Solicitor up and running.' And there was something else. And just like Siobhan I was released and sure and born anew. I was going forward with my life. I was moving on...

Except for a small matter of unfinished business. Darragh. If I *was* going to move on, then he might want to come with me... Angela had said that love was all that mattered and I couldn't let him slip through my fingers... again.

* * *

There was a light breeze in the warm air as everyone went about their early-evening Saturday business, my stomach filled with the flutter of a thousand butterflies. This is what people do who are brave, I thought. People who aren't scared to live fully. People like me. Okay, so I still felt scared. But being scared was just another thing I would have to learn to accept about myself.

What if he wasn't there? I began to jog.

Teolaí was just ahead, customers sitting out under the awning, drinking their wine, and a new waiter, someone I recognised from Lorenzo's party, was flirting with a group of women. The sun was strong and I put my hand above my eye to see properly.

Did I want to do this? Now, was my opportunity to walk away.

But there, walking towards me, was Darragh. He stopped and was staring straight at me, a puzzled look on his face, wondering and curious, but now... smiling... and I could feel my face smiling back, my heart full, my hands reaching for him as we rushed towards each other and then we were in each other's arms, like we'd never been anywhere else.

'I'm sorry,' I said. 'I'm proud of you.' I talked into his neck, making my voice muffled.

But he seemed to hear me. 'I'm proud of you.'

We were both safe and tight and I had the feeling of being exactly where I should be at exactly the right moment in the universe, as Siobhán would have it, as though the stars had aligned.

'I love you,' he whispered.

'I love you too.'

'I don't want to do this without you,' he said. 'I didn't then, and I don't know. It was horrible leaving...' He looked at me. 'Do you understand?'

I nodded. 'I understand.'

'I missed you the moment I left,' he went on. 'I knew it would nearly kill me, and it very nearly did. I am so sorry to have abandoned you. I am just so sorry.'

'It's all right. And it doesn't matter.' It didn't. I wouldn't change a thing, because if I did, we wouldn't be here right now. I realised I loved my life, everything. Even the not so good bits. And more than anything, I loved the way I felt with Darragh. Always had.

And we kissed. And it wasn't a Siobhán and Lolo behind the fridge kind of kiss, it was something else entirely, something I'd been missing, better than before, better than ever, something that was just perfect.

And when we looked up, there was a huge cheer from all the customers, whooping and clapping and taking pictures on their phones. Francisca blew us a kiss and clapped as hard as anyone.

Darragh's arm was around me and mine around him. 'I am never letting you go again,' he said. 'Never.'

'Me neither.' When you love someone, you don't ever let them go. Real love doesn't change or diminish, you just find ways of managing it and I felt so lucky to have so much love in my life.

He pulled me closer to a soundtrack of more cheering and put one arm in the air. 'Thank you!' he said, laughing. 'This is the wonderful Milly Byrne who is back in my life. I feel very lucky...' He kissed me again. 'Very lucky indeed.'

But I was feeling the most lucky – all the love I had, all these wonderful people in my life... alive and dead, they all felt very present and very close indeed. Love is all you need.

EPILOGUE
TWO YEARS LATER

It was a glorious day for a wedding. The bride wore a beautiful grey silk dress, with a bright pink feathered fascinator (chosen by her sister). Everyone said how beautiful and unusual her bouquet was – like an entire Irish garden in a bunch, everything from roses to lavender to fuchsia to yellow Irises. But the buttonholes on the groom and best man featured succulents.

'You look amazing,' I said, kissing Mum.

'Thank you,' she said.

'She's the most radiant bride there's ever been,' said Harold, holding onto Mum's hand as tightly as possible. 'She is radiant in *perpetuum et unum diem*, forever and a day.' He beamed at her. 'My Kitty.'

The last two years, they had become inseparable, selling both family homes and buying in the same street as Angela. Packing up was sad and Sarah and I had stood on the road waving off Mum, who was driving behind the moving van to her new home, but it was time to let the house go. We had our memories tucked away with us. And Sunday lunch at Mum and Harold's new house was now a pre-requisite for all of us, even though Angela was usually the one ordering us all around.

'Have you got the rings?' Harold said to Horace, who had removed his fleece and was wearing a very smart navy suit. He looked quite handsome.

Horace rolled his eyes. 'How many times?! Yes! Yes, I've got the rings. Yes, I've got your speech. Yes, I ordered the cars.'

He'd brought along his girlfriend, Samantha, with whom he'd just returned from Shetland where she was finishing her PhD on the effects of guano on different types of rock. They were perfect for each other.

'Come here,' said Horace suddenly, wrapping his arms around Harold, almost lifting him off his feet. 'Everything is going to go perfectly. You are a lucky man.' When he released his father to the ground, Harold's glasses were steamed up and skewed. Horace then hugged Mum. 'He's a pain in the neck,' he said, 'I don't know how you put up with him.'

'Quite easily,' said Mum, beaming at both of them. 'I find him a pleasure to put up with.'

Horace rolled his eyes at me. 'I think they might be happy,' he said. 'Do you get that impression?'

'I think so,' I agreed.'

'Coming! Coming! Please don't panic!' Auntie Angela ran down the stairs. 'I had forgotten my lipstick, and my water spray and mini fan. I don't want to be overheating.' She bounded up to Mum. 'Now, have you got your something old, something new, something borrowed, something blue?'

Mum nodded. 'My old wedding ring, here.' It was dangling round her neck. 'My new dress and I've borrowed your fascinator, Angela. And I have this blue cloisonné bracelet that Mrs Murphy gave Milly before she died. So, I'm all set.'

Sadly, Mrs Murphy had died six months earlier and had left her estate to the new development, hoping that her story and the legacy of the building would be given back to the people of the city. I had continued my Wednesday meetings with her in the basement of Daphne's hotel, visiting her and Frederick every week and bringing along a little cake for the two of them. Mrs Murphy liked Bakewell tarts and Frederick, it turned out, liked custard slices. All the cream, I presume.

On one of our last meetings, she gave me a bracelet that she had worn on her wedding day. I'd worn it every day since, sure it had brought me luck and so today I'd lent it to Mum.

Daphne was working hard on the project, raising money and sponsors and turning Number One, Merrion Square into an amazing citizens's palace, as she called it. The day Mrs Murphy died, Frederick returned to Daphne's kitchen, never to wander off again. And he didn't go back to his previous name of Pussy Galore. He would be forever, Frederick.

And I'd also seen Ryan in town, the week before. Pushing Lottie in her pram after a hospital check-up, I heard someone call my name. 'Hello,' Ryan said. 'And who's this?' He bent down to look at Lottie. 'She's beautiful.' He stood up, slightly awkwardly. 'Well,' he said, 'you'll be glad to know I resigned from Dublin Investments. And I'm on my way to Goa.'

'Goa?' It didn't sound very luxurious.

He nodded. 'I fancy doing something very different. I'm going on a yoga holiday. It's quite basic...'

'Not the best for the best, then?' I teased.

He blushed. 'God, I talked a lot of rubbish, but I've obviously done a lot of thinking. And... well, I moved out of the coach house and left Mum to it. It was time I stood on my own two feet.'

'Great.'

'And you're well?'

'Very,' I said, telling him quickly about setting up on my own, Lottie's birth.

'And who's the lucky man?'

'Darragh O'Toole,' I said.

'Ah... yes, of course.' It was as though something finally made sense for him.

'It's good to see you,' I said. 'Good luck in India.'

We hugged. 'Good luck, Milly,' he said. 'And when I come back, maybe I could take you and Lottie for a milkshake or whatever it is babies drink.'

'I'd like that,' I said, 'I'd like that very much.'

* * *

Angela turned to me. 'Right, now tell the truth. Hat or no hat? I have to look my very best for my sister's wedding day. Being cancer free is a responsibility. You have to look better than okay. You have to look as though you are thriving.'

'You definitely look as though you are thriving.'

She nodded and then twirled in front of me, once with a huge straw hat, and then without. Her short cropped grey hair (model's own) made her look twenty years younger.

'Without,' I said, just as Mum said, 'with.'

'I'll need a third opinion,' said Angela. 'Where's Sarah?'

'In the kitchen,' I said. 'Feeding Arthur.'

My lovely godson was now eighteen months old and was at the stage where he loved bananas, disco dancing and his granny and granny Angela more than anything in the world. Mum and Angela took him for two days a week, while Sarah, who had finally left nursing, was back in college and Hugh was at work.

'Granny Angela!' said Arthur when he saw her.

'Now, Arthur,' Sarah said. 'Granny Angela needs you to make a very important decision. With the hat, like... this? Or without the hat, like... this?'

Arthur studied her very carefully, and then said, after a moment of deep refection, 'Without!'

'Well, without it shall be!' Angela kissed the top of his head. 'He's going to be a doctor like his father,' she said. 'Brains to burn, that one.'

'Or maybe a pharmacist like his mother is going to be?' said Sarah.

'That's the problem with both parents who are gorgeous and clever,' said Angela. 'You can neither of you take credit for your child's genius. Ah! And here is the lovely Hadriana!'

Hadriana was just coming in with a large dry-cleaning bag. 'Sorry I'm late,' she said. 'My flight was delayed and then I had to pick this up and... and...' She smiled at us all. Hadriana seemed to quite like us all now, and had taken to chatting quite normally and even, on occasion, laughing. She'd totally accepted Mum as her stepmother and had even adopted Angela as her surrogate aunt.

'I'll make you a cuppa,' said Angela. 'You go upstairs to change, everyone is using the front bedroom.'

'Thank you, Angela,' said Hadriana, 'but I'll just wriggle in here. No one minds, do they?'

'*Paul* is on his way,' said Angela, meaningfully. She and Paul had met, not at Sexy Sixties Singletons, but in a cancer support group. He was devilishly handsome and had just gone through six months of chemotherapy. But they said that the best therapy had been meeting each other. Every evening, they walked the pier in Dun Laoghaire, Angela's voice carrying right across the bay. Paul's voice was even more transmittable. He'd taken to calling them 'the two foghorns', both of them delighted to have found a kindred spirit.

'You look lovely, Milly,' Hadriana said. 'Your dress is beautiful.'

'Thanks.' Catriona had lent me something designer and flowy. I'd picked it up the previous day and had stayed for a cup of tea with her and Lydia, who had turned into something of a terror, now being two and a half. Catriona now worked from home three days a week and, on the days she was in the office, she had lunch with Lydia in the crèche on the first floor of her building.

'By the way,' I said to Hadriana, 'I sent the letter to the record company about your copyright. I think we've got a good chance of getting you a better percentage.' Milly Byrne, Solicitor was on the case.

'Thanks.' She put an arm around my shoulder and gave me an excited squeeze. 'Darragh's outside,' she said. 'Struggling with the baby seat.'

'It's so heavy,' I said. 'Neither of us can get used to it. I'll go and give him a hand.' I had missed my little Lottie. We'd been apart for only two hours and I think I must have thought about her every second.

Darragh caught my eye and smiled. 'She's just woken up.' And in the baby seat was my beautiful baby, three weeks old and the sweetest and most wonderful thing.

'Hello, Lottie,' I said. 'Hello, my lovely girl.'

Calling her Lottie or Charlotte was a no-brainer – she was named after Charles, her grandfather. I liked to think of him as her and Arthur's guardian angel.

'We missed you.' Darragh kissed me. 'How are you doing?'

'Doing well,' I said. 'I don't know what I'll be like at 10 p.m. tonight, but Angela says she will be on the floor until midnight. She's asked the DJ to open with *Dancing Queen*.'

Darragh and I had moved into a tiny three bedroom house just behind Teolaí and round the corner from my old flat with Siobhán. We'd adopted a shaggy and sweet little dog called Jess who would sleep under our bed at night and stayed glued to me all day while I worked in my office in the spare bedroom. Milly Byrne was up and running. There were no property developers, just ordinary people who needed help. I had to take a bit of time off to focus on lovely Lottie, but everything seemed manageable. And I had the world's best partner in Darragh. This time around, we were older and wiser and had a better understanding of life. And we could talk more about our lost parents and everything that had happened in our past made us stronger together every day.

Whenever I passed the flat, I would remember the old days. Siobhán Facetimed me every afternoon from New York. She was seeing an artist called Pablo Fiasco who, she said, turned subway trains into political statements.

George was currently in the sixth round of *The Great Irish Bake-Off*, last week he had wowed everyone with his 'showstopper' featuring the Guinness Brewery Gates made from sponge cake and marzipan. He even had a marzipan Arthur Guinness. He got star baker and 10,000 new followers on Twitter. He'd even found time to make the cake for today's wedding. I'd picked it up yesterday – four tiers with tiny meringue swans on the top. A triumph.

'Everyone into the kitchen,' called Angela. 'I would just like to make a rallying call! Just a quickie to set us on the way, to wish the lovely couple luck!'

I lifted Lottie out of her carrier and held her close, my lips against the fuzzy down of her head. Darragh stood with his arms around me, his chin on my shoulder.

'Well, today,' said Angela, 'my baby sister marries the lovely Dr Harold Hawkins. And our families are joined together to celebrate their friendship, companionship and love. Let us not forget our absent friends, those who are with us in spirit.'

Sarah locked eyes with me and we remembered Dad, knowing how much he would – weirdly – have enjoyed today. This family, which a year and a half ago, seemed dwindling to nothing, was now a full and noisy houseful.

'And let us all have a wonderful day!' ended Angela.

I kissed Lottie's little head again while Darragh held me close, his lips against my ear. 'I love you,' he said.

I felt fortified and invincible, bathed in the sounds and the warming glow of love which filled the room, Darragh's arms around me and the soft sweetness of Lottie's downy head. We were getting married later that year. Francisca had invited us to use her family's estate in Tuscany. 'I will look after everything,' she had told us. 'You two just turn up, yes?'

Siobhán said she would come back from New York for it and had said, bravely, that she didn't mind facing Lolo again. 'He was my catalyst,' she said. 'Without my Italian love rat, I might still be sitting on the sofa watching *EastEnders* with George.'

'May I just say something?' said Harold, still holding Mum's hand. 'A small but rather, in my humble opinion, wonderful phrase – *amor omnia vincit*. Love conquers all. To my beautiful Kitty and to our wonderful family. *Amor omnia vincit!*'

'*Amor omnia vincit!*'

If only we could press pause and linger for a moment longer, I thought. But the day was moving on. The cars would be arriving soon and there would be the flurry of family and noise and people grabbing bags and coats and cameras, anticipation filling the air.

'Right everyone!' said Angela. 'Are we ready? Kitty! Harold!' She began bustling us out. 'We've got a wedding to go to!'

And I looked around at my Darragh and my Lottie... and over at Sarah and her little family and to Mum and Harold and to Angela and Paul... and around my neck was my sparkling drop of joy, and I held it and thought of Dad. We were lucky to have him. And on this happy day, right here, right now, I had everything I could ever have wished for because drops of joy never lose their sparkle for too long. And love, as we all know, conquers all.

ACKNOWLEDGMENTS

Thank you...

As always, my deepest appreciation to my unwaveringly supportive agent, the ever fabulous and tremendously kind Ger Nichol and to my fiendishly clever and talented editor, Caroline Ridding, and her amazing team at Boldwood Books.

And to my family and *all* my brilliant friends whom I love and adore and am lucky to even know, but particularly to Caryl Beynon, Louise Halfpenny Karen Wilson.

But most of all to my clever, interesting and funny Ruby. The very best person I will ever meet.

MORE FROM SIÂN O'GORMAN

We hope you enjoyed reading *Life After You*. If you did, please leave a review.

If you'd like to gift a copy, this book is also available as an ebook, digital audio download and audiobook CD.

Sign up to Siân O'Gorman's mailing list for news, competitions and updates on future books.

https://bit.ly/SianOGormannewsletter

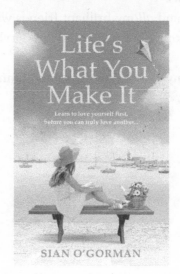

ABOUT THE AUTHOR

Sian O'Gorman was born in Galway on the West Coast of Ireland, grew up in the lovely city of Cardiff, and has found her way back to Ireland and now lives on the east of the country, in the village of Dalkey, just along the coast from Dublin. She works as a radio producer for RTE.

Follow Sian on social media:

facebook.com/sian.ogorman.7
twitter.com/msogorman
instagram.com/msogorman
bookbub.com/authors/sian-o-gorman

ABOUT BOLDWOOD BOOKS

Boldwood Books is a fiction publishing company seeking out the best stories from around the world.

Find out more at www.boldwoodbooks.com

Sign up to the Book and Tonic newsletter for news, offers and competitions from Boldwood Books!

http://www.bit.ly/bookandtonic

We'd love to hear from you, follow us on social media:

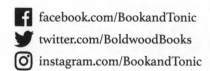

facebook.com/BookandTonic

twitter.com/BoldwoodBooks

instagram.com/BookandTonic